The
Lessons
of Victory

The
Lessons
of Victory

by
THE RIPON
SOCIETY

**The Dial Press, Inc.
New York 1969**

Table of Contents

Preface

In the flush of success, the winner's long-time supporters are inclined to ridicule any attempts to understand the appeals and prejudices, the dynamics and constraints that contributed to the outcome. Yet, if the Republican Party is to learn from its experiences in 1968—if it is to avoid the same disaster that brought down the Democratic government in 1968, that could end the Republican Administration after one term—it must carefully study the reasons it was able to win the Presidency only four years after one of its worst defeats, and why it almost lost just three months after the opposition did its best to commit political suicide. The Nixon Administration's programs for governing the nation and the President's attempt to win a broad mandate for his government must be based on the lessons of 1968.

As Republicans, the members of the Ripon Society hope that this book can contribute to an understanding of the recent campaign. The study is divided into four parts. The first examines the significant events of 1968 that contributed to the Republican victory in November. The second examines the political blocs that are so important to American politics and contrasts the wide gap between the Republican opportunity in 1968 and the victory on November 5. Part III looks at the constellation of election results in the fifty states, both in terms of the local candidates who were elected and with respect to the strength of the national ticket. Finally, in

Preface

Part IV, the Society examines the future of the GOP and attempts to conclude, from the preceding analysis, the steps that our party must take to build itself to majority status—a goal that its campaign strategy of 1968 precluded.

Many members and friends of the Society have contributed to this work. Over a hundred correspondents, from all fifty states, submitted reports on the campaign and the election. Listed below are those who were of major assistance in drafting chapters (where an individual made the predominant contribution to a particular chapter, it is so indicated) or who participated in the editing process that molded these chapters into the four parts and then into a book; to them I owe my sincere thanks:

Christopher W. Beal	John R. Lazerek (12)
Robert L. Beal	Michael S. Lottman
Michael F. Brewer	A. Douglas Matthews
Robert W. Davidson (14)	Michael R. Merz
Terrence E. Dwyer (13)	Howard I. Reiter (6)
J. Montieth Estes	Samuel A. Sherer (9)
Marc J. Glass	Steven F. Stockmeyer
Howard F. Gillette, Jr.	Richard A. Zimmer
William J. Kilberg (7)	

To Evelyn Ellis, Martha McCahill, and Nancy Morton, I would like to express my special appreciation for untiring assistance in preparing the manuscript. The Society also wishes to express its gratitude to NBC News for making available the results of its election-night precinct samples in several states.

As a Republican organization, the Ripon Society has, since its inception in Cambridge, Massachusetts, in December 1962, tried to provide the GOP with political ideas that contribute to the American dialogue. The group of teachers, lawyers, businessmen, law and graduate students that first gathered over six years ago took its name from the birthplace of the Republican Party, Ripon, Wisconsin. They met then, one member said, because they were tired of apologizing to those who represented the world of ideas for being Republicans; and they were tired of apologizing to fellow Republicans for being interested in ideas. From the outset, Ripon members have seen as their most important contribution to American politics a bridging of the gulf that has separated much of the GOP from the intellectual and professional community for the past fifty years.

Our goal is to make the Republican philosophy relevant in the rapidly changing environment of the twentieth century, and to contribute the new political concepts demanded by the complex governmental structure of this heterogeneous country. We believe that the Republican Party can speak creatively and responsibly to a troubled and bewildered world. And we believe that it must. When the margin between sanity and chaos is as thin as at present, we dare wish only the maximum wisdom for any powerful institution.

With our ideas we seek to attract new members to the Republican fold, especially the young—Americans who see the need for change and seek a vehicle that permits them to make a meaningful and constructve contribution to the political progress of America. For if the Republican Party is to be viable in the future, it must actively and systematically involve those who will shape tomorrow's world. It must learn to excite intellectuals, minority groups, laborers, and urban dwellers. It must win the confidence of those who are not at home in the politics of a passing generation, the new middle classes of our suburbs, the moderates of the new South, and of course the young. And it must understand that it is ideas that will make the difference in the long run.

The Ripon Society wants to help Republicans achieve

Preface

these goals. For Ripon believes that the Republican Party can break new ground in American politics and serve as a flexible instrument for exploring the challenges of the decades to come. It is our hope that this book will help the Republican Party determine its political priorities and governmental policies over the next years.

Robert D. Behn
Editor

The Ripon Society
142 Eliot Street
Cambridge, Massachusetts
February 1969

The
Lessons
of Victory

PART I.   The Political Year 1968

It was, in many ways, an election year like 1920. For almost a decade, a truculent, moody nation had been promised too much, had dared too much, expected too much—and it had seen its hopes and ambitions mocked and crushed. As in 1920, an ugly and apparently futile foreign war dramatized the emptiness of America's idealism; at home disorder and drift undermined her traditional confidence in the ultimate triumph of intelligence and control. In the opinion of many Americans, it was time for a "return to normalcy," and the only political question was who could best provide it.

As in 1920, the Republican Party based its appeal—and won the election—almost solely on the fact that it was the party out of power. To be sure, it nominated a much more able candidate for President this time than it had forty-eight years ago, but in both cases the strength of the candidate lay in his general acceptability to all factions rather than his strong appeal to any one of them. The candidate for Vice-President, both then and now, was an obscure governor who seemed to have no strongly offensive characteristics and who had created a tough law-and-order image for himself through a single well-publicized crackdown on militant dissidents.

The Democrats, as was the case in 1920, found that their biggest handicap was the unpopularity of an incumbent President whom they had hailed just a few years earlier as one of their greatest heroes. Their candidate for President, in both elections, was faced with the dilemma of running both as a representative of the incumbent administration and as an alternative to it, and now as then he failed to escape the quandary. Interestingly enough, the most popular figure to emerge from both the 1920 and 1968 campaigns was the vice-presidential candidate of the losing Democratic Party: Edmund S. Muskie in 1968 and Franklin D. Roosevelt in 1920.

Of course, there were dramatic differences between the two elections, and none was more striking than the difference in the Republican victory margin. After all, the smashing 60.4 percent Harding victory in 1920 had brought Republicans to power in numbers that only the Great Depression could substantially diminish. In 1968, a similar sweep had been predicted. Even the cautious London bookmakers rated Nixon's chances at 10 to 1. Richard Rovere summarized the judgment of just about every knowledgeable observer when he wrote in the New Yorker fewer than four weeks before the election that

> Unless all the auguries are mistaken, Nixon will win with a huge electoral majority and Humphrey will be fortunate if he is able to get as many electoral votes as George Wallace.

The only real question, it seemed, was whether the expected Nixon landslide would sweep Republicans into control of the House of Representatives or leave them a hair short of it. In any event, the Democrats' New Deal coalition was at last going to be shattered in this watershed election. For the first time since the 1920's, the Republicans would become the majority party. The unpopularity of the incumbent President, the agonizing Vietnam war, and the spiraling domestic disorder seemed to assure that conclusion.

Indeed, alienation was the dominant national mood. A well-recognized phenomenon in the black and college communities, it also characterized the Los Angeles defense-plant worker, the farmer's wife in Iowa, and the suburbanite in the Northeast—though for these there was no violent manifestation. Nevertheless, the drama of 1968's political battle was set on a stage where all the minor but ultimately decisive characters were groping blindly for a meaningful reference point on which to base their decision. Everyone was searching for a believable leader, one who would not be found deceiving once he had removed his mask of the campaign act. The response of the political personalities and parties to this national mood and to each other is the story of 1968.

CHAPTER 1. NIXON'S NONCAMPAIGN

"Nixon's the One" was the campaign slogan, and it perfectly epitomized the entire campaign. It made no specific appeal; it told nothing about the candidate's fundamental nature; it projected no strong or memorable image. But it did let people know that Richard Nixon was running for President.

This noncommunicative nature of the slogan was, of course, the fundamental reason for its selection, for it said nothing that could offend any voter, took no position with which anyone could disagree. The same was true of other slogans: "This Time, Nixon" or "This time vote as if your whole world depended on it." Similarly, the candidate talked again and again about how the Republican Party had never been so united, though he never went beyond the face of unity to examine the substance that could bring together Senators Strom Thurmond and Jacob Javits, or John Tower and Edward Brooke. The very secret of unity, after all, was the flimsiness of that substance.

During the campaign, the Gallup poll showed that the electorate rated the Republican Party as better able to deal with the nation's problems by a 3 to 2 margin—an impressive reversal of the 2 to 1 ratio by which the Democrats had dominated just four years earlier. If that 3 to 2 margin, achieved in the absence of substantial Republican electioneering, could only be maintained until the fifth of November, then the victory proportions of 1920 could be repeated. Accordingly, the Nixon battle plan in many respects called for a 1960's equivalent of the confident front-porch campaigns that characterized Republican politics two and three generations earlier.

The biggest difference between the election scene of 1920 and that of 1968 was the sawdust crusade of George Corley Wallace. Wallace's presence on the presidential ballot in all fifty states created a strategic problem for Nixon that did not face Harding in 1920; the Alabamian's candidacy created a second way in which the electorate could register the amorphous feeling of protest by which it was so clearly possessed. The specter that haunted Nixon and his advisers from August to November was that Wallace would so split the protest vote that Nixon would be denied an electoral-college majority.

The Nixon camp was convinced that a majority of the voters, controlling a majority of electors, would inevitably vote against the "ins." This conception was rooted in the experience of the winter and early spring campaigning in the primary states, New Hampshire, Wisconsin, Nebraska, and Oregon. Nixon had sensed the mood quickly and hastily formulated his central appeal. "When you're on the wrong road, you take a new road," he told cheering throngs again and again. And he undoubtedly noticed that, at this early stage, there were few who seemed to care very much about just where the alternative road was going. Americans agreed far more on the need for change than on the specifics of change, the Nixonites concluded. The springtime successes of the Democratic insurgents Eugene McCarthy and Robert Kennedy were taken as further evidence for this same assumption.

"A new road—any new road," spoke the voters, according to the Nixon analysis. Because Wallace alone, after the Democratic convention, threatened his monopoly of these anti-Administration voters, most major campaign decisions—including the decision to avoid a television debate—were made in response to the threat of Wallace.

Another way of expressing this central assumption in the GOP calculations is to say that the swing votes in the 1968 election—those that were still transferable as late as September and could be altered by the last ten weeks of campaigning—lay mostly between Nixon and Wallace. The Opinion Research Corporation of Princeton, New Jersey, which took extensive surveys exclusively for Nixon among 7,000 voters, substantiated this assumption; it concluded that 81 percent of those "leaning" toward Wallace in the North and 55 percent of those "leaning" toward Wallace in the South indicated that they might vote differently by the time the election rolled around in November. Consequently Wallace dominated the thinking of the Republican strategists.

These then were the assumptions on which the Nixon strategy was based. The strategy itself was not simple or unambiguous, nor was it adopted or followed without dispute in the Nixon camp. But its presence was felt at almost every turn after the Miami Beach convention. Its chief advocate was Nixon's law partner, John Mitchell, whose authority as campaign manager ensured that it would be implemented effectively.

The essentials of the strategy went something like this: Give as many positive signals as possible to the potential Wallace voter and avoid giving negative signals to everyone else. (It is only fair to note that had Senator McCarthy headed the third-party challenge, a literal interpretation of this analysis would have required substantial overtures to the peace vote and demands for a new Secretary of State would have been heard in place of demands for a new Attorney General.)

What were the positive signals to the Wallace voters that would not be overtly offensive to other groups? It must be stressed initially that they were *not* racist appeals. Nixon was extremely careful to avoid that unhappy trap. He did, however, allow his once strong civil-rights image to be blurred and scrambled. Much of that process occurred at Miami Beach, where the unsuccessful Reagan candidacy succeeded in moving Nixon rightward.

The boasts of Reaganites after the convention were largely correct; their operation was the lever that forced Nixon to a closer alliance with Strom Thurmond than Nixon had planned. Thurmond saved the nomination for Nixon, and Nixon knew it. So for that matter did the whole world. If Nixon had given not an inch away to Thurmond, many voters would still believe he had—and would at the very least find it impossible to erase the mental picture of Nixon and Thurmond, hands tightly interlocked and raised high in the air, receiving the cheers of their party together on the Convention Hall podium. It was a picture that would not win Negro votes.

This picture was further sharpened by Nixon's assurances to the Southern caucus at Miami Beach that he had endorsed open-housing legislation unenthusiastically and only for tactical reasons. And he further reinforced the signal by saying later on a Southern regional telecast that he would not use federal money or threats of its removal to eliminate racial imbalance in schools. He later and quietly answered Northern critics of the statement by distinguishing between overt and de facto segregation and limiting his hands-off attitude to the latter.

Nixon's early acceptance and his later dropping of the word "justice" from his law-and-order pleas are another symbol of the counter-Wallace strategy. So was his occasional belligerence on matters of foreign affairs—some of which brought out cries about the "old Nixon" late in the campaign. On one occasion, for example, Nixon carefully and gratuitously denied that President Johnson had arranged the bombing halt in Vietnam for political reasons, a denial that did far more to spread the suggested charge than to suppress it. On another occasion, the Republican candidate charged the Administration with playing politics with peace, but gingerly focused the charge on the President's assistants and exempted the President himself. He assured his audiences that Johnson and Humphrey were not traitors on so many occasions that he created the impression that he expected people to think they were. As the Democrats feinted to the left to win the peace vote, it became extremely difficult for Nixon to resist the temptation to move right and assume for himself an even greater share of the hawk support.

But for the most part, the "signals" to Wallacites were not directly on race, or integration, or war issues. There were other, safer ways to project the impression of toughness and no-nonsense, of a willingness to crack down on whatever targets he could find for America's frustrations. Thus, the Pueblo was used as a token of America's disgrace, a symbol of Johnsonian weakness. The Supreme Court and the attorney general were whipped again and again—and on them was blamed America's domestic disorder. In "thousands of cases all over the country," criminals run free because of Supreme Court rulings, Nixon asserted in Ohio (a performance that reportedly disappointed even his closest advisers).

These appeals were useful, however, for they helped to project the hard-headed approach for which the nation apparently hungered. They preempted the appeal through which Wallace was realizing his greatest successes. But the critical point in 1968 was that any signals that Nixon made to the right came through clearly, not only to potential Wallacites but to all voters in a day of instant, universal communication. What was said in any one locale was said to a nationwide audience. And the rough-and-ready Nixon image was the one that most voters of all dispositions took to the polls with them on November 5.

Part of the reason that Nixon's larger audience dwelt on a few hard-line signals was that the campaign gave them so little else to focus on. This was a direct result of the second element in the strategy: the desire to avoid needless offense to anyone by making strong appeals to no one, the desire to appear all things to all men.

One implication of this strategy of nonalienation required that Nixon keep clear of special-interest groups. According to columnists Rowland Evans and Robert Novak, for example, Mitchell scotched one plan to have Nixon appear with labor leaders in Pennsylvania, though their willingness to support the Republican candidate had been regarded as a considerable coup. Plans for the candidate to speak on campuses or in ghettos were also vetoed, one by one. Reporters finally began to play a game that paid a dollar to the first of their number to spot a black face in a Nixon crowd. The only Americans who were singled out for special notice by Nixon were the most generalized kind of groups: the young, the aged, or—most usefully—"the forgotten American." The phrase was carefully chosen and defined—"those who are not breaking the law, those who do pay taxes, those who do go to work, those who do support their churches and their schools"—so that almost everyone would wish to identify with it. Nixon would bring Americans together again by appealing to their most common denominators. By and large he would not speak directly of the conditions that separated his countrymen.

The same technique was applied to foreign policy. In August, the Gallup poll reported that a majority of the American people considered Vietnam the most important issue facing

the nation; it far outdistanced the next ranked issues—
crime and civil rights. Yet other polls showed that Nixon
had significant support from both doves and hawks in the
electorate. Understandably afraid that any clear position
would lose more voters than it would gain, Nixon declared
the issue "off limits."

> I do not believe a presidential candidate now should
> say, "This is what I will do in January." I believe
> that if you really want peace, then you have to respect
> a man, look at him, look at his judgment and back-
> ground, and base your decision on which man you
> would rather have sitting at that conference table . . .
> Foreign policy is my strong suit.

It was a game try. What was not appreciated in the effort
to avoid an unpopular position was the likelihood that no
position might be the least popular position of all. The reason that danger was overlooked was the all-pervasive assumption that the anti-Administration voters were "locked
in," that they cared little about alternatives and would vote
Republican simply because "any change was better than
none." After all, the great mass of voters had actually been
joined in making this sweeping claim by such unlikely and
prestigious Nixon supporters as columnists Walter Lippmann and Joseph Kraft.

But as the weeks passed and the fall came, the basic
concern of many voters changed. The question that the
electorate was asking itself switched from "Whom should I
vote for?" to "What kind of President will Nixon make?
What kind of change will we get with a Nixon Administration?" A Gallup poll taken in mid-October found that those
who thought that Nixon would be elected comprised 59
percent of the electorate—a bloc three times the 18 percent
who believed in a Humphrey victory.

The result of this extraordinarily clear assumption was that voters began to measure Nixon, not against Hubert Humphrey or Lyndon Johnson, but against an abstract ideal of the Presidency—much as George Romney had been measured against a larger-than-life ideal a year earlier when he got out in front too far, too soon. The issue was no longer Lyndon and Hubert—for or against, continuity or change—with Nixon as the vague alternative, a convenient receptacle for all manner of anti-Administration feeling. Now suddenly it was Nixon in the spotlight and Nixon on the defensive. "What will he do?" people asked, and an avoidance strategy would not satisfy them.

Yet as October lengthened and Humphrey closed in, Nixon seemed frozen to the strategy of September. He continued to take his left flank for granted, though Humphrey was luring voters away by the droves. He continued—and even intensified—the battle with Wallace, winning some support, but precipitating a large fall-out of supporters to Humphrey even as he did so. The appeal from toughness was amplified. He would increase the non-Vietnam defense budget by $20 billion, he said, and the professional military would be given a greater hearing in White House councils. (The latter statement was made only days after the publication of Robert Kennedy's widely read article on the Cuban missile crisis, which illustrated again the trigger-happy tendencies of many of the generals.) He threw over an earlier prohibition and began attacking Wallace directly, not for his views but because he couldn't win, implying—as Senator Thurmond had been saying throughout the South—that Nixon provided an equivalent political alternative. He explained the differences between himself and the Alabamian bantamweight in these terms:

He's against a lot of things. He's against the rise in

crime. He's against the conduct of foreign policy, of what's happened to respect for Americans throughout the world. I'm against a lot of these things. The difference is—I'm for a lot of things.

It was a fair comment, though it played down other important distinctions. The essential problem, however, was that Nixon had deliberately not developed in a consistent and aggressive manner any clear public image of those things he was for. The American people, by his reckoning, knew better what they didn't like than what they liked. The negative appeal was a broader and safer way to rally a confused and divided public.

Nixon's assumption about the high transferability of the Wallace vote was not mistaken. The Alabamian's vote did crumble late in the campaign, falling 10 percent from what the polls had earlier accorded him. Of that, perhaps half went to Nixon, allowing him to win some critical border states and Southern electors. What was mistaken, however, was the assumption that the "protest" vote was "locked out" from the Administration candidate, and that it would never support Hubert Humphrey unless Nixon committed some major blunder. True as that assumption seemed in the wake of Chicago, it was discredited on November 5 when the Vice-President won the support of millions of voters who only a few days or weeks earlier had been leaning Republican. The significance of that reversal among protest voters is indicated when one remembers that Nixon received the same percentage of votes on November 5 (43 percent) that he had polled throughout the campaign (and for that matter, the same percentage he was polling six months before the election). This happened despite the last minute crossover from Wallace.

The only explanation is that even as he gained perhaps

five percentage points at Wallace's expense, he lost just as many voters to Humphrey along with the remainder of the third-party fall-back and the entire pool of "undecideds." [1] And because each vote lost to Humphrey narrowed the Humphrey-Nixon gap by two (adding to the Humphrey vote at the same time it subtracted from Nixon), the Democrat was able to close a wide gap during the fall campaign and turn the election into a virtual stand-off.

It is important not to overlook the possibility that Nixon might have been unable to hold onto the vote he eventually lost to Humphrey, even if he had run a campaign oriented toward the more moderate voters. It was possible that "those damn liberals" would never support Richard Nixon. It was possible, of course, that he would then have lost votes on both the right and the left, and with them the election. It can be argued, after all, that the orientation of the Nixon campaign was only an excuse for these voters to switch to Humphrey, that they would not have stayed with the Nixon-Agnew ticket whatever the direction of the campaign. Those who argue this line have no doubt but that the best campaign strategy was one that attempted to salvage Wallace voters, which would offset the automatic losses.

Of course, such an argument is the perfect example of a self-fulfilling prophecy. By claiming that Nixon could not hold many moderate or liberal votes, the planners justified a strategy that helped to alienate those very votes. Whether they would have disappeared anyway cannot be answered conclusively, of course, because political systems offer no opportunities to run controlled experiments to test political theories.

[1] This type of analysis represents only the aggregate result of changes in voter preferences. Opinion Research reported to Nixon that, between early September and early October, 20 percent of the electorate changed their presidential preferences though the total statistics remained about the same.

The polling data do indicate, however, that at an early point in the campaign these voters were available to Nixon. Post-election studies—some commissioned by state Republican parties—show that hundreds of thousands of votes slipped to Humphrey in the final few days and hours. It is our conclusion that Mr. Nixon eventually lost millions of votes that he might have had and that a primary reason for this was that his campaign tried so hard to offend no one that its very blandness became offensive. In August, particularly just after the Democratic convention, a great many Americans decided that in 1968 Nixon would surely be "the one," that his election was guaranteed, and that, on balance, this would be a happy result and one to which their vote would contribute. They believed then in what Nixon himself called the "New Nixon." But somehow—and the responsibility is not easily placed—they lost track of that strong and attractive figure during the campaign, so that by the time they actually entered their polling places on the first Tuesday in November, they had reconsidered everything.

The specific desire to win votes from Wallace while taking the remainder of the electorate for granted dictated the fall's campaign planning. But it should also be recognized that although this strategy and those who believed in it were dominant in the end, there were other men and other motives operating in the Nixon campaign that were not completely obscured. They tended to be most visible in spring 1968, when the candidate's most prominent rivals were Governors George Romney and Nelson Rockefeller and went into partial eclipse about July when Ronald Reagan emerged as the most important threat. They were displayed from time to time throughout the fall, never enough to reverse the over-all thrust of the campaign, but always enough to add some ambiguity to the Nixon image. And, happily, they have reemerged in much more important ways since the election.

These motives and themes, generally recessive but still important, were those of the "New Nixon" so much discussed by the press as his intraparty power mounted early in the year. The "New Nixon" emphasized reconciliation at home and peace abroad. His image was thoughtful, searching, confident, generous. When he analyzed problems, the analysis was complex. "There are no easy answers," he would say, while outlining the matter at hand in a measured and careful way that gave the impression that if answers could be found, Nixon would somehow find them. For example, he calmed and wooed and finally won a college audience in Stevens Point, Wisconsin, during the primary campaign by answering a hostile questioner with a skillfully extemporized briefing on Latin American affairs. His office distributed far and wide his excellent *Foreign Affairs* article on "Asia after Vietnam." He endorsed controversial ideas popular with nonvoting students, such as a volunteer army and the eighteen-year-old vote, and he presented strong briefs in support of his conclusions.

On the political level, his aides approached state convention delegates with a conscious desire to avoid arm-twisting and "political overkill." Their easy confidence helped reduce intraparty tensions on all levels and paved the way to a first-ballot nomination.

The New Nixon maneuvered gracefully at Miami Beach, preempting the Reaganites with a strong but balanced law-and-order statement. He moved quickly to similarly deny the liberals an issue around which to rally by calling for a reduction in the American military effort in Vietnam and for more attention to the social and economic plight of that war-torn country. George Romney's promised floor fight on Vietnam became unnecessary and the smoothly programmed convention proceeded without incident and with remarkable consensus.

Throughout the spring, both the candidate and his staff sought out disaffected groups, listened to their advice, and used it to develop interesting new programs. This was particularly true with respect to the black community. After meeting at length with such Black Power advocates as CORE leaders Floyd McKissick and Roy Innis, the Nixonites presented their own program to promote a new "black capitalism," which would give Negroes "a piece of the action" in the "exciting adventures of private enterprise." The proposals themselves were made in two radio speeches, collectively entitled "Bridges to Human Dignity," which were delivered on April 25 and May 2. One outlined the general concept behind black capitalism and the other presented a long list of specific proposals. The cumulative impact was enormous; "Bridges to Human Dignity" brought praise even from the most hostile Nixonophobes. It may well have been the most successful single move in the entire Nixon effort.[2]

It cannot be said that the Nixon organization ever abandoned the black capitalism initiative. Nixon referred to it in his acceptance speech, his office distributed the "Bridges" text in generous quantities along with flyers showing the excellent press reaction. A good advertising campaign was prepared and executed, built around the theme of black capitalism. But here, nevertheless, as in so many other areas, the promise of the spring withered in the colder air of autumn. It was still visible and one could still believe in it, but somehow the life had left it, and, in the black com-

[2] Credit for the development of the black capitalism proposals has been loosely parceled out, but it appears that Nixon aides John McClaughry and Raymond K. Price played the principal roles, the former in the conceptual stage, the latter in writing the radio addresses.

munity in particular, other less attractive images had taken its place.

"Bridges to Human Dignity" was just one of Mr. Nixon's radio successes. Recalling that the candidate had (according to public opinion surveys) scored much higher with radio than with television audiences in the 1960 debates with John F. Kennedy, and with an eye to the amazingly inexpensive price of network radio time, Nixon planners employed a great deal of Nixon's best rhetoric through this medium. This was in both the spring and the fall, but there was an essential difference between the two promotions. The spring radio addresses were played up as major campaign pronouncements. The speeches were well placed; texts were released in advance; each radio appearance was widely advertised; reporters were encouraged in a variety of ways to make each speech into an important and newsworthy happening.

But in the fall, particularly in the last two weeks of the campaign, the radio speeches were regarded more and more as a tactic for projecting an image of thoughtfulness, less and less as a serious attempt to persuade wavering voters. Each was condensed to a few minutes, and the series was presented at the brisk rate of one per evening. The radio speeches were now used less to present new ideas and more to repeat old themes. It appears that the Nixon-Agnew Campaign Committee did not spend a single penny in preadvertising them. Amid all the excitement of the last two weeks of the campaign, most of these radio speeches were almost completely overlooked by the press. Nixon himself, as the polls showed his lead diminishing, would call attention to the fact that he was going nationwide every evening on the issues ("for the first time in history" he would emphasize), but his comments could not counter the impression that he was reluctant to talk about these issues more visibly.

Also late in the campaign, when Nixon was being attacked (sometimes unfairly) on all sides for his lack of specificity, he issued two large compilations of campaign rhetoric to further prove that he had not been evasive. One was called "Nixon on the Issues" and was billed as proof that the candidate had taken firm positions on 227 specific issues during the campaign, excerpting passages from speeches and press conferences on each issue and spreading them across 194 pages. (Nixon himself had been using the figure of 167 issues in his stump speeches, but his estimate evidently was conservative.)

Members of the press corps generally regarded the document as an insult to their intelligence, and they had a certain point. "Issues" are not coins, to be neatly stacked and counted. The number of items covered is far less important than the quality of what is said. Does one set up the "Middle East" or "Vietnam" as a single entry, or is each merely a heading for a constellation of six or seven smaller issues, as it was in the Nixon count? Could the candidate fairly claim to have addressed sixteen separate issues under the general heading of "crime"? Was his comment that "the President must take an activist view of his office" really so strong and concrete that he could claim another specific position on another distinct issue (this one labeled "an activist Presidency")? Or was his statement that "the next President should set in motion a searching, fundamental reappraisal of our whole structure of government" really so bold and forthright that it validated his claim to have thereby addressed the issue of "government reorganization"? Of course not, and these anecdotes only begin to illustrate the questionable nature of the whole project. No wonder the press filed the document away with some embarrassment. And yet there was Nixon—waving his copy defensively, convinced that he had now laid to rest the accusation that he had not spoken to the issues. In the process he only reinforced the impression that almost destroyed him: that he still confused form and substance, that he still mistook quantity for quality.

Nixon's alternative answer, when pressed on the paucity of his positions, was to say: "Of course, Hubert has taken twice as many positions as I have, because he's been on *both* sides of *every* issue." And then everyone would laugh politely.

The second compilation of Nixon rhetoric was far more impressive and will undoubtedly become a valuable historical document. Entitled "Nixon Speaks Out," it presented thirty-four addresses and statements, almost all of which had been first delivered in radio broadcasts. Issued on October 25, with relatively little fanfare, it was nevertheless the best attempt in the late campaign to revive the image that had been so pronounced four and five months earlier. Few read it during those hectic days, but those who did were reminded of their springtime hopes—and given a dramatic measure of how far those hopes still were from fulfillment.

Here, for example, was the May 16 speech, "A New Alignment for American Unity," which imaginatively sketched the outlines of the new political coalition that Nixon would build. The Republican Party would be the majority party for a generation to come, the most important governmental instrument in thirty years. Old Republicans, new liberals, new Southerners, black militants, and the "silent center" would join together in a new alliance, motivated less by economics and more by ideology, united in their common demand for a greater sense of participation and impact in a mass society that seemed to be growing away from them.

And here, too, was the June 27 speech, "Toward an Expanded Democracy," which sensitively discussed this growing alienation and its roots in the lost sense of community and control. Here "the forgotten American" theme took on real meaning, as in Nixon's important observation that "the white man in the Boston suburb shares many of the same frustrations as the black man in the Chicago ghetto," or that "The protesting college students . . . speak not only for the student revolt, but for the frustrations of Americans everywhere." But that was in June. In November, it was hard to find a place where the Nixon campaign was repudiated more decisively than in the Boston suburbs—where he lost many traditionally Republican towns that had voted for him over favorite son John F. Kennedy in 1960—the Chicago ghetto, and among college students—whether they were protesters or not.

"Nixon Speaks Out" also carried the text of the candidate's thoughtful discourse on order (March 7), on international partnership (March 28), on the American spirit (an excellent campaign speech delivered to a mere handful of people at Colonial Williamsburg on October 2). It contained some of the neglected radio speeches of the closing drive, including a ringing effort on the potential for voluntary public service, and reprinted some of the material Nixon had submitted to the platform committee in Miami Beach, most importantly his promising and widely hailed Vietnam statement—his only "specific" Vietnam statement of the entire campaign. The convention acceptance speech was included here, too. And so was a speech which some critics have described as one of the best examples of presidential campaign rhetoric since the days of Adlai Stevenson, Nixon's analysis of "The Nature of the Presidency."

Delivered on September 19 on both the NBC and CBS radio networks, "The Nature of the Presidency" speech received wide attention and even reproduction in other media. A statement of personal philosophy, it presented a disciplined, depersonalized approach to high office that contrasted in a refreshing way with the highly personal style of the incumbent President. It projected the future President as a wise and reflective leader, shrewdly tapping the very best men and women available for the task of government, allowing them considerable freedom in the application of their talents, releasing the nation's creative energies through a process of decentralization, establishing the Presidency as a place of moral leadership, where over-all priorities are set and general goals determined.

"The Nature of the Presidency" speech was the best and the last full-dress campaign appearance of the "New Nixon."

What was it, then, that drove out the good image Nixon had worked so hard to manifest? Did an increasingly hostile press corps suddenly refuse to project all that was positive in the Nixon approach? It seems unlikely. Rather these positive elements were drowned out for the most part by a different Nixon image, a considerably less impressive one. For this was the Nixon of the sock-it-to-'em stump speech, the oversimplified analysis, the all-too-easy answer. It was the Nixon of partisanship and defensiveness. On many issues, it was an evasive and cautious Nixon, determined to sit tight and rock no boats. When he did speak out, he was the hard-line Nixon; his foreign policy suddenly degenerated into preoccupation with weaponry (to close "the security gap"), and his domestic analysis focused myopically on such scapegoats as the Attorney General and the Supreme Court.

Unlike 1960, it was not a series of accidents or slip-ups, lapses or departures from "the game plan" that confused Nixon's image and cost him early support. Rather, all these blurring elements were deliberately chosen, conscious parts of the Nixon strategy. The "New Nixon" was not incidentally obscured during fall 1968, so much as he was intentionally and temporarily repressed.

The Republican candidate in 1968 was a man of considerable talent, attended by other talented men. Just where all that ability would break through into public view may have been in question at the start of the campaign, but one could safely predict that it would break through somewhere. As things worked out, the sit-tight strategy precluded any great public impact on a substantive level and determined instead that the most glittering triumphs of the campaign would be triumphs of technique.

It can be said, in fact, that the technical virtuosity of Nixon and his campaign team often stole the show from the candidate's message. Presumably, that message was the ultimate reason for the entire exercise, but there were many occasions in 1968 when that relation almost seemed to be reversed. This was partly the fault of extraordinary caution on substantive matters, partly the result of an extraordinarily energetic campaign organization.

Working largely with a different group of people than those who had accompanied him in 1960, and with frequent opportunities for "shakedown cruises" beginning in fall 1966, Nixon slowly assembled and then carefully tuned his electioneering machine. In this process, he reportedly applied the lessons he had learned from reading and rereading Theodore H. White's *The Making of the President, 1960* during his years in the political wilderness. Whether that story is apocryphal or not, Nixon did correct a number of errors he had been chided for eight years earlier, and, as usual, he did so thoroughly and with extreme literalness.

Had he worn himself out in the 1960 campaign? This time he would go to the opposite extreme, resting sometimes three, and always two, days a week. His pace was deliberate all autumn long. Every campaign swing included many hours for reclining in the Florida or California sun. The physical and mental weariness that in the past had heightened Nixon's irritability and shortened his famous temper was largely avoided. In fact, of the ten last campaigning days, five were spent in the seclusion of his New York apartment. "He made Cabot Lodge in 1960 look like a veritable dynamo!" said one journalist.

Had Nixon made too many decisions by himself in 1960 and delegated too little work? This time he would delegate almost everything. John Mitchell and others made many decisions that Nixon might never have approved had he known of them beforehand, though he dutifully supported them after the fact. On at least one occasion—the mailing of an insensitive letter to securities dealers suggesting lighter federal controls if Nixon won—the candidate found himself accepting without murmur the public outcry that followed.

Had Nixon been inaccessible in 1960, particularly to members of the press? This time around, incredible efforts would be made to placate traveling reporters. They were wined and dined and continually courted. Whenever a few would complain about the paucity of press conferences, a press conference would be quickly arranged.

Finally, Nixon would also avoid the decision that was most clearly to blame for his 1960 defeat, his agreement to debate his opponent at a time when he was leading in the polls. Nixon treated the prospect of a debate like the plague, even when his avoidance itself became a damaging issue and despite his confidence and that of his advisers that he could easily best any representative of the unpopular incumbent Administration.

In the application of past lessons, as in so many other areas of political behavior, Nixon and his followers showed an extraordinary faith in procedures. They trusted rules, respected forms, and almost worshipped technique. *Life* magazine cited this tendency as a reason for endorsing the Republican standard-bearer; his Administration would be cool, orderly, and neat. But, said *Life*, such qualities as vision, spontaneity, and passion—warmer and admittedly sloppier values—were less important in the Nixonites' scheme of things.

The disposition to value form over content, quantity over quality, was a prevailing characteristic of the 1968 noncampaign. Nowhere was it more evident than in Mr. Nixon's nonspeech. This was the carefully put together stump oration that the candidate delivered over and over again, with little variation, from August to November. He himself described it as a boring exercise, complimenting both his wife and the press on their ability to sit through the thing day in and day out. If he had to listen to the speech like that again and again, said Nixon, "I'd go up the wall myself!"

Essentially, the standard stump speech was a long series of applause lines, each applause point signaled by a rise in pitch and a rush in tempo. An enthusiastic reaction was guaranteed by placing bevies of screaming teen-aged "Nixon girls" around the speaker's podium. "We yell when our leader signals us," said one, proud to be part of this perfectly stage-managed spontaneity.

That reactions to the speech would never be negative was also guaranteed. The Nixon girls, for example, were also used to screen out both the sight and the sound of the kind of youthful protesters who were giving Hubert Humphrey such a hard time. The capacity of these protesters to mar even one of Nixon's glittering happenings was so feared that when the tour reached Boston its managers canceled every one of Nixon's public appearances. At many rallies, including the climactic appearance at Madison Square Garden on Halloween night, anyone wearing a beard was systematically turned away from the proceedings, whether he was a New York Republican Club regular with a ticket or not. It was the only meeting in GOP history, said one angry Republican leader whose friends had not been admitted, that would have excluded both Abraham Lincoln and Jesus

Christ. But for all its precautions, the Madison Square Garden rally was still disrupted by unruly dissidents. In this case, they were members of the Young Americans for Freedom and other conservative groups that came by the busload in order to boo long and hard the appearance of Nelson Rockefeller and Jacob Javits and the very mention of Mayor Lindsay's name. Even the announcement of a bombing halt in Vietnam was greeted by jeers and hooting. It was hardly a comforting sound for the nationwide television audience, and it did not help Nixon's candidacy. Ironically, his appeal did get a shot in the arm on a rare occasion when leftist radicals did make their way into a rally. In Syracuse, late in the campaign, Nixon allowed a group of demonstrators to sing "The Sounds of Silence" to his audience and then scored points with all observers by patiently answering a list of questions they had submitted.

The rhetorical climax of the Nixon stump speech illustrated the essential hollowness of that particular exercise. Face flushing, voice rising, Nixon would rock a bit more noticeably, heels to toes. And then, with a short punching gesture, he would shout, "And so, my friends, I say to you tonight, that in this campaign we're going to take off the gloves and *sock it to 'em!*" Cheers! Bedlam! Hysterics!

And that was it. The point was taken no further.

Socking it to 'em consisted of one thing and one thing only and that was—quite precisely—yelling to your audience that you were going to sock it to 'em. Nixon was the one in 1968 because Nixon was the one. The party was united around the idea that the party should be united. And socking it to 'em meant shouting "sock it to 'em" at the top of your voice.

Given this rhetorical void, it was predictable that the spotlight would focus on the choice of Governor Spiro Agnew for the vice-presidential nomination, the decision not to debate, and, finally, on the sheer theatrics of the GOP campaign.

Almost every facet of the Republican campaign machinery deserved attention and commendation in 1968. One example was the series of hour-long question-and-answer sessions that were televised live on a regional basis throughout the autumn. On each occasion, Nixon smoothly handled a series of questions from a widely mixed group of lay panelists. It was obvious to all that the questions were not prearranged.

But it was also obvious that very few of the questions were incisive or difficult. Despite the assurances of the moderator Bud Wilkinson that "the gloves are really coming off this time," few panelists really pressed Nixon. Part of the problem was that the interrogators could not follow one question by asking another. Then, too, their backgrounds and inexperience often precluded their asking important questions. A retired fisherman in Boston managed to befuddle the candidate with an inquiry about the use of domestic fish in the school lunch program. "Well, I like fish!" Nixon allowed in his answer. And that was about as close as anyone came to stumping the expert.

And, of course, that was the point of the series, skillfully produced for Nixon by CBS television executive Frank Shakespeare to demonstrate Nixon's technical proficiency. Nixon can speak without notes; Nixon can think on his feet; Nixon is an "expert" on the "issues." Above all, Nixon thrives under pressure. This "crisis pschology," on which Nixon dwelt so much, was clearly a part of the whole campaign appeal, but it was most dramatically presented in the regional telecasts.

On each occasion, Nixon would boldly march into the pit of "the arena." Like his hero, Theodore Roosevelt, he talked of how he lived only for "the battle."

At any rate, Frank Shakespeare and the production of the television specials received more publicity in the end than anything Nixon said on them. For these were not situations where the candidate was to be put on the offensive—to make headlines or to excite audiences. In fact, the intention was just the opposite—to show how skillfully Nixon could avoid making headlines and how expertly he could de-fuse even the most explosive questions. It was the same "avoidance" psychology that had created the defensive cast of the whole campaign, a quality that thoroughly perplexed both strategists and observers who had expected a more constructive and aggressive performance by the party out of power.

There was no doubt but that Nixon could handle this art form well, mixing a few facts and figures with a host of generalities. After all, he had always relied heavily on verbal facility, the essential skill of any good lawyer. He was proud of his ability to develop appropriate language for any situation. He was practiced in the art of bridging differences, obscuring disagreements, of reconciling apparent conflicts, all through carefully chosen language; one should not have been surprised to see him utilize that skill in his presidential campaigning.

Perhaps for this reason, he avoided formats that might make it difficult for him to use such patronizing talents. He would not debate Humphrey, it was decided, though many believed a debate would be just the thing to put Nixon on the offensive again. When, finally, he did go on against trained reporters on "Face the Nation" in the last week of the contest—over John Mitchell's protests and, reportedly, at the insistence of Congressman Melvin Laird—it turned out to be his single most damaging appearance.

If form and technique intentionally overshadowed content in Nixon's use of television, the same thing was true of his traveling operation. A crew largely composed of former military officers, armed with walkie-talkies, made it their business to run a logistically perfect "tour" and—in what is a notoriously sloppy business—they succeeded beyond anyone's wildest expectations. Once again, they almost stole the show from their employer—"the body," as they called him in their own special jargon. "That was a good drill," the tourmasters would say after a smoothly executed operation, and most of the events were just that, timed to the minute and sparing no effort to leave the desired image on press and public in each locality. Yet once again, the image manifested was primarily that of an efficient campaign machine. The medium had truly become the message.

There were many technical wonders in the campaign. For example, 5 million letters went out "personalized" with a Richard Nixon signature, written with a water-based ink that would be sure to smear when tested by a skeptical recipient. The letters were mailed from the Nixon-Agnew Citizens' Committee by computer in the week before the election—each one personally addressed and bearing its own, individually affixed law-and-order postage stamp.

Advertising was another technical challenge that was impressively met. Both radio and television commercials used the effective Nixon voice, usually in passages from the acceptance speech. *The Washington Post* columnist David Broder commented in early October:

> Certainly the Nixon commercial—with his voice speaking quietly against the vivid montage of riots at home and warfare in Vietnam—is a classic example of "image" over "meaning." This reporter has yet to meet anyone who can recall what the unseen Nixon is saying: all they know is that conditions look terrible and he seems to promise a change.

It's all very slick and effective, and to disparage it is perhaps to rail against the inevitable.

Testimonials from local and regional GOP heroes were strategically employed in television spots. A half-hour commentary film on Nixon's life, produced by Warren Wallace and featuring informal, shirt-sleeve reminiscences by the candidate, proved one of the most appealing weapons in the Republican arsenal. The comparable Democratic effort, the so-called "mind-changer" film made for Humphrey, was more widely seen and heralded, but its impact was muffled at least partially by the Nixon performance.

By and large, the Nixon managers saw to it that no one would ever say of their candidate, as was so often said of Barry Goldwater just four years earlier, "If he can't run a campaign, how can he run the country?" With Nixon, in fact, it was the other way around. His electioneering effort often seemed to argue exclusively that he was qualified to be President simply because he *could* run a technically competent campaign.

If proficiency was the thing communicated as well as the mark of communication, what could the American public conclude from the message it received in 1968 from the Republican Party? An observer could fairly surmise that a vote for Nixon was a vote for a President who would be politically sensitive and subtle, for a cautious man, one who respected a variety of viewpoints and who belonged wholly to no interest group or ideological persuasion. Unless he was dissuaded by the Agnew choice, the observer could conclude that Nixon respected highly competent men and detailed, advance planning.

From the style of the Nixon campaign, one could also tell something about what might be missing in a Nixon

Presidency. An observer would quickly note, for instance, that Nixon was very rarely seen in a truly spontaneous moment. To be sure, the candidate was acutely aware of the dangers of appearing contrived, but his response was to contrive the appearance of spontaneity. His stump speeches and television shows were carefully staged to emphasize the fact that he was not using notes, and complex subjects were treated only on radio. The fetish over note-using echoed his bitter complaint that John F. Kennedy had somehow cheated by bringing notes into the 1960 television debates. He strongly criticized politicians from both parties who relied on prepared texts and teleprompters. Of course, the memorized speech and mechanical gestures could not be filled with life merely by dragging the lectern away from the podium. What Nixon needed was some evidence of feeling and of surprise—the sort of thing that happened when he confronted a group of deaf children one busy day, a rare moment that provided a highlight of the personal campaign.

Gloria Steinem, in a blistering and often unfair critique in *New York* magazine, represented the reactions of some to the campaigning Nixon when she dubbed him "Plastic Man." "If it can be learned, Nixon will learn it," she concluded, "but if it has to be understood, Nixon—and possibly the whole country—may be in deep trouble." This analysis was seemingly and unknowingly validated by the campaign staff and its chief, John Mitchell, for as many reporters pointed out, they constantly described their work as that of "programming" the candidate.

The New Yorker also spoke to the stylistic problem, the air of contrivance, the absence of passion.

Not many voters, we think, expected to be offered solutions this year; all of us already knew the two major candidates, and all of us understood the deadly com-

plexity of the two major issues—war and race—too
well to expect a sudden unravelling of our fears. What
we did long for in a secret, half-sensed way, was some
evidence in some candidate of a new center for hope—
not a speech or a position paper but perhaps only a
turn of phrase or a knowing silence that would suggest an essential complexity, courage, patience and
contemporaneity. This is style, and for many Americans style has become the essential private metaphor
that makes daily life bearable. For them, it has become
almost impossible to pay attention to people who don't
share this resource, who aren't with it.

For both Nixon and Humphrey, the writer concludes, the
primary problem was aesthetic.

None of these descriptions, it must be emphasized, is fair
to the man Richard Nixon, nor were they necessarily intended as descriptions of his essential nature. They comment rather on the image of Nixon that his campaign
projected, an image that screened him from the public,
represented him unfairly, and almost cost him the election.

In the end, of course, he won the election; his gamble
paid off. Many were put off by the campaign, to be sure,
but in the final reckoning, there were just enough who voted
for Nixon despite it. Massachusetts Senator Edward Brooke
expressed this attitude best (though he did not necessarily
share it) in an introduction of Nixon before a Republican
audience in Boston. He listed the drawbacks of Humphrey
and Wallace and then, smiling at the GOP candidate, he
concluded, "And so, I guess that leaves only you, Dick."

Brooke, who had traveled with Nixon for a period in
September, made the remark facetiously. But the sentiment,
ironically, was the very one that the Nixonites themselves
had attributed to the American electorate all along. They
were convinced from the start that the only way Nixon

could win a national election was by getting people to vote against the Democrats.

The tragedy of 1968 was that it was the perfect time for a wise and experienced man to seize the imagination of an American public hungry for strong leadership. To be sure, Nixon had been badly scarred by over two decades of public controversy. But at the end of the troubled summer of 1968, he was in a position to fill a great void in American life. It was clear then that a bold campaign and sweeping mandate would establish him in unarguable terms as President of all of the people.

But those who planned Nixon's campaign sold him short. They underrated his potential. They accepted a defensive premise and built everything on it. As a result, the allegiance of many who might once have supported him was forfeited, and the enthusiasm of many who did support him was compromised. The Nixon who was to emerge as President was worthy of better.

CHAPTER 2   Agnew vs. Muskie

Perhaps the best way to understand the type of man Richard Nixon wanted for his running mate is to look at the man who stayed in the running longest before Spiro Agnew was selected.

Massachusetts Governor John A. Volpe had been long associated with the moderate gubernatorial wing of the party. He had no significant enemies within the GOP, nor was he likely to arouse strong antagonistic emotions between the convention and election day. He would weld the bond of unity between the ticket and the sometimes recalcitrant governors, while giving no negative signals to any great part of the electorate.

All these attributes were shared by Agnew.

Many close Nixon advisers actually left their meetings with Nixon the night after his nomination thinking that Volpe had been selected. Why the nod went to Agnew over Volpe is uncertain, but the reasons that Agnew and Volpe emerged as the top two contenders are clear. They tell a great deal about the Nixon strategy in 1968.

Nixon's nomination on the first ballot at the Republican convention set off a series of intensive meetings at the Hilton Hotel to deliberate on the selection of a running mate. It was evident that Mr. Nixon had come to Miami Beach with a wide-open mind on the vice-presidential question. During the previous week, his talents had been devoted to winning the nomination and writing his acceptance speech. He apparently had given no extensive thought or study to the matter of his running mate.

Nixon's first meeting after the nomination was with a relatively large group of personal staff members and a few Republican officials who had been closely associated with his campaign. Those present at the first meeting in Mr. Nixon's hotel suite during the early morning hours were:

John N. Mitchell
H. R. Haldeman
Robert F. Ellsworth
Richard G. Kleindienst
Peter Flanigan
Leonard Garment
Frank Shakespeare
Herbert G. Klein
Maurice H. Stans
Ed Nixon
Pat Hitt
John Sears
Charles K. McWhorter
Rose Mary Woods

Linwood Holton
Howard H. Callaway, Jr.
Wayne Hood
Rep. Clark McGregor (Minn.)
Gov. Walter J. Hickel (Alaska)
Gov. Tim Babcock (Mont.)
Fred LaRue
Richard Moore
Glen A. Olds
Sen. Roman L. Hruska (Neb.)

Nixon opened this session by saying that he hadn't "brought any names to Miami Beach" and asked the group for suggestions. By the time they finished, about a dozen names were on the table, including such familiar ones as Governors Reagan, Romney, and Volpe; Senators Howard Baker of Tennessee, Mark Hatfield of Oregon, and Charles Percy of Illinois; and three that had been mentioned less frequently, Senator Robert Griffin of Michigan, Representative George Bush of Texas, and Maryland's Governor Spiro Agnew. Nixon suggested that two criteria be used to guide the discussion: competence for the Presidency and the ability to unite rather than divide the party. This vetoed Bush on the basis of his relative inexperience (one term in the Congress). His listeners assumed that the second qualification excluded those whom Nixon had been known to refer to bitingly as "the glamour boys"—specifically Reagan, Lindsay, Percy, and possibly Romney and Hatfield. Evidently, Nixon felt these potential candidates would lose as many votes as they would win; perhaps more importantly he had no wish to hitch his campaign to a more glittering star after having engineered one of the greatest political comebacks in decades. It was far better, in Nixon's opinion, that his running mate be a lightning rod to draw criticism away from him. "I think if I want to win this, I'm going to have to win it on my own," the candidate concluded. The meeting broke up about 2:35 A.M., when a new group of party leaders was ushered into the Hilton's Penthouse B.

The second group was a select body of party chieftains who had been summoned from the convention floor. It included:

House Minority Whip Leslie C. Arends (Ill.)

Sen. Karl E. Mundt (S. Dak.)

South Carolina Republican Chairman Harry Dent

Florida Republican Chairman William Murfin

Former Sen. Barry Goldwater

Rep. W. E. Brock III (Tenn.)

Rep. Donald Rumsfeld (Ill.)

Cook County Board President and Illinois gubernatorial candidate Richard Ogilvie

Rep. Samuel L. Devine (Ohio)

Former Atty. Gen. Herbert Brownell

Former Gov. Thomas E. Dewey

Gov. Louie B. Nunn (Ky.)	Sen. Strom Thurmond (S. C.)
The Rev. Billy Graham	Rep. John J. Rhodes (Ariz.)
Lt. Gov. Robert H. Finch (Cal.)	Sen. Paul J. Fannin (Ariz.)
Ohio Republican Chairman John Andrews	Sen. Hiram L. Fong (Hawaii)
Gov. James A. Rhodes (O.)	Sen. Jack Miller (Ia.)

An examination of the list reveals that it consisted principally of Nixon's preconvention supporters, a group heavily weighted in favor of the conservative wing of the GOP. Mundt, Goldwater, Brock, Thurmond, and John Rhodes could hardly be balanced by pragmatic moderates Donald Rumsfeld and James Rhodes and aging liberals Brownell and Dewey. Needless to say, Nelson Rockefeller had not been invited, nor for that matter had any active exponent of progressive Republicanism. Though several governors were under consideration, the Chairman of the Republican Governors' Association, John Chafee, was not consulted. Above all, the group was not one that was likely to make an inspired recommendation, and the temperamental bias that it introduced into the decision-making process may have been critical. This factor in the second meeting appears to have been a turning point in the selection process, and—one could say—in the entire panorama of events on Richard Nixon's way to the White House.

Initially, the meeting took on the aspect of a victory party with the ordering of drinks and the exchanging of congratulations. When the group got down to business, Nixon again set the standards that the running mate had to meet. First, Nixon wanted a man with national acceptability; second, he preferred someone who was knowledgeable on urban affairs; third, he thought it might be good to choose a mate with an "ethnic" background; finally, he felt that a bow in the direction of the moderate camp would be desirable, preferably with a moderate who had supported Nixon.

The group's members first sank their teeth into the names that had been bandied about Miami Beach all week. Liberals, such as Lindsay and Hatfield, had dominated the discussion, in large part because Rockefeller and Reagan public agents had tried to use them to scare away some of Nixon's Southern support. The ploy had been somewhat effective; as it turned out Southern votes had wavered, and an emergency conference between Nixon and Thurmond had been quickly arranged on the Monday just after Nixon arrived in Florida from New York. At the meeting, the Southern senator let Nixon know that he was holding the line for the former Vice-President under immense pressure and that he wanted Nixon to fully appreciate the difficulty of his position. In return, as Thurmond aide Harry Dent reported in a postconvention interview, Nixon assured Thurmond that he would not push any vice-presidential nominee down Southern throats. Thurmond returned to his critical role on the convention floor, reassured, as Dent put it, that Nixon was someone "he was willing to tear shirt for even more so" (sic).

On the following day, Nixon said to a caucus of Southern delegates, "I am not going to take, I can assure you, anybody for the Vice-Presidency that is going to divide this party." Accordingly, when Thurmond, with Goldwater's support, objected vigorously to Lindsay, the New York mayor was effectively out of the running, despite strong support from Rhodes, Brownell, and Miller. Ogilvie backed Percy, but the Illinois senator was also unacceptable to the archconservatives. Mundt described him as overly ambitious. Some Southerners argued for Reagan, but Finch assured the group that his governor would never accept the position.

Rumsfeld plugged for Griffin as an ideal compromise, but the suggestion generated no enthusiasm. Gradually, the bright stars from either end of the ideological spectrum were disqualified, leaving a rather murky middle ground that again centered around Volpe and Agnew.

The sun was already up when Nixon went to bed for a brief nap. At 9:00 A.M. he entered a third meeting in the Jackie of Hearts room of the Hilton Plaza. The following men were present:

House Minority Leader
Gerald Ford

Rep. Rogers C. B. Morton (Md.)

Republican National Chairman, Ray C. Bliss

Chairman of the Republican Senatorial Campaign Committee, Sen. George Murphy (Cal.)

Sen. John G. Tower (Tex.)

Texas Republican Chairman, Peter O'Donnell

Wisconsin Republican Chairman, Ody Fish

Chairman of the Republican Congressional Campaign Committee, Rep. Bob Wilson (Cal.)

Senate Minority Leader Everett M. Dirksen (Ill.)

Lt. Gov. Robert H. Finch (Cal.)

Ford plugged hard for Lindsay; he saw an opportunity for a Republican House in the Ninety-second Congress and had already determined that the majority of marginal seats were in the North and East where a progressive image at the top of the ticket was necessary for Republican success. Southerners Tower and O'Donnell pushed Reagan, or failing him, Tower himself. Dirksen crushed any remaining chances for his senatorial colleague Charles Percy and instead argued for Howard Baker. Unfortunately, the fact that Dirksen's daughter was Baker's wife took some of the weight out of the minority leader's recommendation, and the group never really focused on the Tennesseean. Meanwhile, the Secret Service was told by someone to be ready to guard Lindsay, Reagan, Percy, and Hatfield. Later, Hatfield was dropped and Volpe added. Just before noon, Agnew's name was put on the list.

The third meeting ended at 11:05 A.M. and was immediately followed by a fourth, which was limited to the very closest group of Nixon advisers—Finch, Tower, Morton, Ellsworth, Mitchell, and Haldeman. Nixon allowed that his first choice all along was Finch. Finch himself believed that the selection of an old friend who was not nationally prominent would smack of nepotism, and Nixon accepted the judgment. Hatfield was dropped, most probably because of outspoken dovishness, religiously based pacifism, and a strong civil-rights image. Hatfield had hoped that these would be offset in the South by his Baptist affiliations and the fact that he was well known there as a result of his frequent church-related appearances. But he hoped in vain.

Now the procedural problems of making such an important decision in a few hours began to take their toll. The discussants were too tired to reach out for new names (such as Pennsylvania Governor Raymond P. Shafer, who later in the fall became an after-the-fact favorite of the campaign staff). The time of the scheduled press conference to announce the choice had already passed, and some participants were getting edgy. It was not feasible to reassemble the earlier groups in order to check out the names of such non-politicians as John Gardner, reportedly Melvin Laird's first choice. To their own amazement, therefore, the group left Nixon with the two names that had survived the weird obstacle course, Spiro Agnew and John Volpe. Finch left the meeting with the impression that the choice would be Volpe. Nixon retired to another room to make his first and perhaps most important appointment.

Afterward, Nixon said that the decision "was very, very close." Agnew himself said he was "rather shocked" when he got the news and was already preparing to check out of his hotel to begin a short vacation. Volpe's reaction was "I knew up to the last half hour that I was in contention . . . I'm somewhat disappointed." The rest of the party and nation was taken by complete surprise.

Once again, Nixon had worked so hard to please everybody with his choice that he wound up pleasing almost nobody. He made a great deal of the fact that he consulted over one hundred people on the matter, yet most notable about the process were the names that were not consulted. "I must have been the one hundred and first," said Nelson Rockefeller, who took the choice of Agnew as a personal insult and came close to leaving Miami Beach in a huff that very afternoon. The Maryland governor had, after all, been chairman of the Rockefeller effort in the spring, and many felt he jumped camp because his pride was offended when Rockefeller failed to call him before announcing his temporary withdrawal from the race on March 21. "The most important un-made phone call in history," was how one Rockefeller supporter described it.

Other outraged progressives who had been ignored in the process (chiefly Governors Shafer and Chafee) reacted by organizing a bolt, one which might have succeeded if John Lindsay had consented to spearhead it, but finally managed only to delay the convention for an hour and give 186 vice-presidential votes to George Romney. Some Nixon people even regarded the exercise as a necessary and healthy catharsis.

But the wave of protest was by no means limited to the left side of the GOP; it took in moderates and conservatives as well. "You're kidding," said Ray Bliss when he learned the news that traumatic noonday. "Who the hell were these

one hundred people Dick Nixon was supposed to have
talked to?" grumbled Melvin Laird, the power behind the
GOP throne in Congress and later Nixon's choice as defense
secretary. "He blew it, goddamn it, he blew it!" cried a
former Goldwater aide who had recently joined the Nixon
bandwagon.

As Agnew himself put it, he had been selected because he
was "less offensive to all Republicans" than anyone else
whom Nixon could come up with. And there was the
glamour issue, previously referred to. After 1960 there had
been underground murmurings that the Nixon-Lodge ticket
would have won if the ranking had been reversed, and
Nixon was determined to prevent a repeat of that humilia-
tion. Commented one Nixon aide to a reporter, "You don't
want 'Guys and Dolls' coming on before 'Death of a Sales-
man,' " apparently not realizing what his comment seemed
to say about Nixon. Also helping Agnew was the burst of
publicity he had received in the spring when he chewed
out moderate Negroes for tolerating militants. Strom Thurmond didn't have to open his mouth for people to know
that Agnew was "less offensive" to him than Volpe. It was
also suggested by loyal Republicans, groping for an explanation of the choice, that Agnew would have a strong
appeal in suburbia, the heartland of America in the 1960's.
Said one Nixon aide, "This guy is made for 1968. He's Joe
America. Follows the Colts. Drinks beer. Comes across
honest." He was right—but he had no idea just how bluntly
honest "Joe America" Agnew would turn out to be.

An interview that the Maryland governor gave to *The
New York Times* just after his nomination presented him
as a strong, middle-of-the-road American. The governor
identified himself with Negro and white moderates who con-
demn all violence and work for racial justice through tradi-

tional channels. He denied that personal pique had caused his shift from Rockefeller to Nixon, citing instead the riots after the assassination of Martin Luther King. He favored the Fortas nomination, he noted.

Most remarkably, the GOP vice-presidential nominee advocated a federal takeover of all welfare programs, something Nixon had not spoken on. On the other hand, Agnew said he opposed federal bloc grants to state and local governments as advocated in the Republican platform. He was also against federal programs that would guarantee income to the poor or jobs to the unemployed. He repeated his plan to establish satellite cities financed jointly by government and industry and designed to provide low-rent housing that would attract slum residents out of the core cities. He said that he favored greater communication with youth and a greater role for them in the responsibilities of society.

Nor was this the only time that Agnew spoke of positive solutions to the nation's problems. His endorsement of a uniform national-welfare system and the creation of satellite cities was repeated on several occasions. He vigorously urged a high level of business involvement in urban problems, especially in the employment of members of minority groups. "These people cannot simply be invited to come around for a job interview—they must be wooed, they must be actively recruited, often in their own neighborhoods," he said. And he disagreed with his running mate regarding an institution that became one of Nixon's favorite whipping boys: "I don't have as much of a quarrel with the Supreme Court."

Agnew's record as governor supported this moderate image. During his single term, Maryland had adopted a fair-employment practice code for state agencies and the first fair-housing law south of the Mason-Dixon line. Agnew had broadened the state's public accommodations law to include recreational facilities and taverns, and had pushed through a graduated state income tax and a tough antipollution law. He had initiated a reorganization of the executive branch and introduced professionalism into Maryland's governmental structure.

But Agnew's political life had been too short, his rise to governor of Maryland too easy to permit the development of the political sophistication necessary for a long fall campaign. He had come too far too fast, and he was not prepared, just six years after his entry into partisan politics, to face the relentless scrutiny of the national press corps and the television cameras.

Agnew had become governor of Maryland, after all, largely because the divided Democrats had nominated for the post a highly unacceptable maverick who had run on the backlash slogan "Your home is your castle." Four years earlier, in 1962, Agnew had run for Baltimore county executive and had won only because the Democrats were so badly divided. As a matter of fact, on the same night Richard Nixon was conceding his narrow defeat by John F. Kennedy for the Presidency in 1960, Spiro Agnew had also been conceding defeat. He had run that year for a local judicial post and had finished fifth in a field of five.

A central assumption of the Nixon battle plan was that "law and order" would prove the most salient issue in the campaign, and Agnew's physical presence, his direct manner of speech, and his springtime crackdown on racial disturbances seemed to make him an ideal participant in that strategy. He was directed to spend most of his time in the areas where Wallace threatened to be most successful, and there is evidence that in these places he may have added strength to the ticket.

Though Nixon had met Agnew only infrequently and briefly before he chose him as his running mate, he had formed his own clear impressions about the Maryland governor. "He's a proud man, a tough man," he had said in the spring, and these were words he repeated in defense of Agnew in the fall. "There can be a mystique about a man. You can look him in the eye and know he's got it. This guy has got it," Nixon had said when he introduced his running mate, and there were many who were disposed to take the statement as a literal description of the way in which Nixon had made the judgment.

This is not to say that the judgment was incorrect. For Agnew, whatever his other problems, never lost his proud bearing or his tough, candid manner. His whole image seemed to say, "This is the way I see it; let the chips fall where they may." It was in many ways a refreshing style, and it had an appeal to many who were also attracted by George Wallace's directness.

Agnew's problem, of course, was that the chips that fell when his ax swung were large ones. He was continually making points by simplification or exaggeration—and what he intended as hyperbole was often taken literally. (Barry Goldwater had the same problem in 1964.) In the Agnew rhetoric, Humphrey was Neville Chamberlain ("soft on inflation and soft on law and order"), whereas Nixon was Winston Churchill. His inexperience also led him to use words and phrases carelessly and without appreciating their potential consequences. How else could one account for his description of Humphrey as "squishy soft on communism"? When asked on nationwide television, "Isn't civil disobedience in the spirit of Jesus, Mahatma Gandhi, Dr. Martin Luther King and Henry Thoreau?" Agnew answered, "The people you mentioned did not operate in a free society." The resulting impression was that he was both shallow of background and slow of wit.

This is not the place to repeat the list of Agnew's verbal "bloopers." Suffice it to say that a new word, "Agnewism," was coined and was even picked up in European languages as the fall progressed. By the end of October, some newspapers were running collections of "Agnewisms," and it was not unusual for a radio newscast to start, "Spiro Agnew's done it again."

Nor were the bloopers something the frantic Nixon staff could control, though they tried desperately. In the first place, Agnew's pride—on which Nixon had so long remarked—was offended by the notion that tutors dispatched by the Nixon office should be telling him what to do. And he was doubly insulted when new teams kept replacing old ones in an effort to tighten the reins. He did submit to extensive coaching at the start of the campaign and used carefully prepared material in his formal addresses. But the comments that did the most damage were all informal, thrown out casually in press conferences or in conversations. To all this should be added the fact that the press corps was waiting to seize on the slightest slip and inflate it into prominence. The result was that the Agnew tour quickly got out of hand and became something of a sideshow.

Why all the concern for Agnew's slip-ups? Why did they become more important, say, than Eisenhower's complicated syntax or Johnson's Texas accent? In part, at least, because these verbal blunders became positive tokens of what was essentially a negative condition. The basic problem was simply this: Agnew bore no pre-eminent qualifications for the office for which he campaigned. He had no public following; indeed, the public resented what Senator Hugh Scott agreed was a somewhat "cynical" effort to foist a complete unknown on them. Surely, they would give him a chance to prove himself in their eyes. But when he showed no important indications of unusual competence, the public was all too ready to seize on *any* indication, however trivial, of his inadequacy.

The Democrats chose their vice-presidential candidate with greater ease than the GOP. There were no all-night meetings, and, in a convention spoiling for a fight, there was very little protest against the final choice. Humphrey's decision was made a great deal easier, of course, by Senator McCarthy's distaste for any kind of compromise and by the unavailability of Senators Edward Kennedy and George McGovern. Everyone knew that the defeated liberals had spurned the nominee's olive branch, and no one could charge that Humphrey had failed to consider their interests. The result was that Humphrey's choice was almost entirely his own with little outside pressure. The possible candidates in the final analysis were Governor Richard J. Hughes of New Jersey, Senator Fred R. Harris of Oklahoma, and Senator Edmund S. Muskie of Maine. This time the nod went to the relatively obscure northeastern senator. "I guess Humphrey picked me because I'm so average," said Muskie, mirroring Agnew's response to his own vice-presidential candidacy.

Despite his relative obscurity, Muskie brought some noticeable strengths to the ticket. He was the first national nominee of Polish-Catholic extraction, a qualification that would help neutralize the Wallace appeal among lower-middle-class ethnic groups that accounted for so much of the "white backlash" phenomenon. Muskie had also demonstrated his talents under fire in the Senate for many years and had strong credentials among insiders. Moreover, he augured to balance the rather volatile Humphrey style of campaigning with a cooler and quieter approach on the stump.

There was no a priori reason why Muskie's edge over Agnew should have become so important in the campaign.

His record was good, but not exceptionally exciting. It was not that of a crusader, but rather of one who had co-operated with the party establishment and rarely rocked the boat. In many ways, his selection reflected the "old politics" way of doing things—balancing the ticket and avoiding offending large blocs of voters.

Perhaps the major distinction between the selection of Muskie and that of Agnew was the personal relationship between the two halves of each ticket. Nixon had only met Agnew the previous spring, and during the subsequent months of traveling in pursuit of the GOP nomination, Nixon had little opportunity to assess the qualifications of the Maryland governor. In contrast, Humphrey and Muskie had long been colleagues in the Senate and seemed to have developed a rapport. During the traumatic hours following the deaths of both Dr. Martin Luther King and Robert F. Kennedy, Humphrey had sought the quiet support of his old friend. Whatever the actual rationale for either decision, certainly Humphrey had a firmer basis for a human assessment.

And as September wore on, the presence of Edmund Muskie was slowly felt. More than anything, perhaps, the secret was in his almost painfully unemotional manner and his repeated insistence that men reason together with a sense of their own fallibility. Amid the turbulence of 1968, it struck a note that was even more refreshing than Agnew's tough candor. Day by day, more Americans turned away from the evening news summaries saying, "You know, this Muskie fellow seems like a decent guy."

More than any other man in the 1968 sweepstakes, Muskie demonstrated a quiet confidence in the American people and in his own ability to contribute to their progress. He appealed not only to those who advocated the "new politics," but to those who longed for a quiet "return to normalcy." Columnist David Broder, widely experienced and usually skeptical, said of one Muskie speech that he would "swap" it "for all the other political speeches I have heard this year." In it Muskie stated:

> Without understanding, how do we make a free society work? It isn't an easy thing to do—to understand another human being, perhaps someone 3000 miles away, perhaps someone of another color. Today Americans are deeply suspicious of other Americans, deeply distrustful of each other. But somehow, we must learn to take risks on one another . . . At the risk of sounding like a preacher, the single most important word is trust.

The senator from Maine didn't need a slogan saying "Trust Muskie"; it happened naturally. "Trust" became the watchword of the Muskie campaign, much as "tough" was the watchword of Agnew's. Both struck sensitive nerves in the electorate, but those who responded to Muskie outnumbered those who warmed to Agnew. In the Louis Harris poll taken among 1899 voters during the period from October 8 to 10, the Democratic vice-presidential candidate was preferred over the Republican by 41 to 24 percent. In the South, the locale for which Agnew's appeal was groomed, Muskie led 27 to 21 percent, with LeMay taking 28 percent of respondents. There was absolutely no demographic group listed by Harris (the breakdown included education, age, and size of home town) with whom Agnew rated above Muskie; even suburbia rejected the Maryland governor. And even among Wallace voters, whose conversion was such a high-priority item for the Republican ticket, Muskie received slightly more first-place votes than Agnew—though here General LeMay, of course, ran far ahead of both of them.

It will never be possible to describe exactly how much

the candidacy of Spiro T. Agnew hurt the Republican ticket
in 1968. But the evidence seems clear that it did considerable damage to GOP drawing power. "I had firmly determined to vote for Nixon," said one active Republican after
the election, "but Agnew's name just jumped off the ballot
at me." Nor was the Maryland governor's impact limited
to last-minute switches. From September on, his name was
indeed a household word, far more familiar than Nixon had
expected—or desired. The Democrats—and the press—
quickly concluded Agnew was the weakest link in the GOP
chain. It was a judgment that may in the end have saved
Nixon by sparing him the brunt of attacks from the opposition. At any rate, it was here that the Humphrey organization concentrated its fire. Television spots showed
only Agnew's face accompanied by sound-track laughter.
"Spiro who?" appeared on buttons and bumper stickers.
Newspaper advertisements asked simply, "Can you imagine
a President Agnew?"

Often the critics went too far. When, for example,
George Ball resigned his U.N. ambassadorship to work for
Humphrey's election, he described Agnew as "a fourth-rate
hack politician." This prompted Mary McGrory to write,
"That's unfair to fourth-rate hack politicians." One winces
at such extremes, even as columnist Joseph Kraft winced
when *The New York Times* tried to blow up once again a
tired and petty scandal charge involving Agnew's financial
holdings in Maryland. Agnew's qualifications for the second
highest office in the land had been previously so thoroughly
discredited, Kraft observed, that the *Times'* awkward vendetta seemed rather like "criticizing Mussolini for being fat."

The most interesting and effective "anti-Agnew" columns
and advertisements had an additional refinement that is also
worthy of comment. Recognizing that the top of the ticket
wins or loses the vote, they did not merely ask voters to

reject Agnew. Rather they cited Agnew as a reason for rejecting the man who had picked him. Agnew's selection, they claimed, was a reflection on Nixon's judgment, wisdom, and much-discussed "coolness under fire." "Nixon's first appointment," read some advertisements, and that point was perhaps the most telling. "It just shows what happens when you keep Dick up all night and then ask him to make an important decision," said one associate of the candidate.

Certainly Nixon could not have predicted the extent of Agnew's coming blunders, nor were the blunders a definite indication of Agnew's competence. But at the very least, the nomination must be viewed as reflecting a somewhat casual attitude toward the second spot on the ticket. Whatever else could be said for Agnew, there were few who could claim at the time of his selection that he adequately filled the criterion supposedly foremost in Nixon's mind, the capacity to be President. And the point was particularly evident to the voters in view of the long series of statements in which Nixon had listed the qualifications he would employ in selecting his running mate—the man would have to be a good campaigner, experienced in urban problems, and *above all* fit for the nation's highest office. He repeated the criterion even as he made the thunderbolt announcement at the Hilton Hotel on August 8. And he dwelt on it later in the campaign, frequently repeating his litany about choosing a man with the best credentials to succeed him.

> I know Ted Agnew well . . . He has real depth . . . tremendous brain power, great courage and an unprejudiced legal mind. He has vigor and imagination . . . He is the man who can best work with me . . . He has attributes of a statesman of the first rank.

Nixon loyally stuck to his guns even when Agnew must have been ready to abandon the fiction. It was a loyalty that grew out of Nixon's own experience as a much criticized running mate for General Eisenhower, and a loyalty which Agnew would gratefully return to the newly elected President.

Interestingly enough, it was Nixon's personality—not Agnew's—that became the center of controversy late in the campaign during the mini-battle with *The New York Times.* The *Times* charges had done little damage to his running mate until they were raised on "Face the Nation" (the first such televised press interview for Nixon in over two years). They would probably have been passed over there as well had not the much feared Nixon temper chosen that moment to surface. In an angry counterattack, he announced a probable lawsuit against the newspaper, accused the *Times* of practicing the lowest form of gutter journalism, yet failed in his emotion to deny the charges in any detail. Important and admirable as it was for him to rally to his running mate's defense, the performance raised the specter of the "Old Nixon" in the minds of thousands who couldn't have cared less about the specific question that he had been asked. The upshot of the episode was that newspapers across the nation ran the previously obscure *Times* editorial as a news item and noted the lack of an effective rebuttal. In the final analysis, Agnew's vulnerability as a candidate may have been most significant as a reflection on Nixon.

Ironically, Nixon himself was the first modern, visible Vice-President. The public's recognition of the responsibilities of the office, coupled with the technological development of the national news media, meant that Agnew could no longer be as unimportant to the ticket's popularity as John Nance Garner had been to Franklin D. Roosevelt in 1932 and 1936. Since Garner, the public expectation had changed. F.D.R.'s death, Eisenhower's illness, and particularly the murder of John F. Kennedy had brought home the importance of the Vice-Presidency. And if recent reminders were needed, the assassinations of Martin Luther King and Robert Kennedy had illustrated again the perilous tightrope walked by America's political and social leaders. The fact that Nixon, Humphrey, and President Johnson had all served in the post gave it added luster. It was extremely important to many voters in 1968 that their new Vice-President have independent prestige and a capacity for inspiring confidence. It was also important that he at least appear to have been chosen with care and deliberation. Somehow all this had been obscured in the Miami Beach discussions during the night of August 7 and the morning of August 8.

The fact that Agnew might prove himself in office—as many believe he did in the first few months—was not persuasive to voters who felt that potential Vice-Presidents should be proven quantities before nomination. Given that feeling, there was little Agnew could do to avoid a fiery baptism.

Chapter 3. The Failures of Republican Moderates

We go back now to before the Nixon presidential campaign, and before the Miami convention that confirmed the vice-presidential candidacy of Spiro Agnew. Despite all the talk in recent years about the power of the "Eastern Establishment" in the Republican Party, GOP moderates have not been able to produce a sense of common cause or a united crusade on the national level since the days of Thomas Dewey. Not since General Eisenhower won the presidential nomination in 1952 have Republican progressives participated successfully in those intraparty maneuverings that culminate in the quadrennial nominating convention. More and more, the nominations of Willkie, Dewey, and Eisenhower appear as brief progressive interludes between periods of conservative Republican dominance.

The reasons for these recent failures of GOP moderates were many and have been much analyzed. Perhaps most important was the moderates' inability to use to better advantage those eight years when they actually held the Presidency. By and large, the 1950's saw the GOP's progressive wing turn so fully from intraparty affairs to the work of government that it lost control of the party machinery. During Eisenhower's second term much of that machinery fell into conservative hands. Only impassioned appeals for party loyalty stilled an incipient conservative revolt against Richard Nixon in 1960 (a lesson not lost on the former Vice-President eight years later). By 1964, the "right" was in full control of the nominating machinery, and their power extended as well to other Republican institutions. The so-called "syndicate" of old friends still ran the Young Republicans—and used that organization as a central network in the Goldwater drive. The women's auxiliary was also proudly conservative. That same old guard dominated the GOP leadership in both houses of Congress, and conservatives worked their will on the national committee. And to all of this, the dedicated conservatives added a pervasive network of educational organizations: magazines, newspapers, radio stations, book clubs, study groups—all working day in and day out to propagate the simplistic and appealing doctrines that produced their enthusiasm and sense of commitment.

Meanwhile, the progressives often could still win local and statewide elections, most significantly at the gubernatorial level. But such victories did not confer on them automatic control of the party apparatus; their conquests were usually personal ones gained independently of (and sometimes in spite of) the official party structure. Above all else, GOP moderates lacked the ideological zeal and cohesion that characterized the right. The moderates were simply too moderate to make the intellectual and emotional commitments necessary for success over the long haul. Their specialty was a cool, technocratic approach to government; they had little taste or relish for the nastier, grubbier side of politics. As a result, their triumphs were triumphs of glamorous personalities or glittering records of public service. Voters gave their support again and again to individual progressive Republicans. But they did not for the most part consider themselves as converts to an ongoing political affiliation or philosophical creed.

In the early and mid-1960's, the Republican Governors' Association increasingly became the focus of progressive

Republican ambitions. Organized primarily by Idaho's Governor Robert Smylie in 1962, the RGA brought together an impressive group of innovative administrators who excelled in handling the intricacies of modern government. Its stars were such men as Romney, Scranton, Hatfield, Volpe, Chafee, Rhodes, Love, two Andersons, Rockefeller. (It should be noted, though, that Rockefeller's staff provided the major impetus behind the RGA's work.) Meanwhile, such senators as Case, Javits, Scott, Aiken, Smith, Cooper, and Kuchel also demonstrated the moderate Republican potential. During the four years that followed the traumatic Cow Palace convention, the moderate wing added more names to its personality parade. At the gubernatorial level, Shafer, Evans, Cargo, McCall, Knowles, Levander, Agnew, and another Rockefeller, Winthrop of Arkansas, were added. In 1965, John Lindsay became mayor of New York, and in 1966 a bright crop of freshman senators went to Washington —Brooke, Baker, Griffin, Hatfield, Percy. But on the precinct and county level, the strength of the moderates did not grow appreciably after 1964. Nor had the progressives yet developed a greater sense of mutual confidence and common goals. Their ability to exchange information and to consult on strategy was still limited. There were some good cards in the hand the Republican moderates held at the beginning of the political year 1968, but there were some weaknesses as well. And then, to compound their difficulties, the moderates began by playing their hand poorly.

GOP progressives entered the preliminary stages of the 1968 presidential sweepstakes with a wealth of potential leaders. Throughout 1967, they floated a number of trial balloons. Senator Charles Percy's name was frequently mentioned at GOP gatherings during the spring and summer of that year; Duff Reed, Senator Thruston Morton's roving aide

with carte blanche, was one who pushed the Illinois freshman. Others talked of Senator Mark Hatfield. There were
rumors that New York's Mayor John Lindsay might be
urged into running. A boomlet for retired General James
Gavin surfaced during the summer and then faded after
the general proved unwilling even to change his registration
to the Republican line. Later, just before the filing date for
the Wisconsin primary, some were arguing for Senator
Morton to enter the race and keep progressive options open.
But none of these possibilities was considered seriously—the
potential strength of these and other men was never put to
any test.

Although there was a general belief in 1967 that Lyndon
Johnson was unbeatable, a more immediate obstacle was
present. The constellation of primary states has an inherent
bias, for in New Hampshire, Wisconsin, Nebraska, and
Oregon, the voters, particularly in the GOP, have a chiefly
white-Protestant, nonurban orientation. By holding primaries in such states, the Democrats are forced to look for
candidates with appeal outside their established political
base; these same states merely reinforce GOP insularity. To
progressive Republicans, whose key to success is an ability
to win the support of independents and swing Democrats,
the primary route is fraught with special dangers. One man,
however, did seem to have the small-town style that would
appeal to GOP voters in the primary states, and he combined the style with a proven record as a campaigner and
administrator in a major industrial state—George Wilkens
Romney.

Speculation on presidential contestants usually begins
with the congressional and statewide elections that come
two years before the actual election. In 1966, a number of
progressive Republicans won victories, and among these
were the significant reelection triumphs of two big-state

governors, New York's Nelson Rockefeller and Michigan's George Romney. Before the 1966 elections, when there was already talk that Romney would make a good presidential candidate, Melvin Laird had—rather gratuitously—stated that Romney would have to win big in Michigan and demonstrate his coat tails at the senatorial and congressional level to qualify as a presidential contender. Romney met these requirements easily, adding five new Republicans to Michigan's congressional delegation and ensuring the election of Senator Robert P. Griffin, whom he had previously appointed to fill an unexpired term. With that triumph behind him, Romney viewed himself as a presidential candidate, and with the intense sense of devotion that so characterizes the former Michigan governor, he began almost immediately to pursue his new goal.

In 1966, too, Nelson Rockefeller won a third term, despite the fact that his low rating in New York only a year earlier had brought widespread demands that he step aside. But two years of good political homework throughout the state, a superb advertising campaign, and a weak opponent made Rockefeller the senior governor in the nation and a presidential possibility whether he liked it or not. The New York governor held a unique position in the Republican Party that prevented him from merely retreating into the background.

On the national level, the moderate wing of the Republican Party had been for the last eight years under Rockefeller's guardianship. In good times and bad, the moderates had looked to "Rocky" for national direction; on those occasions when he failed to provide it, they were left with no option but to retreat from national politics and concentrate instead on state and local challenges. On those occasions when he vacillated over whether or not to accept a leadership role, other moderates who might have carried the torch found themselves waiting to react to his lead. When he did lead actively, he often led very well, but his "troops" were too dependent on him to act significantly on their own. For a full decade, Republican progressives had relied almost entirely on Rockefeller to do their fighting for them in the national arena. He was the only one with the staff or the heart to play the national game.

Because Rockefeller was the unofficial leader of the moderate wing, if any moderate wished to assert national leadership he had to do it with at least the tacit approval of the New York governor. Now, in 1967, Rockefeller—certain that an open run by him for the nomination would be hopeless—supported, completely, the presidential ambitions of his gubernatorial colleague, George Romney. That blessing had two implications: (1) It made it impossible for other candidates to get going; (2) It made Romney appear to be a Rockefeller stalking horse. Indeed, Rockefeller's power was such that his affectionate embrace turned into a crushing bear hug that probably hurt the Romney candidacy as much as it helped it.

When Romney moved out front with Rockefeller's support, there was no other power center from which alternative moderate candidates could emerge. The money and moral support, the publicity, and later the criticism were all focused on one target, Romney. Indeed, the Rockefeller endorsement was accompanied by a strong Rockefeller discouragement for other potential entrants. One Republican activist referred to the arrangement as "Nelson Rockefeller's nonproliferation treaty."

One of the reasons for this decision to put all the moderate Republican eggs in one basket in 1968 was what moderates took as the lesson of 1964. Then, they were convinced, they had divided their early strength among too many candidates. This time they would go with only one. But this conclusion, it can be argued, resulted from a misreading of the 1964 experience, and consequently it duplicated the 1964 mistake rather than benefiting from it. For in 1964, the front runner, Nelson Rockefeller, had also been agreed on *too early*. In both years, the leader at the start had proved wanting in the long pull, and the precious primary months were used to scramble for new candidates rather than to test a well-identified field and narrow it to the strongest survivor. It was Nelson Rockefeller's nonproliferation treaty, as much as anything, that left the progressive wing without a candidate when Romney withdrew from the race before the New Hampshire primary.

Why, having been handed the single basket in which all of the progressives carefully placed their political eggs, did Romney fail? Of all the moderates, it had been argued, his direct and fervent style was the most likely to appeal to the small-town voters in such states as New Hampshire, Wisconsin, Indiana, Nebraska, and Oregon. Romney's record was splendid, his personality ideal, his commitment total. There was some question about his feel for foreign policy, but he quickly built up extraordinary staff support in this area. Why, then, did everything go so completely wrong?

The answer to that question would be worth exploring at greater length than this analysis can provide. Certainly the reasons are more complex than Romney's suggestion that he had been "brainwashed" by the Johnson Administration on the Vietnam issue. They stem from the fact that Romney got too far ahead too soon—that he became, therefore, the sole focus of public attention and of barbed questions from a press corps made uncomfortable by his personal and intellectual style. This stylistic clash was well demonstrated in October 1967, when Romney and Governor Ronald Reagan of California both held press conferences aboard the *Independence* en route to the governors' conference in the Virgin Islands. The Michigan governor faced a tough and even bitter grilling whereas his California colleague merely exchanged jokes and genial pleasantries with the reporters. After attending Reagan's conference, Romney's loyal helpmate Lenore asked several members of the journalistic fraternity, "Why weren't you as tough on him as you were on George?" They knew she had a point and some admitted it. Later, David Broder of *The Washington Post* put it this way:

> I often thought, for example, as I saw Romney during his presidential campaign, surrounded by our circle—men a generation younger than he, many of us with cigarettes in our mouths, drinks in our hands, and cynicism in our hearts—that he must have felt as helpless with us as I would feel if my fate or future as a journalist were being decided by a committee of Romney's colleagues among the elders of the Mormon church.

Though the press often places a premium on style, this was by no means the entire Romney story. Romney also failed because many Republican moderates were not persuaded of his presidential capacities, particularly in foreign affairs. Some such as the progressive former Kansas Congressman Robert Ellsworth were so convinced of this that they went over to Nixon very early in the game. Others, who gave Romney a longer hearing, found that press-conference confusion and such remarks as that about "brainwashing" confirmed their worst suspicions. Romney's own embargo on all foreign-policy talk looked defensive, whereas the same tactic employed by the more experienced Nixon looked prudent and wise.

In part, too, it must be said, Romney collapsed because

he could not build alone and overnight the sense of crusade and the grass-roots organization that GOP moderates had lacked since the days of Thomas Dewey and Herbert Brownell.

Finally, Romney failed because his candidacy was untenable as long as the power of Nelson Rockefeller was so great. Rocky had been too important to progressive Republicans for too long a time to be dismissed now. He had carried the burden quite exclusively, and he could not suddenly withdraw and be forgotten. Behind the substance of Romney, there lurked always the shadow of Rockefeller, and neither man could do much about it.

It must be said too that there were moments when a glint in the Rockefeller eye contributed to the impression that in the end he would eventually be a candidate. Romney in his sensitivity, and the press in its wishful thinking, may have overestimated their importance. But when Rockefeller said in January 1968 that he would accept the nomination "under certain circumstances"—a change from the verbal formula he had earlier used—both the Michigan governor and the journalists interpreted the remark as a clear sign that the rug would eventually be pulled out from under the Romney candidacy. The news stories in turn triggered a further reaction with the public, and the bottom dropped out of Romney's already anemic polls.

Romney had begun to fade in the late summer and fall of 1967, and the more Rockefeller tried to prop him up, the more visible the New Yorker became. Some reports said that Romney's campaign received several hundred thousand dollars from his benefactor's family. When Rockefeller also took to the stump in his colleague's behalf, tongues wagged more furiously still. Yet if Rockefeller had failed to speak out (and his advisers made this clear to him), he would undoubtedly have been charged with forsaking his candidate to the wolves. There was no clear "right way" for Rockefeller to play it.

With the fall of his poll ratings, Romney tried to use the Vietnam issue to draw a distinction with Nixon, but his credibility had been too badly undermined. Even his announcement in Hartford, Connecticut, of an unusually perceptive and well-balanced Vietnam program could not reverse the sentiment. Nor could the Tet offensive, which so helped Eugene McCarthy in his race against Lyndon Johnson.

From the start, Romney's strategy had been to emphasize his electability. Like Rockefeller many months afterward, he decided that, above all else, the party wanted a winner in 1968. He was deeply concerned by the direction in which the country was heading, but he recognized that his campaign slogan would have to ignore the issues that divided him from many conservatives and stress instead the all-consuming goal that united the party. And so the bumper stickers and letterheads and buttons emerged carrying the words, "Winning is the name of the game."

If the progressives placed all their eggs in Romney's basket, Romney in turn had placed all of his in the basket marked "opinion polls." This essentially defensive strategy backfired when the polls collapsed beneath him. By late February 1968, Romney's own private surveys in New Hampshire showed that he would win only 19 percent of the vote to 73 percent for Richard Nixon. The Michigan governor knew it was all over. He pulled out of the race on February 28. The Republican governors were convening the next weekend and could presumably move to fill the gap. It was, of course, too late for anyone to challenge Nixon in the nation's first primary, only thirteen days away. On March 12, Nixon won 79 percent of the Republican vote in New Hampshire. Rockefeller placed second with 11 percent—all on write-ins. Richard Nixon had won his first election since the California gubernatorial primary in 1962.

In retrospect, the most dramatic failure of the GOP left in 1968 was that it never properly played its trump card—its telling ability to win elections. Certainly the Republican-only primary contests were not the best game in which to play that card; the strength of the GOP progressives lay in their appeal to independents and swing Democrats. Still, Richard Nixon had not won an election on his own in eighteen years, and whatever his hopes, the stigma he carried had to be reversed in the primary contests; he himself admitted that if he did not win in the primaries he would be out of the race. Nixon appeared willing to put his money on the line, and though the bet was not so risky as it might have been, it was a sufficiently dangerous course to convince many Republicans that if Nixon could survive intact he would deserve the nomination. The focus of the delegates' attention, then, became the primaries rather than the opinion polls, a forum that would still seem to have given the progressive forces a decent chance of upsetting the Nixon bandwagon. It was this chance which was forfeited completely by the "oh-so moderate" Republicans. But they blew their chances sky high. Nixon, expecting the fight of his life, at least in New Hampshire, Wisconsin, and Oregon, escaped without a single scratch or bruise. "He didn't even have to work up a sweat," said one progressive observer. "He saved money, energy, commitments, exposure, everything. We just handed it all right to him."

Throughout the primary months, Republican progressive forces mounted not a single sustained, respectable campaign. The "miracle" of Eugene McCarthy was never matched in the GOP, though one would think in a party out of power containing so many bright young liberals, the potential for a McCarthyesque "happening" should have been great. Even the lesser miracle—that some viable representative of the progressive wing would emerge from the primaries with some significant chance of nomination—proved impossible. Admittedly, the primaries presented some large obstacles, but they also presented significant opportunities. And no one even tried.

After his withdrawal, Romney expected Rockefeller to enter in his stead, as did most Romney supporters. After all, it had been the New Yorker's apparent willingness to consider the race that had sealed Romney's doom. But having helped to keep everyone else out of the contest, Rockefeller now refused to enter it himself. He refused to retract his affidavit of noncandidacy in Wisconsin, and on April 2 Nixon polled 81 percent of the Republican primary voters there (with perhaps one quarter of the state's GOP, almost all of them potential Rockefeller backers, crossing over to the Democratic ballot and voting for Senator McCarthy). Nixon had cleared the second primary hurdle with ease.

But there still remained Oregon—and there a progressive Republican would have a chance of winning if he campaigned actively. Rockefeller had done so in 1964 and he still maintained a strong Western following. Oregon Governor Tom McCall was solidly in his corner. Moreover, Ronald Reagan's name would be on the Oregon ballot and that would help split the conservative support. With Robert Kennedy now coming on strong, Republican loyalists were more desperate than ever to nominate a sure winner, for very few of them could believe that the Republicans would win in a Nixon-Kennedy race.

Late as it was, then, Rocky was still viable. Then came March 21; Rockefeller—after intensive discussions with his staff and GOP leaders—met with the press and announced he was not a candidate.

There seems no doubt that, in the meetings in Albany and New York City that preceded the March 21 press conference, Rockefeller was seeking the presidential nomination. The questions were, "Can I win it?" and "What strategy should I follow?"

George Romney's withdrawal had been entirely unexpected, and Rockefeller and his staff were not prepared for the spotlight to focus on them so quickly. Faced immediately by the primaries in Nebraska and Oregon, there were those in the Rockefeller circle who saw them not as an opportunity but as a stumbling block. Nebraska was a Nixon stronghold, of course (on November 5, the state would give him the highest percentage in the nation). And according to state laws, Rocky could not stay out of Nebraska unless he also stayed out of Oregon.

Even in Oregon, there were heavy risks. In 1964, Rockefeller's victory there came only after a dramatic and expensive campaign. Barry Goldwater had done so poorly in the early opinion polls in Oregon that he made a decision to concentrate on California and minimize the psychological effect of an Oregon loss. Goldwater's absence allowed Rockefeller to use the slogan, "He cared enough to come," and the New York governor was able to fight the contest on nonideological grounds. Even then, Henry Cabot Lodge —who had won an upset, absentee, write-in victory in the New Hampshire primary—led in the early polls. Rockefeller finally had to argue that he should be backed because Lodge was not on the California primary ballot; if Rockefeller was not able to win in both Oregon and California, Goldwater would easily win the GOP nomination. After a hard drive in the closing week of the campaign, Rockefeller (33 percent) did edge out the Saigon ambassador (29 percent), and, yes, Richard Nixon (16.8 percent), who with no public effort did about as well in Oregon in 1964 as did Senator Goldwater (17.6 percent).

In 1968 a group of well-known and respected Republicans had spent months of hard work organizing and collecting signatures to prove Rockefeller's popularity in Oregon.

They had been highly successful in their efforts and had presented the New York governor not only with a long list of signatures but also with an offer to help him in the state primary. It was a unique opportunity; a man who had no national organization, let alone a state organization outside of New York, was being handed the services of a working, proven, local group in the only remaining primary state in which he had a possibility of winning. (Thomas E. Dewey won only one major primary in 1948; that was in Oregon where he trounced front runner and earlier primary-winner Harold Stassen and then went on to win the nomination.) But the Oregon group could only promise a 50 to 50 chance of victory, and that only if, in mid-March, Rockefeller energetically entered the race. At this same time, Nixon was intentionally poor-mouthing his primary prospects in a calculated effort to increase the persuasive impact of a Nixon victory on suspicious party pros. Independent polls in Oregon, however, showed throughout the spring that Nixon was leading or tied for the lead.

Altogether, the Oregon primary placed Rockefeller in a difficult bind. If he entered and lost he was finished. If he entered and won he might violate the dictum of Republican unity and revive the old animosities of the GOP right, whose organizational strength gave it veto power over the presidential nominees.

A second major consideration was the degree of open support available from his fellow governors and other party leaders.

In mid-March four governors (Chafee, Agnew, Shafer, and McCall) had openly indicated that they favored his nomination, and all had promised assistance. Many senators and congressmen had urged him to run, including Senator Morton, a former national chairman who had impeccable credentials as a Republican regular. The House and Senate Class of 1966 contained many potential supporters, and many others who were willing to remain neutral despite Nixon pressures at home.

Given the fact that he had remained aloof from Republican circles for so many years, Rockefeller's position was not altogether depressing. For the better part of the last four years, after all, Rockefeller had withdrawn from intraparty activity. Ignoring most non-New York Republicans, he had consistently refused to travel the banquet circuit, to help in raising money or in winning votes. He made few trips out of the state for any purpose, and even within New York he spoke mainly about state problems and only rarely issued statements on national and international matters. He publicly ignored the Vietnam war for almost three years (in fact, it was only six weeks after he became a presidential candidate that Rockefeller commented on the war in any detail).

In short, Rockefeller, first struggling for his political life within New York State and later putting all of his chips on his colleague from Michigan, had done very little to keep his presidential options open. The tedious but important work of cultivating political friendships, performed so assiduously during his 1964 campaign, was ignored. The network of allies around the country fell into decay. When Rockefeller decided to seek the Presidency one more time, it was almost in spite of the fact that he had been the second most popular candidate in both 1960 and 1964. Convention delegates naturally put a heavy emphasis on partisan service. The contrast between Nixon's and Rockefeller's rapport with local party leadership was a significant factor in the New York governor's inability to later pull delegates away from the 1960 nominee—not so much because Nixon had collected a series of binding political IOU's, but simply because Nixon was accepted as a loyal and familiar Republican who "deserved" the nomination. It is true, of course, that personal attention to the cold-chicken dinner circuit was not necessary for Eisenhower to win the nomination in 1952. But it should be recalled that it was the Dewey party machine that obtained the nomination for Eisenhower that year, a machine that had been kept well-tooled and well-greased since 1948.

Still, the New York governor demanded active and open support from most of his fellow moderates in the Republican Governors' Association as a prerequisite for an open candidacy. But now the old plague of the moderates returned with a vengeance. With their political base founded almost solely on personal popularity with the voting masses (Democrats and independents as well as Republicans) rather than on the ideological commitments of GOP regulars, many governors—particularly in the West where the absence of a traditional party machinery eliminates the possibility of coopting party control—found that home state politics precluded quick endorsements. As a result, these potential Rockefellerites were cautious and that made Rockefeller—twice burned in earlier quadrenniums—cautious as well.

The final blow may have come at the breakfast with GOP senators which was hosted by Thruston Morton two days before the withdrawal announcement. One senator argued that he should get into the race not because he would win but because he would bring more publicity to the GOP, which had been overshadowed by the excitement of Kennedy and McCarthy on the Democratic side. The appeal to altruism brought an icy response from the philanthropist governor; he had carried the burden with little help in 1960 and 1964 and still remembered the cuts and the bruises he and his family had suffered. He was not going to be put through all that again without some indication of widespread support —and certainly not if the purpose of the whole exercise was merely to set him up as a party cheerleader.

What he may not have sufficiently appreciated during this

time of decision was that the most valuable political support often comes in negative form, that is, when clever politicians withhold their public support from *any* announced candidate. Many governors said "No" to Rockefeller, and that disappointed him, but what he may have overlooked was that they were also saying "No" to Nixon. After Rockefeller's withdrawal, an aide to Morton summed up the situation this way:

> The simple thing is Rockefeller refused to believe the truth, the truth being that the breadth and depth of the support for him in the Republican Party across the country was very substantial and growing.

But Rockefeller felt he had no obligation to bail the moderates out again—and certainly not if they didn't want him. "Make 'em come and ask you to run," was the way one Rockefeller adviser put it. And it was this view, despite vigorous staff disagreements, that prevailed in mid-March.

There was another factor in the decision. Although the press and many Republicans refused to believe that Ronald Reagan was a serious candidate, Rockefeller's staff perceived him as such, and the Californian's strength entered their calculations. They expected a Reagan candidacy to be in full bloom by the time of the Miami Beach Convention, and assumed the California governor would drain away key support from Nixon in the South. Thus, Rockefeller need not stop Nixon alone; Reagan would help. And if Nixon proved strong enough to get the nomination without a large bloc of Southern votes, nothing Rockefeller could do would deny him the nomination. Of course, during the debate in March no one could predict, or even speculate, that Strom Thurmond's ultimate loyalty would be with Richard Nixon, not Ronald Reagan, nor that Nixon's homework in the South would produce such dividends.

So it was that Nelson Rockefeller elected not to enter the Oregon primary, and because all presidential candidates are automatically on the Oregon ballot, that meant declaring that he was *not* a candidate. The decision, however, did not preclude his becoming a candidate later. Some Rockefeller advisers say that they merely saw Oregon as too risky a step to take on short notice and that they recommended, therefore, that the political cauldron be allowed to bubble for a couple of months while moderate support for a Rockefeller candidacy slowly surfaced. They claim now that the governor always thought it highly probable that he would jump into the race later. This indeed was the very course suggested by Ohio's Governor James Rhodes, who had tried to broker a Rockefeller-Reagan ticket as early as the December 1967 governors' meeting.

Whatever the intentions of Rockefeller and his staff, the declaration of noncandidacy on March 21 was irremediably abrupt. The failure to give advance notice to key promoters (the only governors contacted before the announcement were Rhodes and Nelson's brother Winthrop) let his associates down with such a thud that some, such as Spiro Agnew, never rejoined him. And the suddenness of the announcement was only one problem. The other was that Rockefeller let it appear—as he had in 1960—that he was out of the race unconditionally and for good. He sent out 398 telegrams to backers across the country asking them to "cease and desist" from further advancing his presidential candidacy. Many, such as Massachusetts Congressman F. Bradford Morse, read this statement as a final withdrawal and moved quickly to Nixon. It was hard for those who still hoped for a Rocky revival to argue with that telegram or fault the logic of the many who now gave up on the New York governor.

It is true that Rockefeller made it clear at his press conference that he would accept a convention draft. However, in his effort to avoid the Oregon primary, his actions over-stepped the bounds of what could be considered either politically prudent or legally essential. Whatever his sup-porters would later decide about the meaning of March 21, it would seem that Nelson Rockefeller had turned his back on the Presidency on that day and that his efforts to turn around later on were made far more difficult by the public and the party reaction to that message.

Now again, as in June 1964, GOP moderates found them-selves without a candidate. This time not even a Bill Scran-ton could emerge from the wings to make an idealistic if quixotic plunge into the competition And rather than trying to cook up some new hurried and hopeless candidacy, many moderates now sensibly resolved that this time they would go with the winner in order to help determine the direction of the party platform and the fall campaign. This time they would not be left behind. Their decision was made easier by the fact that the only alternative to Richard Nixon was Ronald Reagan and that his support seemed to be growing in the South and West. Although they might have preferred a more liberal candidate than Nixon, most moderates still respected the former Vice-President and suddenly saw that even he might be able to defeat the divided Democrats. They moved to Nixon not so much because he excited them, but rather because he increasingly appeared a likely nominee and a possible November winner. In sum, by the time Rocke-feller was ready to announce his candidacy, on April 30— a decision that may have been partly motivated by the assassination of Martin Luther King and the rioting that followed it—he had created an impression of indecisiveness and had lost further valuable time and still more valuable grassroots support.

Rockefeller's low write-in total in Oregon on April 28 was in fact widely interpreted as a decisive defeat. Nixon's 73 percent victory in the face of the active Reagan promotion and a major write-in campaign, seemed to wind things up for Rockefeller. For once and all, Nixon had cast off his loser image. He had run the primary gauntlet and had escaped untouched.

Rockefeller's reentry into the presidential sweepstakes on April 30 was accompanied by a stunning, unsolicited write-in victory over Nixon supporter John Volpe, who ran as a favorite son in the Massachusetts primary. Emmet John Hughes, Rockefeller brain truster, manager, and jack-of-all-trades, confessed on hearing the news that he didn't even know there was a primary that day. It was symptomatic of the Rockefeller campaign, perhaps, that some of the best things that happened to it were a product of the governor's high reputation and long record of service, not the result of organizational acumen. At any rate, Rocky was off and running, but he had a long, long way to go.

Still, three months remained until the convention—and the opportunity to win delegates was there. The New York governor now launched a massive campaign toward that end, one that was probably more successful than most would have predicted, but one hobbled by certain inherent liabilities, not the least of which was the absence of a "tight-ship" operation and the kind of tough, centralized decision-making that had characterized Rocky's 1966 reelection effort.

In his appeal to GOP regulars, Rockefeller had to face his failure to cultivate them over the years and—after his refusal to actively support Goldwater in 1964—the suspicion that he was not a "real" Republican. Some party officials feared that he would not handle patronage through them and that he would give too many jobs to independents and Democrats. (Ironically, the same officials were bitterly making the same complaints ten months later about the new President, Richard Nixon.) Many were also fearful that

Rockefeller would not make an effort to build up the party, that under him it would drift and atrophy as it had during the 1950's. The constant appearances of Emmet John Hughes during Rockefeller's campaign travels gave substance to this fear. For Hughes was anathema to many Republican regulars, apart from ideology, partly because of his "kiss-and-tell" book on his White House years under Eisenhower and partly because he refused to identify himself as a Republican and often accepted the label of Democrat.

At some point during the spring, the Rockefeller strategists had decided that the best way to reach the convention delegates was through a campaign that focused on public opinion polls. They reasoned that Rockefeller could never be nominated unless the delegates were convinced that he would win whereas Nixon would lose. The argument concluded that the convention would be so impressed with Rockefeller's late July rating in Louis Harris' and George Gallup's crystal balls, that they would almost beg him to run.

The preconvention drive, therefore, once it got under way, included all the trappings and paraphernalia ordinarily associated with a fall campaign: public speeches and rallies, books on the issues, mass-media advertising, fliers, pamphlets, posters, and bumper stickers. The occasion for these materials, however, was not a fall campaign, with its target of an open public election. For at the convention a predetermined group of 1,333 delegates would select the party nominee. Rockefeller's only hope was that the success of his public appeal could somehow be translated into delegate support.

His route was fraught with peril. Perceptions of public opinion are notoriously inexact, and many delegates saw only what they wanted to as they watched the famous Rocky blitz move into high gear. Though the candidate said he was "going to the people," many argued that it was hypocritical for him to do so after having failed to participate in the only real means available in the American democratic process to have the people make their voice heard by the delegates—the primary contests. Moreover, the polling figures in late July could never be said to differentiate accurately between the potential of a Rockefeller and a Nixon campaign during the brutal fall months.

Finally, the opinion-poll strategy required that the candidate "open up" on his opponent. There would be time for reconciliation later, but Rockefeller could not hope to gain a comparative advantage with public opinion if he gave the impression that there were no major and significant differences between himself and Nixon. If it came down to a matter of who "deserved the nomination" in a personal sense, Nixon was the one. But the "opening up on Nixon" had to be subtly managed lest Rockefeller appear a spoiler, smearer, and wrecker, and possibly the scapegoat for a Nixon defeat in November 1968 as he had been for the Goldwater defeat four years earlier.

Despite all these constraints, Rockefeller managed to put together impressive strength during the early summer. In fact, it can be argued that had he read his position more confidently in March and initiated a cautious but deliberate drive then, he might actually have stopped Nixon and won the nomination. Once he opened the throttle, he ran strongly. To be sure, the Rockefeller campaign was characterized more by dynamic media salesmanship than by quiet delegate persuasion. In part, that was because both the candidate and the press found it the more emotionally satisfying method, particularly after the assassination of Robert F. Kennedy in early June. Rockefeller instinctively moved to fill the gaping vacuum that tragedy had left, and the public was responsive.

It was true, of course, that the poll strategy did not

eliminate the necessity for personalized pursuit of delegates, but merely created the principal ammunition to be used in that pursuit. The delegates could not be expected to respond to the polls by themselves; personal contact was required to exploit Rockefeller's public strength and Nixon's purported unpopularity.

For this reason, Rockefeller scheduled a series of intimate meetings with delegations in all parts of the country. Most of them were quite successful—if not in winning new converts, at least in cementing old alliances and neutralizing old enemies. Many a Nixon delegate came away from the private sessions finding it a whole lot harder to hate the New York governor and prepared to switch over to him if his own candidate faltered.

The governor's performances before individual delegations were particularly helpful to him later. Ohio held to its favorite son status right to the end, at least partly because Rockefeller's appearances convinced Rhodes and key Ohio delegates of his potential electability. In Illinois, he was said to have "loosened up" several delegates, even though he entered this Nixon bastion two weeks after its June 11 primary. One prominent downstate delegate, in fact, who had been counted as leaning to Nixon, emerged from the Springfield gathering and announced that he was now uncommitted (though Nixon's forces were eventually able to bring him back into line). Even South Carolina delegates came away very impressed from their meeting. One man was heard to comment that although he still wouldn't vote for the New York governor at Miami Beach, he would have no problem supporting him in the fall if he were nominated. At Miami Beach itself, delegations received repeated personal visits from Rockefeller and continued to be impressed. He sent his brother David Rockefeller to the Texas caucus, where the younger Rockefeller received a standing ovation.

Rockefeller's personal pursuit of delegates contrasted sharply with Nixon's decision to remain aloof and entrust such work to subordinates. On one occasion, Nixon summoned Midwestern delegates to Chicago—they had to pay their own expenses and were reimbursed later—where he gave them the standard campaign pitch. Then the delegates and their wives were queued up and funneled past the candidate who shook their hands, said a few cordial, predictable words, smiled for the camera, and then greeted the next delegate. The whole episode brought back memories of the awkward 1960 campaign.

Still, in the tired post-mortems following the Republican convention, some Rockefeller supporters concluded that too much attention had been paid to the public and too little to the party, that more concern for the "old politics" of delegate hunting might have garnered more votes during the balloting. As one Reagan strategist said of Rockefeller: "He's appealed to the people; and the people don't nominate Presidents. That may be sad, but it's a fact.

Several Rocky staffers estimated that only 6 percent of the total campaign budget was spent in direct attempts to win delegates. (The largest share of the campaign funds was spent on television advertising.) Commenting on the two delegate operations at Miami Beach, one reporter confided that he never thought he "would see the day when a Nixon campaign effort would out-spend Nelson Rockefeller." A similar discrepancy in resource allocation was evident in staffing; only a small percentage of all the Rockefeller campaign personnel was directly involved in delegate contacts. As a result, there were constant slip-ups and a great deal of improvisation, particularly at the convention itself. Research aides wound up giving press briefings; Professor Henry Kissinger found himself buttonholing delegates on the convention floor (and loving every second of it). On the important evening of Monday, August 5, the opening day of the convention, when Strom Thurmond, Barry Goldwater, and John Tower were making the rounds of delegates holding the South for Nixon, few Rockefeller operatives were to be seen in the aisles of the convention.

The reason that Rockefeller's comeback fell short, however, has far more to do with the polls themselves than with the way his campaign was organized. Just as the Nixon people would later assume that the public mood of September would hold until November, so the Rockefeller people failed to appreciate the impact their own indecision in March and April would have on the June and July poll ratings. Moreover, they underestimated the recuperative powers of Nixon's public image, carefully nurtured with dignity and poise during the uncontested primaries. The "wishy-washy Rockefeller," as the Nixonites labeled him, was still more popular than the "New Nixon" in the nation as a whole, but the margin was less than was expected. Moreover, with Bob Kennedy now dead, the likelihood of a Nixon victory in November was much increased and the pressure for a Rockefeller selection less pronounced among party regulars.

Throughout July, the polls were of only limited help, much less useful than any of the Rockefellerites had expected. Then, on July 29, they backfired entirely, almost causing the Rockefeller campaign to fall apart just as it seemed to be gaining steam. Senator Percy had surprised nearly everyone, most of all the Nixonites, by endorsing Rockefeller a few days earlier; Illinois leader Richard Ogilvie was thought to be wavering, and there was hope that the bandwagon might at last begin to roll. But on the Monday of the preconvention week the Gallup poll for mid-July was released showing Nixon leading both Humphrey and McCarthy; 40 to 38 and 41 to 36, respectively. In contrast,

Rockefeller ran even with Humphrey (36 to 36) and only one point ahead of McCarthy (36 to 35). The impact on the morale of the Rockefeller staff was devastating, and in the lobby of the Fontainebleau Hotel at Miami Beach, it was hard to find anyone who believed that there was much left to stop Nixon. Not only had the Gallup survey failed to prove that Nixon could not win, it failed to even show that Rockefeller could.

Two days later, the Rockefeller staff—desperate for success on the field which they themselves had selected for the nomination fight—prematurely released Lou Harris' latest polling figures. These results for late July indicated that Rockefeller led both Humphrey and McCarthy by six percentage points (40 to 34 in both cases), whereas Nixon trailed Humphrey by 36 to 41 and McCarthy 35 to 43. The contradiction presented by these two critical surveys required the oracles themselves, Mr. Gallup and Mr. Harris, to issue a joint statement declaring that "each poll was an accurate reflection of opinion at the time taken." Gallup polled from July 19 to 21, Harris from July 21 to 26. The two pollsters agreed that a Nixon-Humphrey contest "today would be extremely close," whereas Rockefeller "has now moved to an open lead over both his possible Democrat candidates." Many thought that the Gallup poll reflected a highly transitory burst of Nixon enthusiasm among progressive Republicans following his endorsement by General Eisenhower—an analysis that would also explain McCarthy's abrupt decline, because he drew much of his support from this same group.

But the damage had been done. Rockefeller had failed to establish the premise that he alone could win. Still, the New York governor valiantly continued to play the game to which he was committed—the battle of the polls. On Wednesday of that same week, Leonard Hall, an important

Rockefeller adviser and former Republican National Chairman, presented a poll taken specifically for Rockefeller by Archibald Crossley. Of nine key industrial states (California, Illinois, Maryland, Massachusetts, Michigan, New Jersey, New York, Ohio, and Pennsylvania) with 226 electoral college votes, the New York governor led Humphrey in all; Nixon, however, led Humphrey in only five, trailing the Vice-President in Maryland, Massachusetts, Michigan, and Pennsylvania. One reporter asked the critical question immediately, "How can Rockefeller dare release a poll showing that Nixon will carry California, Illinois, New Jersey, New York, and Ohio?"

New York Congressman Charles E. Goodell continued the fight with yet another poll showing Rockefeller stronger than Nixon in three key congressional districts: Ohio's Twenty-second (Cleveland), Michigan's Second (Ann Arbor), and New Jersey's Second (Atlantic City). The point here was that the Rockefeller victory margin would be crucial to a Republican majority in the new Congress. But the Rockefeller forces were clearly grasping at straws; they had failed to establish the crucial premise—that Nixon's ability to win in November was in doubt.

In addition to his standing in the polls, Rockefeller's fortunes were also dependent on the success of Ronald Reagan's delegate procurement. The scenario envisioned by the Rockefeller strategists required that Reagan pull Southern strength from Nixon. Reagan on the right and Rockefeller on the left had to cooperate tacitly until they denied Nixon the prize; then they would go back to being mortal enemies. In April 1968, William Rusher, publisher of *The National Review,* told some liberal Republicans that he thought Rockefeller and Reagan would be informally allied for two ballots and then (with an ominous grin) that "we would see" which side had prepared the best on the following ballots. Both candidates entertained the possibility of a more formal compact at some appropriate point in the proceedings if it proved necessary. Neither made any overtures, however, for fear of dampening the enthusiasm of their own, more idealistic supporters.

It would be foolish to argue that Rockefeller could have gained many more Southern delegates had he appealed to them more directly (Claude Kirk's conversion notwithstanding). What may have been possible, however, was the kind of challenge used with some success by Democratic liberals in 1964 and 1968, with regard to their party's all-white Southern delegations. For that matter, in 1952, the nomination of General Eisenhower had been dependent in the end on the Dewey machine's brilliant plan of offering rump Southern delegations to replace those loyal to Senator Robert Taft; the plan was well executed at the opening of the convention and was decisive in securing the nomination. Rockefeller too could have had one of his colleagues confront the convention with integrated delegations. He would undoubtedly have lost such a test vote, but the challenge would have forced Nixon to take a stand on a delicate race-related issue and reduced his room for maneuver. But Rockefeller's abdication of any effort in the South left Nixon much room to maneuver, permitting him to claim a moderate posture in the North and West, even while using Strom Thurmond as his most visible spokesman in the South.

For his part, Nixon tried to turn the Rockefeller-Reagan pincers movement to his advantage. To a significant extent he succeeded, winning Rockefeller supporters by citing the Reagan threat, and vice versa. Indeed, some politicians argued that it was the success of Rockefeller at Miami Beach, and the feeling that if Nixon did not get the nomination Rockefeller would, that kept the entire Mississippi and Florida delegations—and their combined fifty-two votes—

with Nixon. The Rockefeller staff counted on Reagan to win about 220 votes from the beginning. They planned on about 280 themselves and that, when combined with about 200 delegates committed to favorite sons, was enough to stop Nixon. By this test, it can be said that Nixon won the nomination largely because Reagan did not make his quota.[1] This variable—over which Rockefeller had no control— produced the most important deviation in Rockefeller's game plan, and it was mostly the doing of Thurmond, Tower, and Goldwater.

Their success was made possible, however, by the groundwork carefully laid by Nixon. Among the earliest Nixon boosters were many Southerners who had been instrumental in the Draft Goldwater Committee—Texas State Chairman Peter O'Donnell, Jr., and Mississippi National Committeeman Fred LaRue. The missionary efforts of Nixon's fieldmen and the candidate's years of party service were factors that ultimately ensured the solid support of the Southern Republican leadership. True, Congressman James Gardner of North Carolina would break for Reagan, but even he could bring along less than half of his delegation.

Nixon won the nomination, then, largely because he secured the South against Reagan. But who would have won had Nixon been stopped? Both the Reagan and Rockefeller camps had firm figures showing that the *other* could never win—figures needed to peel loose delegates who argued that it was safest to stay with Nixon. In the event of several deadlocked ballots, Nixon might have come back again, or his endorsement would have thrown the nomination to a fourth candidate who shared his centrist dispositions.

Although the delegates at Miami Beach were more mod-

[1] Reagan polled 182 votes on the first ballot before switches; Rockefeller, 277; the favorite sons, another 182. It was not enough. Nixon tallied 692, twenty-five more than needed.

erately disposed than those at San Francisco in 1964, they were on the whole more conservative than liberal. Consequently, Rockefeller's scenario showed that Reagan might come within reach of the nomination on the third or fourth ballot. To the Southern delegates he had used to deny Nixon an early nomination, Reagan would add the Far West, plus a few delegates from the Midwest and the East; by that time he might have enough votes so that one of the big state governors could put him over in exchange for the vice-presidential nomination. It was this fear that Reagan might not be stopped that led some moderates, though not enough to be significant, to stay with Nixon rather than vote for Rockefeller in accordance with their personal preferences. It was a reasonable fear, and it may well have been realized had the balloting gone longer.

This same scenario predicted that Rockefeller's strength would not reach its peak until about the fifth ballot. It was believed that many Nixon delegates would be prepared to move to Rockefeller by that time, joining the bulk of the favorite son supporters. Richard Ogilvie, the GOP gubernatorial candidate from Illinois who had finally announced for Nixon, had promised Rockefeller his support if Nixon was stopped on the first few ballots. Some thought that Senator Tower might make a Rockefeller deal or that when Nixon himself threw in his chips he would favor Rockefeller as the candidate most likely to win in November. But all this was useless speculation. Though it might have been, it never was.

Despite the difficulties with the polls, and the failure of Reagan to pick up strength, the third link in Rockefeller's strategy—favorite son delegations withholding their support from any of the three contenders—was amazingly successful. George Romney and Ohio's Governor James Rhodes doggedly maintained their favorite son status despite immense pressures to release Nixon voters among their membership. Even when it became clear during the roll-call vote that Nixon's running total was ahead of what he needed for nomination and George Hinman sent word to Ohio state chairman John Andrews that Nixon had the nomination, Rhodes did not break. (It is possibly that he was motivated more by a desire to prove that he had the delegation under his control than by his devotion to any ideological cause, but the tenacity of the Ohio governor was nonetheless impressive.)

In fact, one crucial tactical error during the early summer months may have been the decision to have Pennsylvania Governor Raymond Shafer discard his favorite son role, which bound the sixty-four votes of the Pennsylvania delegation to him, and announce his support for Rockefeller. At the time of the National Governors' Association meeting in June, the Rockefeller strategists felt that they needed some added momentum to demonstrate that their candidate was actually catching fire. In retrospect, however, some Rockefeller advisers admit that if the twenty-two Pennsylvania delegates who voted for Nixon had remained committed to Shafer, Rockefeller might have been able to hold on to a couple dozen more votes—the eighteen in New Jersey, for example—that went over to Nixon on the assumption that he had the nomination safely in his grasp.

Whatever their earlier errors, it must be said that in the end the moderate Republicans maintained unity at Miami Beach. Governors Shafer, Chafee, and John Love of Colorado all worked hard to win votes for their New York colleague. David Cargo of New Mexico and Daniel Evans, the convention keynoter from Washington, endorsed Rockefeller despite the most intensive and unsubtle home-state pressures. Of the states in which the GOP moderates have positions of influence,[2] all but eight (Nebraska, Colorado, Kentucky, Oregon, Wisconsin, Tennessee, Washington, and New Mexico) gave Rockefeller substantial support, and three of these (Nebraska, Oregon, and Wisconsin) were primary states. Of those progressive leaders who did move to Nixon, several were lost because of the indecisiveness in March and April, several because of primary results, a few because of personal ambitions, and others as a result of Nixon's divide and conquer tactics or because of home-state difficulties.

It must be remembered that through all of this a great many progressive Republicans continued to see Richard Nixon as essentially one of their own—a judgment that his Administration may vindicate. At any rate, there was no repetition of the clear-cut ideological confrontation that had split the party four years before.

To a man, the Republican moderates rallied to the Nixon-Agnew ticket after the convention. With the chance of a Republican presidential victory and with a candidate whose qualifications they respected and whose views were not nearly so different from their own as Goldwater's had been, they campaigned actively for Republican national victory. There were no defectors, not even neutral observers, in 1968. Of course, degrees of activity varied, and it must be noted that none of the progressive governors (Rockefeller, Rhodes, Shafer, Romney, and Volpe) who stood with Nixon and Agnew at Madison Square Garden on October 31 faced reelection that following Tuesday.[3] One who was not pres-

[2] Massachusetts, New York, Rhode Island, Pennsylvania, Ohio, Michigan, Wisconsin, Oregon, Minnesota, Nebraska, New Jersey, Arkansas, Kansas, Colorado, New Mexico, Washington, Kentucky.

[3] Both Michigan and Massachusetts had changes in their state constitutions since 1964 that increased the gubernatorial term to four years.

ent, and who was up for reelection, was Rhode Island's John Chafee. The reason for his absence became evident in the fact that he ran sixteen percentage points ahead of the presidential ticket in his state, though still losing.

Elsewhere, too, the prospects of progressive GOP candidates were not strengthened by the Nixon coat tails on November 5. Nor did the Nixon strategy require that he be particularly attentive to their suggestions during the campaign. The moderates (as well as such conservatives as Everett Dirksen) were quick to let Nixon know that Spiro Agnew's intemperate statements were hurting the ticket badly, from top to bottom, in their own regions. But the Nixon campaign strategy was firmly established. Most of the moderates' pleas that he modify his own law and order speeches with stronger references to justice were ignored by the candidate. The critical votes lay elsewhere in Nixon's judgment, and as long as he did not have the overt opposition of the Republican left there was little reason for him to court them.

Senator Edward Brooke traveled with the GOP nominee in September; Governor Rockefeller and Mayor Lindsay campaigned for the ticket outside New York as well as in— though the fall school strike in New York City forced Lindsay to cancel a number of scheduled engagements. Senators Percy and Hatfield were active supporters. But as the weather changed, the enthusiasm of some cooled; such campaign appearances became fewer. The Nixon strategy, designed to alienate no one, began to worry Republican progressives who felt that they had been excluded from its councils.

After the election, of course, it was different. Nixon wanted the progressives in his government, and he moved quickly to be sure that they were included, independent of earlier political dispositions or election results. Governor

Chafee—a strong opponent of both the presidential and vice-presidential nominations, became Secretary of the Navy. Elliot Richardson, a Rockefeller delegate from Massachusetts, became Under Secretary of State. Henry Kissinger, a convention-time opponent, became assistant for national security affairs. Erstwhile opponent Romney entered the Cabinet despite the fact that his state decisively went Democratic in November. The political jockeying was a thing of the past; the question was no longer control of the party, but rather the service of the party to the nation.

But the lesson of the past should not be forgotten. Republican moderates cannot afford to let go their grasp of local party machinery, wherever they have obtained it. They must vigilantly apply themselves to the daily business of politics, working always to expand the Republican appeal beyond its minority base. Only in this way can they build a nationwide foundation for future political influence. Though the horizon may be far away, GOP progressives must look, with one eye at least, to the day when they will again have to contest anew for national leadership.

CHAPTER 4   THE CONSERVATIVE CAUSE

The American right wing achieved by indirection in the
1968 election campaign much that the Goldwater crusade,
in its orgasm of ideological purity, failed to accomplish in
1964. The mood of the nation was receptive to conservative
diagnosis—if not to conservative solutions—and the tone
of political debate in 1968 reflected the concerns of conservatives to a greater degree than it had at any time since
the early 1950's. Interestingly enough, this was more the
case with domestic than with foreign-policy questions; law
and order, crime in the streets, Supreme Court permissive-
ness, and the threat of the overmilitant young—these were
the "gut" issues for conservatives in 1968, even though
George Wallace himself found it profitable to liberalize his
stance on Vietnam. The pattern, it might be noted, was
somewhat the reverse of that which obtained two decades
ago when Joe McCarthy combined domestic populism with
international intransigence.

Two fascinating political personalities—governor-turned-
right-wing-populist George Wallace of Alabama and actor-
turned-governor Ronald Reagan of California—provided
the major focus for right-wing aspirations in 1968. Wallace,
the first Deep Southern firebrand to possess a national following, capitalized on the alienation of the Deep South from
the rest of the country and on the fears of many white
Americans over the pace of social change. Against remark-

able obstacles, Wallace launched a fair semblance of a national campaign. His presence significantly influenced the election strategies of both major-party presidential nominees.

But equally interesting as the flesh-and-blood candidacy of Alabama's ex-governor was the shadow candidacy of Ronald Reagan, the hero of the ideological right.

Reagan's arrival on the political scene had come in a highly emotional and effective television plea for funds and support for Barry Goldwater shortly before the 1964 general election. It can truly be said that he sprang forth as a national political figure, phoenix-like, from the ashes of the Goldwater dream. He appealed particularly to those unwilling to concede that Goldwater's philosophy had been rejected in 1964 and who saw Goldwater's failure as a failure of style. In their hearts, they knew that Barry was right, but they now argued that the conservative cause would be much better served if it were led by someone who was not constantly tripping over his tongue and who could project well over television. Reagan's experience in movies, television, and on the banquet circuit made him an ideal media candidate.

Even before the 1964 election returns were fully counted, some perceptive right-wing Republicans were laying plans to groom Reagan for the Presidency in 1968. Early in 1965, a leader of the Draft Goldwater movement was asked: "Whom will you go with next time? Will it be Tower in '68 or Dominick? Will you try Barry again?" The answer was quick and sure, "Ronald Reagan," and in the stunned pause that followed he underscored the assertion: "And just you watch us nominate him." Shortly, *National Review* intellectuals such as William Rusher and William Buckley began to spread word of Reagan's potential. By the time the good-guy actor announced his candidacy for governor of California in 1966, thousands of conservatives across the nation were ready to open their pocketbooks to ensure that Reagan would succeed Pat Brown as governor of California.

Reagan's head start among the fat-cat right and rank-and-file conservatives was sufficient to discourage other entries from that wing of the party in the gubernatorial sweepstakes. Meanwhile, the moderates searched frantically for a candidate who could match his appeal. The possibility that California would provide a strong conservative base in 1968 if Reagan was elected disturbed many Republicans across the land and brought considerable pressure on Senate Minority Whip Thomas Kuchel to run for governor. Kuchel had no stomach for what would surely be a bruising battle, and in the end it was former San Francisco Mayor George Christopher who entered the fight. Mismanaged, underfinanced, and notoriously unglamorous, the Christopher campaign was a failure.

Reagan's road to the governorship was skillfully paved by the campaign agents, Spencer-Roberts Associates, who worked for Kuchel in earlier and later primaries and who also managed the 1964 California presidential primary campaign of Nelson Rockefeller. Reagan, Spencer, and Roberts received a major assist from incumbent Governor Pat Brown, who defended a so-so record primarily by attempting to portray Reagan as the ally of Birchites and extremists. Reagan effectively countered by projecting an image of sweet reasonableness in frequent television appearances. He was the earnest citizen-politician who would apply simple common sense to the problems of government, and the voters were responsive.

Reagan's victory over Brown by a million votes thrust him overnight into the 1968 presidential spotlight. But California's new governor faced several obstacles before he could launch a successful presidential candidacy. First, he had to establish that he was a competent executive; his amateur quality was a plus on the state level, but it would hardly enhance his credentials to become the future Chief Executive. Second, Reagan also needed to make himself far more acceptable to moderate Republicans than Goldwater had been, not only to win nomination but also to have any chance at all in the November election. Third, he had to consolidate support among conservatives, many of whom were still shocked from the 1964 experience and who believed that a unity candidate such as Nixon could restore the Republican Party to national power. Nixon's yeoman service in the 1966 congressional campaign reinforced this inclination.

But the Reagan strategists decided to pursue the top prize whatever the difficulties in order to maintain conservative influence. Almost immediately they began to address a national audience, receiving more press and television play in some weeks than the President. Employing news conferences and televised statements, Reagan soon evolved his own style of confrontation politics. Characterizing complex issues as conflicts between good and evil, he pictured the forces of law, order, and decent middle-class sobriety doing battle with unkempt college students, black militants, and professional bureaucrats. A short film clip on national television of a brash campus militant followed by a minute of calm moralistic putdown from the governor was the perfect way for a telegenic politician to build a national following.

On the programmatic level, Reagan's success was less impressive. He was criticized widely when Clark Kerr was fired from his job as chancellor of the University of California. Many of his early appointments drew heavy fire, as did his inability to curb the soaring state-tax rate. His budget cutting in areas like mental health and education also brought severe criticism.

The result was that Reagan proved unable to convince his home constituency that he was ready for national office.

Shortly before the California presidential primary in June 1968, California polls showed, as Roscoe Drummond noted, that Reagan "loses overwhelmingly in his own state to every Democratic candidate—to McCarthy by 35 percent, to Humphrey by 33 percent, and to Kennedy by 17 percent."

The Reagan presidential strategy recognized this problem, however, and tried to avert it by refusing to move into the open. The Presidency was to seek Reagan—it could not be the other way around. In California, he would merely be the favorite son, protecting the unity of his party by preventing a conflict in the primary. To the national Republican Party, he would appear—in sharp contrast to Nelson Rockefeller —as a sturdy work horse on the cold-chicken circuit, gladly fiiling Republican war chests for future campaigns. In the other state primaries, he would remain a noncandidate, but would refuse to withdraw his name from the various ballots to avoid inconsistencies with his favorite-son position.

Meanwhile, Reagan sought to soften his image with the moderate wing of the Republican Party. In late 1967, he gathered reams of publicity during a week's stay as a Chubb Fellow at Yale University. He also received a favorable reception at various party functions in the East. His political importance and his motion-picture fame made Reagan the number one star on the Republican banquet-and-fund-raising circuit. His set speech—developed during years on the General Electric lecture circuit and on the stump throughout the 1966 campaign, but carefully adapted to the specific occasion—would consistently bring Republican audiences to their feet in roaring applause. He was pleasant, polished, and prudent; he convinced the party that he was not another Goldwater and that he did not, as so many of them put it, "wear horns." As early as May 1967, a *Newsweek* cover story touted him as a presidential contender—and the most exciting figure on the Republican scene.

The Reagan presidential strategy was based on clear understanding of political realities. Following the November 1966 elections, the two leading prospects for the 1968 Republican nomination were Richard Nixon and Governor Romney of Michigan. It was impossible for a complete novice to make a graceful head-on challenge to these established front-runners. If Reagan's candidacy was to be plausible, it would have to appear that he had been drafted.

Reagan's main chance lay in the possibility that a Romney-Nixon clash would scar both contenders and remind the party leaders of the serious liabilities of each. Romney could never hope to win in the South; he also bore the taint of his failure in 1964 to support Barry Goldwater. Still, his whirlwind campaigning technique could be expected to dent Nixon's armor at the very least in Wisconsin and Oregon. One or two primary defeats—plus a poor polling performance—would probably remind the party regulars of Nixon's knack for losing elections. And then they just might remember another Republican who beat Nixon's 1962 conqueror by a million—count them—a million votes just four years later. The intelligent Reagan strategy, a full year and a half before the 1968 convention, seemed to say, "Stay loose, get plenty of exposure in the media and among organization Republicans, let Nixon and Romney cut each other up, and be ready to step in when Nixon falters."

It is not unreasonable to conclude that this strategy almost worked in 1968. Although no one was looking in 1967 and early 1968, certain critical elements of the Reagan scenario were falling into place. Neither Nixon nor Romney was building overwhelming power. But then, in February, the premature collapse of the Romney campaign bolstered Nixon's position substantially. Had Romney given Nixon the intense competition that had been anticipated in the primaries, it is possible that the Nixon bandwagon could have been sidetracked.

When Romney withdrew, Rockefeller and Reagan were forced to play a political "game of chicken." Either could actively have entered the Oregon primary, challenged Nixon, and conceivably emerged victorious. But in the process the new candidate—had it been Rockefeller or Reagan—would have drawn the enmity of the Nixon supporters and thus have improved the position of his silent opponent at the other end of the spectrum. Nixon had carefully cultivated the theme of GOP unity as the key to a Republican presidential victory in 1968. Any aggressive challenge might smack of the ultimate sin—disunity. Certainly Ronald Reagan, the first Republican elected on the basis of the eleventh commandment, "Thou shalt not speak ill of any other Republicans," could not be the one to shatter this Republican creed.

This unity maxim was the invention of Dr. Gaylord Parkinson, party chairman in California and, for a brief while, the Nixon campaign manager. It was first employed during the Reagan campaign in California where it was used to beat down dissident moderates who objected to the Reagan candidacy. Even the powerful argument that Reagan was inexperienced in government was, according to the doctrine, beyond the pale of propriety, and—to their later regret—the Christopher supporters let themselves be cowed into soft-pedaling that contention. (Interestingly enough, the eleventh commandment was not revived during the Kuchel-Rafferty primary of 1968 when the conservatives were underdogs and launched bitter attacks against the incumbent senator.)

But even though the commandment was clearly seen by all party leaders as the peculiar product of certain strategic demands in 1966, it did symbolize the sensitivity to discord that many delegates would bring to the 1968 convention. It was clear that the whole purpose of primaries and conventions would be violated if the party refused to candidly air its differences and rigorously compare its candidates. It was also clear that meaningful debate would be impossible if weaknesses in the position of one candidate could not be discussed by any other. Yet, so traumatic had been the experience of 1964, so nervous and fearful was the party of 1968, that the eleventh commandment became official dogma when, on June 5, the Republican national committee actually adopted it as a formal resolution. Needless to say, the eleventh commandment was designed to favor the front-runner—and, needless to say, Richard Nixon made the most of it.

It may be that Reagan overreacted to the fear of disunity. Many Reaganites thought afterward that he would have drawn much greater support if he had entered earlier—and they observed that the case against Rockefeller and Reagan at Miami Beach was not that they had been divisive, but that they had both been unwilling to enter the primaries. The Nixonites used the eleventh commandment to keep competition out—then switched arguments: The earlier reluctance of the opponents was a reason for disqualifying them. It was a masterful and well-executed strategy.

One reason Reagan did not enter the lists was that from May on, Rockefeller was doing at least some of his fighting for him. Believing that Rockefeller could never receive a nomination from a conservatively oriented convention, Reaganites nevertheless knew that Rockefeller, much more than Romney, had the money, the skill, and the gut-fighting instinct to inflict serious wounds on Nixon.

Meanwhile, the favorite-son status gave the California governor enormous flexibility. It locked up the second largest delegation to the national convention and created ideal opportunities for a demonstration of growing Reagan strength in the free-for-all primaries in Wisconsin, Nebraska, and Oregon. His name would automatically be on the ballot, but he would avoid overt campaigning and formally refuse to encourage efforts made in his behalf (though he had carefully scheduled a number of public appearances in each state long before the primaries). Thus, the California governor could express pleasant surprise at any votes that he received, and the scheduling of the primaries could contribute to the impression that a "prairie fire" was building. Wisconsin, with a strong conservative party faction, was first. In Nebraska, a bedrock of Midwestern conservatism, his support would be even greater, and in neighboring Oregon, to which he had made many "nonpolitical" trips and where he had always been well received, a well-financed, "unauthorized" Reagan campaign would demonstrate that the California governor's appeal was not restricted to conservatives. A first-rate group of Oregon politicians of surprisingly diversified backgrounds and possessing a $300,000 war chest were expected to assure that conclusion.

A large Reagan vote in California on June 4, a week after the Oregon primary, was a certainty. And that event, only six weeks before the Republican convention, would provide the final momentum. All that was needed then was a single Nixon stumble—almost any excuse for his conservative supporters to break with him and join the Reagan bandwagon.

The plan did not go badly. Funds for these unofficial efforts poured in from conservatives across the country. In both Wisconsin and Nebraska, his unofficial supporters used hard-hitting television films that lauded their hero and compared his and Nixon's relative campaign performances against Pat Brown. His modest showing on April 2 in Wisconsin with 11 percent of the vote was followed by an impressive 22 percent on May 14 in the Nixon stronghold of Nebraska. But Oregon, on May 28, was a disappointment. Despite a quantum jump in covert campaign effort, the Reagan showing, 23 percent, was hardly better than in Nebraska.

It seems plausible that the mutual fear that the Rocke-feller and Reagan people had of each other may have in-creased the margin of Nixon's Oregon victory. As talk of a possible Reagan triumph in the state increased, Reagan-fearing Rockefeller supporters scampered to Nixon in sub-stantial numbers. At the same time, Howard Appling, Nixon's wily Oregon campaign manager, successfully per-suaded many conservative Oregonians that a bad Nixon showing in the state would open the way for Governor Rockefeller to sweep the summer convention. The wide spec-ulation early in 1968 of a possible Rockefeller-Reagan ticket together with the reports that Rockefeller hoped that Rea-gan would do well at Nixon's expense in Oregon lent credibility to this argument—one that the Nixon operatives would use again, with great success, at Miami Beach in August.

The smashing 73 percent vote for Nixon was a decisive setback for both Reagan and Rockefeller. It was the mo-ment at which the Nixon strategists became confident of their eventual victory. It was after Oregon that Strom Thur-mond decided to yield to what appeared to him to be the inevitable (and shape it if he could). And many lukewarm Nixonites were persuaded that their leader had finally shed his loser's image.

Rockefeller's open candidacy kept Reagan's hopes alive; it put pressure on Nixon and enhanced the prospects of a major Nixon error. But as the front-runner kept his cool, and as the convention drew closer, Reagan was forced to move more openly. His people began to approach Nixon's more conservative supporters, using the contacts F. Clifton White had retained from his successful delegate hunt four years earlier.

But there were problems. Many delegates protested that they could not desert Richard Nixon for a man who was not even a candidate. Reagan, therefore, took a further step toward open declaration by saying that he would *become* a candidate when his name was placed in nomination. But even this was not enough. And so on the opening day of the convention, Reagan finally announced his formal candidacy —under the guise of a request to do so by former Senator William Knowland and the California delegation. The declaration appeared a defensive move at this stage, however, designed to hold in line a group of delegates (led by Lieutenant Governor Robert Finch) who threatened to bolt to Nixon. It did not provide the spark needed to light the long-awaited "prairie fire."

But it may have come very close to doing just that. Initially, it subjected many Southern delegates to intense cross pressures, particularly when, that very morning, *The New York Times* ran the front-page headline: "Nixon Said to Want Rockefeller, Lindsay, or Percy for 2nd Place." The *Miami Herald* simultaneously indicated that the choice would be among Lindsay, Percy, and Hatfield. Reagan workers distributed copies of the *Herald* article throughout the Southern delegation, telling these uncertain Nixon supporters that they would soon be sold down the river.

The Reagan candidacy fitfully launched and loosely managed—changed the history of the convention despite its failure, a fact that testifies to the inherently conservative nature of the GOP party apparatus. Nixon recognized that condition and his consequent vulnerability to the Reagan challenge. And he moved to meet it. His extraordinarily hard-line statement to the Republican platform committee on the issue of law and order, for example, robbed Reaganites of an issue around which to rally potential supporters. But the most effective defensive weapon was South Carolina Senator Strom Thurmond. Thurmond was living proof of Nixon's conservative credentials. In 1948 he had, after all, been the presidential nominee of the Dixiecrat splinter party. He was the perfect figure to calm fears of a liberal vice-presidential nominee, particularly after he received firm reassurances from Nixon. Ultimately, the only significant defection to Reagan from the Nixon camp came in North Carolina, where the gubernatorial nominee James Gardner felt the strength of the Wallace tide and announced for him.

The first ballot of the convention was the last ballot. The Rockefeller-Reagan strategy of nipping away at Nixon from the left and right was successfully countered by Nixon's strategy of playing both ends against the middle. Rockefeller's strength on that one ballot was about what his lieutenants expected it would be; he lost only about ten delegates at the last minute from Maryland and New Jersey. It was Reagan's estimate that proved unrealistic. The Reagan staff—led principally by White, Californian Tom Reed, and the former Young Republican chairman and Kansas State Senator Tom Van Sickle—did not perform as well as most observers expected. White, who signed on as "adviser" to the California delegation for what was reported to be a six-figure fee, found he could not repeat his earlier success, losing over fifty votes from Reagan's rightful philosophical brothers in Mississippi, Alabama, Florida, and Louisiana. He worked from a trailer marked "Suite 3505A"—an echo of the 1964 campaign—but his major service to Reagan the night of the balloting was to convince party officials that Reagan should be admitted to the podium to move that the nomination be made unanimous.

For White, it was an unusual role, that of the loser. But Reagan had played the gracious loser before, the good guy next door who didn't get the girl, and his performance, as usual, was convincing.

The other candidate on the right in 1968, George Wallace,

rose out of a protest movement that was distinctively Southern, yet managed to develop a nationwide following that left its mark on Nixon's campaign strategy—even as Reagan's advances had influenced the strategy at the convention.

Wallace's Northern backing first evidenced itself in the Democratic primaries of 1964. He surprised almost everyone then by polling 43 percent of the vote in Maryland, 30 percent in Indiana, and 34 percent in Wisconsin, enough to whet his appetite for 1968. Yet it is important to note that Wallace's Northern support did not always come from the same places that supported Reagan or Goldwater. His Indiana followers, for example, voted for Lyndon Johnson against Goldwater in the general election in 1964—and many of them supported Eugene McCarthy or Robert Kennedy in the 1968 primaries. Wallace shared certain issues and themes with the Republican conservatives, but he often attracted a different kind of support and most often it was from the lower-middle-class or blue-collar voter. For these Americans, Wallace was the irreverent, antiestablishment figure in a way that Reagan and Goldwater could never be. He would take the government, as one observer said, and "give it a good shake by the scruff of the neck and whack some sense into it." Many of the Wallace supporters liked Robert Kennedy for the same reason—he did things that the "proper people," the sheltered "do-gooders," the established middle-class types didn't like. Like Kennedy, Wallace would wage war against stuffy, rule-bound bureaucrats.

It would be a mistake, of course, to identify the sources of Wallace support completely with those Kennedy drew on; clearly their dramatic differences on the issues produced differing constituencies. But those constituencies did overlap to an important degree—and the reason, it seems, had to do with their style.

Similarly, it was Wallace's "style" that prevented him

from making inroads among many middle- and upper-class conservatives, despite the fact that his positions on many issues agreed with those of Reagan and Goldwater. In fact, a great deal of 1968's anti-Wallace literature came from the ideological conservatives. Some pointed to Wallace's earlier, populist "liberalism" (chiefly his expenditures of federal money when he was governor of Alabama). They recalled that Wallace was only a recent convert to right-wing rhetoric—and that the impelling force in his conversion was race. Wallace, after all, had once run as something of a moderate and had attributed his defeat in Alabama's 1958 gubernatorial race by segregationist John Patterson to the fact that he had been "out nigguhed." Wallace had then resolved never to be "out nigguhed" again. But on all other matters, Wallace seemed to most conservatives to be using ideology as a means to power rather than seeking power in order to implement conservative ideology.

Many conservative accounts also stressed the fact that Wallace could not win the Presidency and that a conservative vote for him would be wasted. But most importantly, the word was passed among conservatives that Wallace was temperamentally not one of them, that he was a troublemaker and a radical. True conservatives don't incite people to violence, the line ran, often accompanied by a quote from Wallace's speeches. "Anyone lies down in front of my car, that's the last car he'll lie down in front of," the Alabamian would say, or else, "Those protestors oughta to be put *under* a good jail." The raucous, violent tone of the Wallace rallies gave the conservatives' argument against him considerable impact in tranquil towns and pleasant suburbs. NBC's voter sample districts showed that New York senatorial candidate (and brother of the *National Review* editor) James L. Buckley, running with the Conservative Party label, collected one quarter of the votes cast in high-income areas, whereas Wallace polled less than 2 percent in the same areas of the state.

The *National Review* devoted the cover of its October 22, 1968, issue to a "Memo to American Conservatives." All the memo said was, "Please don't throw away your vote by voting for George Wallace." It was signed by Barry Goldwater. Inside appeared two strikingly similar articles —one signed by the 1964 GOP standard-bearer and entitled "Don't Waste a Vote on Wallace" and the other headlined "And Anyway, Is Wallace a Conservative?" and signed by American Conservative Union president and Ohio Congressman John Ashbrook. Only pages apart, the two articles went through the catalogue of conservative arguments in a remarkably similar tone. And at one stretch, the language of the two men was identical, word for word, for several paragraphs, proving—one supposes—that conservative minds tend to think alike.

George Wallace's "Stand Up for America" crusade probably began as a warm-up for 1972. But by fall 1968, Wallace was at least entertaining the possibility that he might win four years ahead of schedule. After all, he already had more support than most political observers had thought possible. He would be listed in November on the ballots of all fifty states, no small accomplishment and the work, in large part, of William K. Shearer. In California and Massachusetts, enormous signature campaigns had been required to obtain formal listing. In Ohio, it took a landmark decision by the U.S. Supreme Court, one of Wallace's favorite campaign targets. Only in the District of Columbia did Wallace fail to get on the ballot. At the same time, Wallace had also been developing remarkably broad-based financial support, with much of the income derived from the sale of campaign paraphernalia. His was the only campaign since the invention of the automobile in which bumper stickers were not given away.

To all of these signs of success was added the most propitious—his recognition as a serious figure in the judgment of the national press. Throughout September, in fact, correspondents and columnists were almost possessed by the Wallace phenomenon—propelling it forward even as they thundered against it. The national press corps began to follow Wallace's travels, in numbers far greater than his modest organization was prepared to handle. To be sure, the Wallace tour featured a noisy, smoke-belching, old plane instead of sleek jets; it offered grimy bottles of Dr. Pepper each morning, whereas the other tours served Bloody Marys. In a strange way, nevertheless, this was where the action was in September, this was a man who was communicating and who was being listened to. Unlike the Nixon and Humphrey operations, the early Wallace campaign knew exactly where it was going. It was "for real."

What pleased Wallace most, however, was that other candidates had begun to steal his lines. He mentioned this phenomenon at every appearance; like Reagan, he could claim that his cause was advanced by his candidacy. Even the senator from New York, Robert Kennedy, had picked up the law-and-order issue in his primary campaigns in Indiana and Nebraska, and the more superficial across the nation were willing to follow the lead of commentators who treated that fact as a coup for Wallace. After voting in Alabama on November 5, Wallace would fall back on this face-saving theme again as he stood on the courthouse steps in Barbour County: "This movement is highly successful already. Both parties are talking like we do."

But the central goal for Wallace—one that also appeared likely of attainment in the early fall—was to prevent both Nixon and Humphrey from winning an outright majority of votes in the electoral college. In such a circumstance, Wallace might well be able to choose the next President. The thought appealed to his fancy, and the more he reflected on it, the more he became possessed with the idea. Accordingly, he even collected affidavits from all of his electors pledging them to vote for him, or whomever he designated, in the college balloting, and he repeatedly claimed he would not let the election get to the House of Representatives, where his personal influence presumably would be lessened.

> I might not have any chance in the House. But you must remember, before you go to the House you go to the electoral college. If we hold the balance of power, we may decide the question in the electoral college because one party may have to make a concession to the people of our country, a solemn covenant to them.

And he lashed out angrily against the "unconstitutional" arrangement, pushed by Congressmen Morris K. Udall and Charles E. Goodell, whereby members of the House would pledge ahead of time to support the candidate with the largest popular national vote. Nor did he like the idea of any agreement between the two major candidates that the winner of the popular vote should be the new President. (Nixon proposed this and pledged himself to the arrangement unilaterally. Humphrey never responded. There were moments on election night when the popular vote was virtually tied, when Nixon may have regretted his confident generosity.)

But there would be no deadlock if Wallace could not carry the South—and there Wallace directed his fire against Nixon, who had conceded the blacks and white liberals to Humphrey. He had difficulty finding his target, however. Nixon remained rather vague in his speeches—and he refused to criticize Wallace directly. Finally, on a regional tele-

vision broadcast, Nixon, when asked of Wallace's comments about running over demonstrators who sat down in
front of his car, suggested that the comment was not fitting
for a possible President. Wallace immediately sought to
make his remark appear as an insult to the whole South,
raising traditional jealousies and resentments. Remember,
his argument would go, George Wallace is the home town
boy who's had the guts to go North and battle for us folks
against the Sodoms and Gomorrahs of the urban North.
Richard Nixon, on the other hand, is a Wall Street lawyer
all set to sweet talk the South out of its inheritance in order
to make a fast buck.

In the North, Wallace also competed with Nixon for
votes—but there his *main* opponent was Humphrey. Traditional Democrats gave him much of his support in the
North, and he wooed them by suggesting that the Democratic Party had forgotten its "common origins." He demonstrated his empathy with the fears of insecure Americans;
he described himself as the candidate of "the barbers, beau-
ticians, cab drivers, and steelworkers." Again he defined
his appeal in terms of life styles and personality types. He
ran against "pointy-headed intellectuals and bureaucrats."
Almost anyone of status or prestige was grist for Wallace's
mill.

Actually, the majority of the Alabamian's supporters were
ordinary folk who perceived much turmoil and change in
the world around them. Some were frightened by it; others
felt directly threatened. For many Americans in 1968, the
things they saw happening in the streets and on the campuses were at odds with the values and beliefs they had held
since childhood; the stable environment they knew and had
grown up in was collapsing around them.

American society has always been dynamic; change and
conflict occur as normal attributes of the national life. In

1967 and 1968, however, the level of conflict and the magnitude of change escalated rapidly. Yet, it seems likely that most Wallacites had little comprehension of the events that were so disturbing them. They were attracted to Wallace because he spoke their language and promised to restore the society to a more orderly state.

Often these were people whom the technological society had passed by, who never made as much of their lives as they thought they ought to have. Wallace would reassure them, buttress their confidence in their common sense, tell them that a college education or a big fancy job would have only confused and spoiled them. And there was always the none-too-subtle implication that Wallace would help them meet the biggest threat they faced, the threat from the blacks, who were below but coming up fast. As one observer put it: "He gives them an array of villains on whom to blame their own troubles. A vote for Wallace may be bad politics, and these people will almost admit that. But it's *great* therapy."

The therapeutic style was best evidenced in Wallace's campaign rallies. "I always wanted to fight the main event in the Garden," the one-time boxer told his Madison Square Garden audience of 16,000 on October 24, and the metaphor was perfect. For here, as at every stop on his tour, Wallace did *not* give a speech. Rather he fought a battle. His opponents—dutifully showing up at stop after stop, loyally playing their parts as if they were paid to do it, dependable and helpful as any straight man or sparring partner could ever be—were the student demonstrators. Dressed in a way that confirmed the worst suspicions of the Wallace crowds, they would scream obscenities at the candidate. The crowd would gasp.

Wallace would counter; the crowd would roar with approval. A demonstrator would lunge toward the stage; boos would engulf him. Wallace would wisecrack—a standing ovation.

At stop after stop, the little morality play would unfold like clockwork. "Is that a *he* or *she*?" "Let 'em alone now because after November, they're gonna be *through*." "Let the police handle it, folks, let the police handle it." The rasping voice would pierce through the din of the hall on the world's most powerful amplifying system, crashing through the bedlam that characterized each rally, drowning out the protest chants, fighting for the attention of an audience distracted again and again by fist-fights and forced evacuations.

At one rally the demonstrators turned the tables, responding to the speaker with shouts of "We want Wallace" and "Kill the Commies." On that occasion Wallace was undone—he proved fumbling and helpless—but for the most part he had his foil and the audience had its bloodletting. And then they would leave the arena, like Romans must have left the gladiatorial spectacles, like Spaniards leave their bullfights. "He really told 'em, didn't he," a pleasant matron would laugh to her sport-shirted rough-hewn husband. And—it just may have been—that having spent their emotions and obtained their therapy at the rally hall, many of those who cheered for Wallace did not need to do so again in the voting booth.

But there were other reasons than the natural waning of hysteria for Wallace's decline in the last weeks of the campaign. An important one was the intensive campaign of labor leaders to reclaim the support of unionists for the man who had been labor's most important legislative friend for two decades, Hubert Humphrey. Factory parking lots from Massachusetts to California had been sprouting Wallace bumper stickers by the thousands. Even some runaway locals endorsed Wallace. Suddenly those who drove the cars were subjected to a barrage of anti-Wallace literature from their state and national labor leadership, and this converted many of them. "Don't waste your vote" was only part of its message. Most effective was an array of statistics that cut through Wallace's rhetoric to the realities of his Alabama record. An editorial in the *AFL-CIO News* observed that Alabama ranked forty-eighth among the states in per capita annual income and in per pupil expenditures in public schools. The *Kentucky Labor News,* official weekly of that state's AFL-CIO, was typical of many labor newsletters when it described Alabama as a hotbed of crime. "The murder rate in Alabama is running 12.9 murders per 100,000 population annually. . . . The rape rate is 11.9 per 100,000 per year."

There was also the positive appeal of the Humphrey record of support for labor's interests—an appeal that grew stronger as the campaign went along. At the same time, Senator Edmund Muskie was bringing over many voters of Eastern and Central European origin—identifying them with his own success and reminding them of the noble dreams of their fathers. But the most important of the factors that slowed the Wallace steamroller and reversed his momentum was his selection of a running mate, a decision that he deferred as long as he could, almost as if he knew that it could only create problems.

Many of his advisers argued that Wallace needed a well-known Northern vice-presidential running mate in order to broaden his appeal. Others said that any identifiable running mate would only dilute his following. Former Georgia Governor S. Marvin Griffin served as a stand-in for the purpose of getting Wallace on the fifty state ballots, but most Wallacites agreed that this arch-segregationist should not be the final selection. A consensus finally materialized for A. B. "Happy" Chandler of Kentucky, a former governor, U.S.

senator, and commissioner of baseball. But Chandler proved unwilling to "play ball" with Wallace on racial matters. His views had moderated since his days as a segregationist politician, and his recent pronouncements were, according to Chandler, unacceptable to a certain "Mr. Big" who supposedly controlled the Wallace campaign. Chandler refused to change his style, and Wallace had to reject him.

The final choice was retired Air Force General Curtis LeMay, a cigar-chomping, former Air Force Chief of Staff under President Kennedy and major architect of the Strategic Air Command. LeMay was better known before his nomination as Vice-President than either Agnew or Muskie had been and presumably he would broaden Wallace's appeal. The presumption, however, was wrong. LeMay, like Agnew, turned out to be a major liability, and for some of the same reasons. No politician, he quickly dispensed off-the-cuff opinions on a variety of subjects. Sometimes he proved more conservative than his boss, sometimes more liberal. The problem was that he spoke out on whatever came to his mind, and the subject that did so most frequently was, predictably enough, nuclear weapons.

Barry Goldwater had learned in 1964 that the nuclear issue is the most explosive one in politics. It took only a few hours after LeMay's selection for the point to be demonstrated again. At his first press conference, LeMay repeated his standard argument that there was little point in building nuclear bombs unless you retain the option of using them. We shouldn't have a phobia on the subject, he said. As if to prove his point, horrified headlines reporting his remarks immediately bloomed like mushroom clouds across the country. Both candidates of both major parties pounced immediately to the attack. *Washington Post* cartoonist Herblock had a field day. From that point on, it was all downhill for Wallace.

LeMay, huge and severe and cold, frightened many voters. Moreover he dimmed Wallace's appeal to "the little man." A World War II air force flight sergeant, Wallace was enthralled by the possibility of having a nationally prominent four-star general under his authority. It seems, however, that many Wallace supporters had difficulty identifying with Curtis LeMay, a man who represented established political and economic power.

It had been safe to register a protest by voting for Wallace in the Democratic primaries of 1964; nobody at that time was going to deny Lyndon Johnson the nomination. It was also safe to say "yes" when asked by a pollster if one were voting for Wallace; pollsters did not elect Presidents. Harvard Professor Thomas Pettigrew put it this way:

> People are very aware of the polls reported on the front page of newspapers, and they take advantage of them. In this day when politicians get in and out of races because of the polls—remember George Romney in New Hampshire?—people are very aware that you can cast your ballot by public opinion and it is safer because the guy doesn't get elected.

But the election itself was a different story. In the peripheral South many anti-Humphrey Wallace supporters switched to Nixon at the very last minute to ensure Humphrey's defeat. It is possible, in fact, that one effect of the bombing pause was to scare many Southern and border-state voters to Nixon because it made a Humphrey victory seem possible. It could also be argued that a later election day would have seen an even greater defection from Wallace to Nixon as Humphrey's success in the opinion polls hit home with Wallace voters. As it was, the Wallace vote in such states as Kentucky, Missouri, North Carolina, Virginia, and South Carolina was significantly below the preelection expectations.

Predictably, he was weakest with middle-class voters; his Snopesian language and bantam-rooster manner did not go over with the young business executives of the New South. Richard Nixon's style was more to their liking.

And, though perhaps not a "true" conservative, Nixon did have the very best of credentials. After all, even the bumper stickers said that the way to "Help Strom" was to "Elect Nixon." Senator Thurmond's all-out support of Nixon may have irritated red-necks, but it persuaded middle-class conservatives, and after a touch-and-go battle it delivered South Carolina.

Wallace carried only five states, and the election was not close enough in terms of electoral votes for them to be crucial and produce the electoral deadlock he had hoped for. Nevertheless, Wallace left his mark on national politics in 1968. After the election, he crowed that his cause was "living because the winner of the presidential campaign said almost identically the same things we were saying in the campaign." He continued, "And I dare say, had this movement not been in existence that would not have been the case."

It is yet to be determined whether the American Independent Party will develop some real power of its own. Organizational meetings in early 1969 were reminders that it would remain a thorn in Nixon's side, and an incentive for him to protect himself on the right. Bumper stickers appeared after the election reading "Wallace in '72," and an "Association of Wallace Voters" announced its intention to coordinate local groups developed during the campaign. "We didn't wind up with a national party," commented one of Wallace's principal aides, "we wound up with fifty state parties."

Still, it seemed in early 1969 that the emotions that fueled the Wallace campaign had played themselves out and were no longer as potent in the calm and quiet atmosphere so carefully constructed by President Nixon. Moreover, Wallace's failure to win a large vote in any industrial state in 1968 was bound to be disheartening for any future effort. Just as Goldwater's most devoted supporters could sustain themselves before November 1964 with thoughts that a massive "silent" vote would rescue their hero, so the Wallace enthusiasts could persuade themselves that the Alabamian would sweep Northern blue-collar areas. This dream was less tenable after the 1968 election. Nor would Wallace be likely to do better with these voters against a Catholic Democrat, such as Senator Muskie or Kennedy, than he did against Humphrey. It should also be noted that a strong Kennedy challenge would be the one force most likely to drive Wallace supporters in the Deep South into support of Nixon.

In sum, it seems clear since the 1968 election that many voters who would support Wallace as a protest gesture have no desire to see him President of the United States. At this point it must be said that the Wallace appeal is still largely a regional phenomenon and that it may well be very difficult for Wallace to sustain the enthusiasm of his supporters for another grueling campaign in the national arena.

CHAPTER 5 The Demise of the Democrats

The Republicans' compulsive allegiance to the eleventh commandment was widely recognized as an understandable reaction to the trauma of 1964. Less widely acknowledged, but equally inevitable, was the Democrats' reaction to their own legacy from the 1964 L.B.J. victory, the politics of spurious consensus.

Democrats have traditionally been less self-conscious than Republicans about their party's inner contradictions. This tolerance of ideological diversity has been one of the fundamental reasons for their electoral success. To be sure, they have paid a price for this diversity; for one thing, they have lived constantly with the unnerving danger of irreparable schism. But, in the past, intraparty disputes were rarely so fundamental that they could not be compromised or ignored; the Democratic Party leadership was always pragmatic enough to put *electoral* victory above ideological differences. How else could one justify a national ticket composed of Adlai Stevenson and John Sparkman, or John Kennedy and Lyndon Johnson?

The Johnson Administration succeeded in breaking this tradition. By embroiling the United States in the all-too-visible fiasco of Vietnam and by subordinating domestic priorities to the pursuit of an elusive victory abroad, President Johnson created an issue that could be neither papered over nor forgotten. By permitting the Democratic national

115

committee to suffocate under the blanket of personal leadership and by impugning the loyalty of critics within his own party, Johnson set the stage for a damaging ideological shootout in which victory for the Administration meant the nomination of a crippled candidate.

In only four years, the Democratic Party decayed from one that had swept the nation with a notably uncharismatic leader to one that lost the Presidency to its most disliked and mistrusted partisan enemy. It is a measure of the depth of Democratic disunity in 1968 that not even the candidacy of Richard Nixon was able to bring order to its ranks.

When the unlikely pretender, Eugene McCarthy, first offered his candidacy on November 30, 1967, few thought he would be more than a minor irritation to L.B.J. McCarthy's only ammunition was moral fervor—not the sort of thing to wrest a nomination from an incumbent. The Minnesota senator lacked even a personal following. After all, Allard Lowenstein, the originator of the "Dump Johnson" movement, had been looking for a candidate since the summer—and McCarthy had hardly been his first choice. When McCarthy finally agreed to carry the torch, many attributed his decision to personal pique against the man who only four years earlier had almost selected him as his running mate. Even the charge of Texas Governor John Connally that McCarthy was only a stalking horse for Robert Kennedy rang true in the closing days of the pre-election year. No one, but no one, was taking McCarthy seriously in his own right.

During fall 1967, the Administration had been building momentum in the war of words over Vietnam. "We are turning the corner," the public was told again and again. The Vietcong could not continue to resist the power that the United States was pouring into the country; they were on the defensive, fighting with teen-age boys and rapidly running out of food. The argument seemed reasonable. As Hubert Humphrey put the orthodox "line" to a group of Midwestern Democrats on January 27:

> Some people say we need more police, that we need more National Guardsmen to keep the country's streets safe. Well, what about the world's streets? Who can maintain peace and security if we can't?

But on January 3, the Vietcong and North Vietnamese struck forty of South Vietnam's cities in numbers estimated at 50,000 in the now famous Tet offensive. Even the American embassy in Saigon was invaded. It was incomprehensible that a fighting force as "demoralized" as the Vietcong was supposed to be could muster an attack of this magnitude. Nonetheless, President Johnson reassured the American people three days later that the offensive against the Vietnamese cities had been "a complete failure," both in military and psychological terms. Later in February, General William Westmoreland reinforced this official position, claiming that the enemy had "suffered a military defeat," though he did concede them "some temporary psychological advantage." At the same time, Westmoreland asked for 200,000 additional troops, a request that other military men described as "panicked" and one that forced the complete review of Vietnam policy that eventually brought the Johnson reversal on March 31.

The American electorate, however, was watching the fighting in the streets of Saigon and Hue from its living rooms. What they saw led a majority to believe for the first time that the war was going badly. The ritual of government reassurance no longer was effective. Many decided the government was either lying or stupid—whichever was the case did not really make much difference.

Meanwhile, with the New Hampshire primary little more than a month away, college students from New England and New York, and from points even farther south and west, poured into New Hampshire to ring doorbells, run mimeograph machines, and address letters. They came "Clean for Gene," shaving their beards and dressing neatly in an exercise that provided a superb outlet for many frustrated energies. The McCarthy campaign became an emotional focal point, not only for those who worked (and those who came to work but were turned away because too many had shown up), but also for those young people generally who finally saw their generation making a significant impact. In proving that America's youth could accomplish something meaningful, the miracle of New Hampshire kept many members of the alienated generation from slipping off to the violent fringe.

Like the candidate himself, McCarthy's campaign was smooth and cool, too cool by far for the professional radicals who spent most of the winter trying to wreck it with ridicule. But it was just right for thousands of New Hampshire citizens who—in the best New England tradition—insisted on being thoughtful and independent. Moreover, the campaign took maximum advantage of the fiercely intolerant response of the state and national party hierarchy. McCarthy adroitly exploited the organization's crude attempt to use signed pledge cards to pressure rank and file Democrats into supporting the President. Similarly, Johnson's cause was severely damaged by radio advertisements in which Governor John King intemperately dubbed McCarthy as a "spokesman for the forces of appeasement," one who was "advocating a policy of surrender which would destroy everything we have been fighting for." In contrast, McCarthy's radio commercial—beamed into every home

every half-hour during the last two days of the campaign—
was a simple one-sentence message.

> Think how you would feel to wake up Wednesday
> morning to find out that Gene McCarthy had won the
> New Hampshire primary—to find that New Hampshire
> had changed the course of American politics!

The appeal came through loud and clear, for as Richard
Goodwin noted, "Many of those who stopped to think
quickly realized that such an outcome would delight them,"
unlikely as it had seemed two weeks before. Johnson's early
readings were that McCarthy would be held with ease to
15 percent of the vote, maybe even less. But on March 12,
McCarthy received 42 percent of the Democratic ballots,
falling short of Johnson's 48 percent but taking twenty of
the twenty-four convention delegates. Though the national
television commentators refused to acknowledge it that
evening, it was a devastating blow for Lyndon Johnson, one
from which he would not recover.

But now Robert Kennedy, understandably reluctant all
fall to undertake what might look like a personal vendetta
against the reigning President, ached to join the battle toward which his instincts so long had moved him. Inasmuch
as McCarthy's victory in New Hampshire proved the party
was already split, he need not bear the onus of being the
party divider. But in return for that advantage, he now had
to pay a heavy price—the revival of his image as a ruthless
opportunist, not only with the old guard but, even more
seriously, with McCarthy's young people. Once they had
been his, the special Kennedy constituency, wooed and won
at countless high-school assemblies and college rallies over
more than a decade. Now some would come along, but as
Kennedy himself said one day, "I've got the B and C kids,

McCarthy has the A ones." "They'll come to you in the end," an aide reassured him. "But it'll never be the same," Bobby is said to have whispered.

Nevertheless, Kennedy's announcement on March 16, only four days after New Hampshire, placed the identity of the Democratic nominee in serious doubt for the first time. No one had really believed that McCarthy could ever pull the necessary strings with the Democratic power brokers; in fact, his endorsement by the Americans for Democratic Action in February had brought the resignation from the ADA of several prominent labor leaders and other Administration supporters. But given the power of the Kennedy machine and R.F.K.'s contacts throughout the fifty states, there would now be a real contest. The impossible was now possible: an incumbent President just might fail to be renominated.

Publicly, at least, President Johnson discounted the New Hampshire results as an insignificant aberration and professed indifference to Robert Kennedy's rapid entry and the subsequent erosion of Administration support among party leaders. Only when confronted by the imminent prospect of repudiation in the April 2 Wisconsin primary did Johnson take decisive action.

For two months the President and his highest counselors had been subjecting their Vietnam policy to the closest scrutiny. Intertwined as always with the changing war situation in Asia was the changing political situation at home. Now, on the last day of March, the results of that review process were announced.

In a prime time Sunday evening television appearance, the President announced a partial bombing halt in Vietnam and the beginning of exploratory talks in Paris—an abrupt reversal of his earlier position. But for the big news, the public had to wait for the closing passage: "Accordingly,

I shall not seek, and I will not accept, the nomination of my party for another term as your President."

The verdict of the New Hampshire primary, the formidable candidacy of Robert Kennedy, the personal attacks that led L.B.J. to believe he was dividing the country, and the forceful arguments of his wife were said to be the major factors contributing to his decision. It is possible that the President had not discarded all hope of a second term, concluding only that if he was to win the Democratic nomination in 1968 it would have to come after other challengers proved unable to build majority support. But more importantly, the President's political retirement accomplished the one goal to which he was overwhelmingly committed, a goal that could be accomplished in no other way. At least temporarily, he managed to separate the Vietnam war from domestic politics.

Gone, for the time being at least, was the one issue that had made McCarthy a presidential contender. Gone, too, was the moral rationale for the Kennedy campaign. (And gone for now was Richard Nixon's secret weapon—the albatross he had planned to hang around the neck of his opponent in the fall.) Nor would Vietnam, the overriding issue of the 1960's, become a central point of debate between the parties in the course of the 1968 campaign, though inevitably the reaction to Vietnam severely hurt Humphrey and aided Nixon.

Hubert Humphrey was not taken by surprise by the announcement, although the March 31 blockbuster did find him on a routine trip to Mexico, an awkward place for an heir apparent to be at the moment of abdication. As the weeks passed, Humphrey and the Administration professionals did not prove to be so resourceful in rallying their party as many Republicans had anticipated. The Vice-President waited twenty-eight days to announce his own candidacy in an effort to finesse the primaries, a strategy that paid off in August but may have hurt him in his later efforts to unify the party. Like Nelson Rockefeller, Humphrey found it difficult to explain his reluctance to battle openly in the springtime trial heats. And like Rockefeller, he found that some of his natural allies were unwilling to drag him into the race until he made an all-out plunge. On April 15, a meeting of seventeen Democratic governors was convened at the instigation of Southerners interested in blocking Robert Kennedy's try for the nomination. In the mirror image of their timid GOP brethren, the Democratic governors ultimately adopted a resolution agreeing "to observe the events of history as they develop in the next few months . . . and then reach a decision of conscience as to the man who should be nominated."

Humphrey entered the race on April 27. His maiden speech epitomized the Vice-President perfectly, for it was warm and sincere and radiant, a bit overblown, perhaps, but still winning and wonderful. It was just about right for almost any time in the nation's life—but in 1968 it came to seem very, very wrong.

> And here we are, just as we ought to be, here we are, the people; here we are in a spirit of dedication, here we are the way politics ought to be in America, the politics of happiness, the politics of purpose, and the politics of joy. And that's the way it's going to be, too, all the way from here on out.

While McCarthy and Kennedy were jointly trouncing Humphrey and his surrogates in the spring primaries and winning the lion's share of the public attention the Vice-President was busy untangling himself from a number of verbal and political embarrassments. On May 17, for example, he suggested that the United States and the North

Vietnamese had agreed to permit the Vietcong to sit in on the Paris talks, only to retract the statement in a subsequent "clarification." The following day, he claimed there was a chance that the crew of the *Pueblo* might be released as part of a package deal involving Vietnam; aides later said the statement represented an "absolute misunderstanding," but they did not deny that the candidate had said it.

Still, as the spring weeks passed, Humphrey's failure to seize the public imagination seemed to make less and less difference. Senators Fred Harris and Walter Mondale, his campaign managers, found they could successfully beat back Kennedy and McCarthy assaults on state and local party leaders. Equally important was the effect of the McCarthy victory over Kennedy in the Oregon primary—an outcome that helped to shatter the myth of Kennedy invincibility (even as the Republican outcome there helped Richard Nixon shed his "loser" image). It was the first election a Kennedy had ever lost in twenty-six electoral tries.

Whether the R.F.K. momentum could have been successfully resumed is difficult to judge. Analysts were still sorting out the impact of his dazzling South Dakota triumph and his less spectacular but perhaps sufficient California victory when gunshots ripped into the heart of American life for the second time in ten weeks—the third time in five years. From June 6 through to November, the quadrennial American political circus played out its script with a brave gaiety. But the exhilaration was gone—what little of it had ever seemed appropriate in 1968—and the word "if" was the fulcrum of countless pieces of political punditry.

If Kennedy had lived . . . even now the subjunctive persists. Though R.F.K. in life was not regarded with as broad an esteem as one might assume in retrospect, the events of summer 1968 could very well have led to his nomination. Humphrey's slippage in the polls, the planned post-California

Kennedy blitz of more than twenty-five states, the senator's slow but apparent success in shedding much of his unfavorable image, his appeal to the working class as well as to the disaffected—these factors might have combined to transform March's flawed but exciting candidate into August's nominee.

What is clear is that Kennedy's death marked the death of all hopes for an anti-Administration Democratic candidate. McCarthy's forces alone were incapable of making a strong bid for the nomination. They did not have and could not obtain even the minimal trust of such party leaders as Daley, Barr, and Tate. Powerful remnants of the machine system that once held most of the giant cities safe for the Democrats, such leaders were concerned with bread and butter issues that directly touched their constituents, issues on which McCarthy and Humphrey scarcely disagreed. Technicians rather than ideologues, the pros could certainly have accepted a peace candidate and, in some circumstances, might even have welcomed one. But they could not accept—and would not even consider—a nominee who seemed to them a self-righteous threat to their power and their methods of operation.

Not only did the Minnesota senator lack Kennedy's rapport with those who controlled large chunks of Northern convention strength, but he also could not command the loyalties of the now bereft Kennedy legions. Whatever common ground had ever existed between the two peace camps had been badly undermined by the increasingly bitter and personal tone of the last primaries. Eventually, one can guess, most of McCarthy's followers might have supported a Kennedy candidacy, but the deep personal commitment of the grief-stricken Kennedy supporters to their now fallen leader made the opposite movement exceptionally difficult. Too many remembered Kennedy's reflection after Oregon:

"I think what [McCarthy] wanted most was to knock me off. I guess he may hate me that much." Even Jesse Unruh, a vociferous McCarthy partisan by the time of the Chicago convention, had been slow to shift his support after the assassination.

Without the support of either the Daleys or the Soren sens, McCarthy was doomed, as he probably had been from the beginning. In early August, McCarthy was forced to cut his payroll by one third. The polls showed him trailing Humphrey by fourteen percentage points among Democrats. Many political observers thought Kennedy—had he lived—would have been a slight favorite at Chicago. But there were now no odds on McCarthy. And there was nothing left to do but demonstrate.

With one potential Democratic peace candidate dead and the other nearly impotent, the Republican convention could afford to sidestep the war issue in the platform and to select a nominee who seemed likely to sidestep the issue in the campaign. The absence of Robert Kennedy from the Democratic field meant less pressure on the Republicans to nominate the only man who then seemed likely to beat him—Nelson Rockefeller. Moreover, the GOP professionals found their fear of March—that Johnson had stolen their best issue when he took himself out of the race—unfounded in August. To be sure, Vietnam as such was no longer an issue between the parties, but L.B.J. still was. For the obvious Democratic candidate bore the indelible brand of the Texas President. Despite Humphrey's homilies ("One does not repudiate his family in order to establish his own identity. Hubert Humphrey as Vice-President was a member of the team. Hubert Humphrey as President will be captain of the team."), he had not yet publicly differed with the President on any issue of consequence. There was the possibility, of course, that Hubert would become his old self, his own man, after the

Democratic convention. But the Republican delegates at Miami Beach didn't let that possibility intimidate them.

The ossification of the Democratic power structure might not have been fatal in November if it had not been made absolutely manifest to the electorate by the fiasco of Chicago. Even if the party leadership was not entirely responsible for the violence outside the convention hall, they could blame no one but themselves for permitting the outrageous episodes that occurred within it. There, suddenly, a Nixon line that seemed a bit abstract all spring took on new and vivid meaning: "How can a party which cannot unite itself hope to unite America?" After the "siege of Chicago," it seemed like a damn good question.

The McCarthy-McGovern forces had decided to spurn all compromise with Humphrey in the hope of winning a clear-cut face-off on the Vietnam issue. In addition, they took up other causes, partly for strategic reasons. The seating of integrated delegations from the South was one example; the abolition of the unit rule another. On the first two days, these tactics produced some significant, if overlooked, successes and struck a sharp contrast with the lethargic Republican display at Miami Beach.

At the GOP convention, to take just one example, there had been no effort to unseat lily-white delegations selected in ways that discouraged Negro participation. Nor had there been any establishment leader opening doors to the future as New Jersey Governor Richard Hughes did when he replied to a questioner (who argued that if Lester Maddox left the Georgia delegation then so should Julian Bond): "This man is a symbol. We've got to have him."

But if the Miami Beach convention did not feel the winds of the future, it did at least proceed with order and a sense of general consent. That was not the case at the Chicago gathering, jammed into the old International Amphitheater only because a fire had destroyed the spacious new McCormack Place facility. "We will be judged by our decorum," said Congressman Carl Albert as he took the gavel. Truer words were never spoken.

The over all impression the public received of the Democratic Party during the last week in August was one of an undisciplined authority of the establishment putting down defenseless dissenting voices. While Carl Albert gaveled the podium to quiet, the peace delegates singing "The Battle Hymn of the Republic" in tribute to Robert Kennedy, Mayor Daley's police force was gaveling the heads of youths who had gathered in front of the Chicago Hilton—both youths who provoked a response and youths who did nothing. Again and again, protesting delegates from Wisconsin were either ignored or were ruled out of order, while Mayor Daley sat and smiled, able to end a session with a quick gesture to the chairman. In the side streets of the city as in the side aisles of the convention, those who held power brutally repressed those who sought to share it. And though his sympathies had always been with the latter group, Hubert Humphrey was forced by political reality to acquiesce to the acts of the former, even to defend them: "We ought to quit pretending that Mayor Daley did something that was wrong," he said. Commented one Democratic loyalist, "Now we have two albatrosses around our neck, Lyndon Johnson *and* Dick Daley."

It must be noted that Humphrey had been prepared to salvage the residue of a shattered consensus by going along with the minority plank on Vietnam. But this hope was stilled when L.B.J. sent personal instructions to hold the line for the committee recommendation. McCarthy-McGovern supporters had attempted to reach agreement between themselves and among other uncommitted liberal forces on a plank that Humphrey could also accept, but Johnson's message made it clear that there would have to be a clean break. The thin threads that still held Hubert Humphrey to his old constituencies were being stretched too far, and many of them were breaking.

The defeat of the minority plank by a 3 to 2 margin marked the final demise of the politics of consensus within the Democratic Party; it gave Nixon strategists a fine excuse to ignore those Democrats whose views had been explicitly repudiated. The GOP thesis was that the Democratic doves who had not yet been alienated by Humphrey could never be swung loose, whereas those doves who had been thoroughly alienated would punish Humphrey by voting for Nixon—on the condition that the GOP candidate only avoid explicit bellicosity.

The peace issue was thus perceived as Humphrey's problem; he could pick up votes on either side of the schism only by forfeiting votes on the other. For the first time in a long while, it was the Republicans' opportunity to be all things to all men, and there was every reason to hope that they would be equal to it.

The Republican tactic of allowing Humphrey to be chopped up by the Democratic whipsaw was remarkably successful at first. Shell-shocked by Chicago, plagued by egregious advance work, taunted by hecklers, and spurned by McCarthy's armies, the Democratic nominee tried to gloss over the war issue by stating that the Democrats' two contending Vietnam planks were "so mildly different" that "I would have no difficulty accepting the minority plank at all." But the next day he qualified that comment: Though he *could* have accepted the peace plank, he said, he would have "felt a right and indeed an obligation" to make his own interpretation and elaboration.

On September 9, the Vice-President asserted that he could "safely predict" that the United States would begin Vietnam troop withdrawals by early 1969. But on the following day, the President himself hastened to assure the American Legion that "no man can predict" when "our men can come home." The comment reflected a tension between the two top Democrats that persisted throughout the campaign. The Humphrey staff felt that the President underestimated how unpopular his Administration was, whereas Johnson saw no reason why his party's nominee should have to be defensive about his policies.

And while it seemed as though Johnson—to use Senator McCarthy's phrase—kept behaving like a football coach who ran off the bench to tackle his star runner, there were many sagacious observers who claimed that Johnson's instincts were better than anyone's during the fall. Take a final position as early as possible on your weak issues (like Vietnam)—the President counseled Humphrey—and then go after Nixon with hammer and tongs. By election day people will have ended their obsession with those things that embarrass you, and they will be thinking instead about the things that embarrass the other fellow. In the end, it was the strategy that Humphrey followed—but his delay in coming to it was fatal.

Still, by early October, the Johnson-Humphrey breach was healed enough for the President to make a nationwide radio speech extolling the virtues of the old Democratic Party. "Nixon is the one man," said the President, "who said that Medicare 'would do more harm than good.'" At the same time, Johnson raised the Democrats' most successful propaganda line, the Agnew question, by recalling that "one third of our twentieth-century presidents did not get to live to finish the term in which they were elected."

Humphrey was competing not only for Johnson's demanding heart, however, but also for his money. Some early resentment was aroused by reports that Johnsonites were raising money for the President's proposed library in Austin, Texas, whereas Humphrey's bankroll remained extremely inadequate. But as prospects for victory increased during October, so did the contributions. A television commercial shown nationwide included a special appeal for funds, and, though only about $15,000 was expected the message produced a return of $300,000. Joe Napolitan's devastating television advertisements, previously almost unused in comparison to the omnipresent Nixon advertisements, were finally, during the last ten days, funded on a basis that matched the Republican expenditures.

In fact, a lot of things were done at the end of the Humphrey campaign that might have won the victory had they been started sooner. During the closing days, for example, the Humphrey-Muskie campaign director, Lawrence O'Brien, was able to revive his old "blitz system" of prodding local political operations. Employed successfully for the Kennedy-Johnson ticket in 1960, the technique required the dispatching of political operatives to areas other than their home territories. Because they were not associated with local factions nor interested in a personal future in the politics of that locale, the outsiders could prod and cajole the local organization into movement that inertia and personal rivalries had previously blocked.

Still, on November 5, the Democratic organization across the country failed to meet its usual standards. In Chicago, Mayor Daley's precinct captains gave less attention to the Humphrey-Muskie ticket than they did to local elections. In Ohio, Illinois, and California, the Democratic vote was below expectations in many dependable districts. The Humphrey staff displayed an acid bitterness toward some of the local

Democratic operations, particularly in New Jersey, Ohio, Illinois, and California. Commented one Humphrey aide:

> The only decent guy in the whole New Jersey operation was Governor Hughes . . . The rest of them didn't do a thing to help us. They squabbled, they wasted the money we put in there, and they sat on their hands. They ought to be put in jail for what they did to us.

New Jersey was important because the race turned out to be so close, but back in September no one would have guessed that the failure of the old machines in three or four cities in three or four states might make all the difference.

What turned the campaign around, most observers felt afterward, was Humphrey's Salt Lake City speech on Vietnam on September 30. A remarkably vague and balanced manifesto, the statement did not necessarily represent any fundamental change in policy. However, the show of good intentions and the display of dovish rhetoric (we must take "risks" for peace) were contrasted with Humphrey's hawkish statements of the spring and summer; it provided a lonely peg on which many doves, increasingly apprehensive of Nixon, could hang their hopes and their votes. Now, as Johnson had all along predicted, the statement, simply because it now was out of the way, shifted the emphasis of the Humphrey campaign from the trouble with the Democrats to the trouble with the Republicans. When that happened, Humphrey began to score points. His obvious emulation of Harry Truman appealed only because he was permitted to characterize his opponent as a latter-day McKinley.

Humphrey's ability to run against the "Old Nixon" resulted in part from the Republicans' inability to keep the "New Nixon" in the public eye. More than that, they were also unable to keep the off-balance Humphrey on the defensive. The overtones of partisan negativism and the lack of strongly voiced alternatives permitted Humphrey to make the most of the only kind of campaign he was emotionally capable of running. Rhapsodizing the long-obsolete virtues of the New Deal and labeling the GOP candidate a "cold-war warrior" and an ally of Southern reaction, Humphrey incessantly returned to the theme: What has the Republican Party ever done for you? "We're going to give him [Nixon] plenty of Medicare and Social Security for his retirement after the election," Humphrey would chortle.

Nixon's letter to Wall Street, his open embrace of the oil-depletion allowance, and his "security gap" charges were all that prevented such Humphrey statements from sounding absurd. At Moravian College in Bethlehem, Pennsylvania, Humphrey even tried to impress an undergraduate audience by bragging about the three tax cuts during the Kennedy-Johnson years. The Democratic nominee was obsolete, but the Republican nominee wasn't telling, or at least he was not making his point heard above the autumn clamor.

The eleventh-hour cessation of bombing, followed by a North Vietnamese agreement to negotiate in expanded peace talks on substantive issues, caused Humphrey, whose spirits had been on the rise for three weeks, to burst into an exuberant confidence. Perhaps, it seemed, peace was just around the corner—or, at least, the American people might be made to think so until November 5. But by the time election day had come around, the South Vietnamese had demonstrated that they could play American electoral politics as well as the next foreign government. Their initial refusal to show up in Paris, the leaked reports that the American decision had "given in" to the Communists, the whole aura of confusion that consequently surrounded the halt in bombing, made the decision appear all too political. President Johnson's long-standing credibility gap made him particularly vulnerable to such suspicion, and this vulnerability blunted the impact of autumn's most dramatic event.

There were Nixon analysts, in fact, who claimed that their man had actually gained strength during the hectic final twenty-four hours. "The bombing halt hurt us," they said, "but the Saigon reaction helped us get the situation turned around."

Still, it is clear that on balance the bombing halt helped Humphrey. Together with the Salt Lake City speech, it lowered the saliency of the war issue and increased the impact of other factors on the balloting. But the halt did not provide enough of a push to put the Vice-President over. The President's action removed the albatross, but it did not bestow the crown.

What brought defeat to the Democrats, then, was not so much internal discord as a leadership too rigid to deal with that discord and to harness the still considerable energies of the party. The leadership's candidate, Hubert Humphrey, was defeated not only by the Nixon electoral strategy, but also by his association with the Johnson Administration, by the destructive impact of the Chicago riots, and by his own inability to project the image of a forceful, confident leader. To many he was the dummy seeking to replace the rejected ventriloquist.

The Republicans, still shell-shocked from 1964, could easily see their own recent debacle reflected in the agony of the Democrats. What they did not always grasp was that the Democrats were learning from their agonies and laying the foundation for long-range strength even as they suffered from temporary traumas. In the short run, the preconvention struggle meant that the Democratic Party captured its full share of attention in the public media and established itself as the only party in which relevant issues were being debated with the intensity they demanded. The Democratic Party remained the party of insurgency in 1968 and even in defeat retained at least the potential respect of many voters who disagreed with its policies but admired the courage shown by many of its members. This phenomenon surely was responsible in part for the stunning general election victories of such doves as Senators Church, Cranston, Fulbright, McGovern, Hughes, and Nelson in states that were generally thought to be hawkish and conservative.

A longer-run benefit of the Democratic turmoil was the politicization and Democratization (with a capital D) of many of the most talented members of a new generation. Some of the younger people mobilized by the McCarthy and Kennedy campaigns were Republicans before 1968; a larger group were nominal Democrats who were not averse to voting Republican at least as reprisal to unresponsive leaders; and the majority was probably relatively apolitical and independent before its involvement in the campaign. But in 1969 it seems that many of these new activists are inclined to look on the Democratic Party as their political home. The belated endorsements Humphrey received from just about every springtime insurgent revealed the basic loyalty the Democrats are still able to draw on under the most difficult of circumstances.

And even those lower-level insurgents who failed to support Humphrey do not seem to have written off his party for good. They foresee a bruising and promising battle for control of the Democratic Party during the next four years, and they have already institutionalized their movement into the New Democratic Coalition and its statewide analogues. They will undoubtedly bring permanent discord into the Democratic ranks, but with that discord they will bring a measure of strength and relevance and the prospect of resurgence.

Nearly two decades ago Samuel Lubell observed:

> Our political solar system . . . has been characterized not by two equally competing suns, but by a sun and a moon. It is within the majority party that the issues of any particular period are fought out; while the minority party shines in reflected radiance of the heat thus generated.
>
> The essential strength or weakness of an American political party is not to be measured simply by the votes it commands, but by the *timeliness* of the elements which compose the party's following.

Humphrey supporters showed their ignorance of that fundamental truth when they complained that antiwar demonstrators should have been picketing and heckling the Republican candidate instead of their own. The Democratic Party was the target for protest because it did hold power and because it was still more representative of the disparate elements of American political life than was the GOP. It was thus an inadvertent compliment to the new President when the radical leader David Dellinger announced that the Nixon inaugural would be the target of a demonstration by his National Mobilization Committee to End the War in Vietnam. It was, in its own way, another measure of the transitional nature of 1968–1969 and of the potential this period holds for the Republican Party.

Dellinger's compliment was prompted by the fact that Republicans are now in power. This fact itself may convince some of the spokesmen for the alienated in America that they should make their battle within the GOP. But more than this will be required to convince newly politicized voters to leave their Democratic home. For even if power alone were a sufficient magnet, power is not yet firmly in the Republicans' grasp. Congress is solidly controlled by the

Democrats, and many members of both parties see the Nixon Administration as a temporary anomaly in an era of Democratic control.

More importantly, power alone is not as crucial a factor as is political relevance; at this time in our history, political relevance would seem to require the unsettling presence in a party of the black, the poor, and the young, along with all the other elements of the political spectrum. For this reason a politically relevant party in 1970 and 1972 must be a diversified party today. Intraparty dissent can help a party more than it hurts if its leadership is tolerant, responsive, and resilient. The Democrats did not appreciate that fact as fully as they might have in 1968; whether the Republicans can do better is still to be determined.

The lesson of the experience of the Democratic Party in 1968 would seem to be clear: Those who hold political power do their party a disservice by stifling discussion of fundamental issues in the name of consensus. And its corollary would also seem clear. President Nixon can realize his dream of rebuilding the GOP only if he encourages his party to follow the advice given a group of Young Republicans by Spiro Agnew:

> Carry the crusade for Republican humanism to places where Republicans have long been reluctant or loath to travel. Get a little dust on your shoes. In fact, start acting like a Democrat.

There are important signs that Agnew's advice may be heeded by his party in the next few years. If it is, then the Republican Party may start acting "like Democrats" in the most important way of all—winning elections, and setting the political pace for the nation.

Part II. Political Coalitions in Limbo

Voting blocs have been the story of recent American politics. Thirty-seven years ago Franklin D. Roosevelt forged, on the anvil of the Depression, the political coalition that has dominated American elections ever since. With the support of the South, the labor unions, the big-city machines, the Negroes, and the Catholics, the Democratic Party has enjoyed nearly continuous control of Congress and the White House. Since 1960, however, the country has been ripe for a realignment of political allegiances. John F. Kennedy was to redirect the thinking of the Democratic Party, and the nation, away from their obsession with the past, the Depression, and the New Deal—but Dallas intervened. Then a "government in exile" waited at Harvard University and other Kennedy outposts around the nation while Lyndon Johnson ran through what was to be the final encore of the politics of F.D.R. But again, an assassination changed the picture.

Even after the death of Robert F. Kennedy, it appeared that the old political ties—ethnic, economic, ideological, and emotional—were inevitably loosening. On October 2, 1968, just a month before the election, the Gallup poll reported:

The 1968 presidential race may go into the record books as one that shattered more traditional voting patterns than any other election of this century.

137

If this meant that the 1968 race would have more impact than even the Roosevelt-Hoover contest of 1932, it was certainly a sweeping prediction. But given the unrest in the country, the presence of a strong third-party candidate, and the attenuation of memories of the Depression, the Gallup observation was not unreasonable. There was wide agreement that the ties that had bound the Democratic Party together were fraying at the edges and that 1968 would be a watershed election, comparable to those of 1860, 1896, and 1932. For the first time since the 1920's, many were predicting the GOP would become the majority party in the United States.

With all this potential for change, the fact that nothing significant happened to alter the structure of America's political coalitions may be the most important single lesson of the year 1968.

Chapter 6. The Lost Opportunity

The three men who faced the American electorate in fall 1968 found that among many major voting blocs there was an almost unprecedented lack of party loyalty and enthusiasm. For a large portion of the public, there was a genuine need for a new Roosevelt, a forceful and dynamic leader who could fuse old antagonists into a new and vigorous coalition, as the master of Hyde Park had done in 1932. And it did not have to be a Democrat this time who put the pieces together; 1968 could have seen the formation of a new Republican majority.

But by the time the shouting had died down and the votes had been cast, the old alignments stood pretty much intact. Hubert Humphrey had brought the bulk of the labor movement back into the Democratic Party, and George Wallace turned out to have less appeal than had been hoped or feared. As for Richard Nixon, his narrow victory was almost a replay of the 1960 election. In short, the Republican Party had lost, for four years longer, its chance to secure the allegiance of a majority of American voters.

The politics-as-usual nature of the 1968 election was reflected in the failure of any of the three candidates to bring great numbers of new voters to the polls. Despite the Gallup organization's prediction of a record 75 million ballots, and despite last-minute forecasts of a close election, only 73.2 million people bothered to vote—60 percent of the 122 million Americans of voting age. This represented a substantial decrease from the 69 percent who voted in

1960, and the 64 percent who cast ballots in 1964. Of the ten largest states, all but Texas and Florida had lower percentage turn-outs in 1968 than in 1960 or 1964, and the drop-off was especially noticeable in the largest cities. In fact, the absolute nationwide total might have been smaller than in 1964 if not for the big increases in the South resulting from Negro registration and the accompanying reaction of backlash white voters. Texas, Alabama, Mississippi, and Louisiana accounted collectively for more than 1 million new votes in 1968, but the increase for the entire nation was only about 1.6 million.

In recent years, according to the best available indicators, political parties as such have been losing their hold on the electorate. Since 1940, the Gallup pollsters have been asking voters to categorize themselves by party, and the proportion of self-styled independents has been rising steadily. As a matter of fact, independents have outnumbered Republicans for the last several years.

There is no precise way to determine the number of ticket-splitters in a given election but circumstantial evidence indicates that the number is rising. For example, the number of states simultaneously electing a governor from one party and a U.S. senator from the other has risen sharply since 1946. In that year, of the twenty-four states that held both gubernatorial and senatorial elections, only one elected a Democrat to one office and a Republican to the other. In 1964, 1966, and 1968, however, a majority of such states split their choices. In 1968, the figure was nine out of fifteen, and a month after the election, the Gallup poll reported that 54 percent of the voters had split their tickets.

Another sign of the instability of party allegiance was the Wallace movement of 1968. Political analysts, such as the late V. O. Key, Jr., and Samuel Lubell, have theorized that third parties represent an effort by members of the established parties to seek out new forms of political expression. In the North as well as the South, George Wallace built a substantial following on his contention that there was not "a dime's worth of difference" between the two major parties. (Like most minor candidates, however, his strength was greatest *before* election day.)

What explains these signs of atrophy in partisan loyalties? In general, parties lose their effectiveness when the issues around which they have been built become obsolete. The major parties as presently constituted were founded around economic issues in the years of the Depression. But by 1968, the great controversies raging in America were not primarily of an economic nature. The war in Vietnam was certainly a different kind of issue, and it split both parties down the middle. Although the problems of urban decay and discrimination have obvious economic relevance, they are not intrinsically economic; rather, they reflect moral and social concerns. Therefore, much of the debate on these issues is couched in noneconomic terms—"crime in the streets," "living off welfare," "Black Power," and so on. It is more like a clash between middle-class and lower-class *cultures* than one involving the familiar question of who gets what and how much.

With these new issues have come several new kinds of political cleavages—cutting across society in new ways, creating strange bedfellows and new hostilities. One of these cleavages might be termed the status cleavage, dividing the nation into three general groupings: those with power—labor unions, big business, farmers, the technocratic elite; those desiring new power relationships—the lower classes, blacks, the student left; and those whom power has left behind—small-town residents and ethnic groups who identify with traditional values. If the two latter groups are combined, they make up a coalition that is alienated from the dominant power structure of America, and especially from the policies of the federal government, leaving labor, farmers, big business, and the technocrats on the other side of this alienation cleavage. Another major cleavage is based on the question of what to do about various kinds of deviant social groups, such as criminals, black militants, campus protesters, hippies, and pornographers. Those who advocate a hard line in dealing with such nonconformists include businessmen, union members, farmers, small-town dwellers, and lower-class ethnics; those who are apt to be more tolerant include the disadvantaged, the student left, and the liberal elements of the intellectual and technocratic elites. None of these new cleavages is directly related to the economic divisions of the immediate post-New Deal period.

The old economic alignments still have meaning for people in poverty, who remain attached to the Democratic Party. Conversely, the very wealthy remain Republican. But the mass of Americans in between are no longer in economic need, and have shifted their concern to questions of status and power. They are shopping for new and lasting party affiliations.

The year 1968 was an excellent opportunity for the Republican Party to attain majority status with the American electorate. In control of neither elective branch of the federal government, it could not be blamed for troubles at home or abroad. In fact, as cited above, the GOP's rating with the public had risen to stunning heights compared with the unfathomed deeps to which it had sunk in 1964. The opportunity was so great that even the Republican professionals could scarcely comprehend it.

Some 10 million Americans went shopping on election day 1968 and bought Wallace. This massive dislocation of normal voting patterns—which could have been much larger if the major-party candidates had not altered their strategies and positions in response to the third-party challenge—has been the subject of much speculation. Did Wallace take votes from the Democrats, votes that may return to the Democrats and oust Richard Nixon from the White House in 1972? Or did the Alabamian take votes from the Republicans, leaving the GOP the task of wooing them back in order to hold the line? Or did Wallace have an equal effect on both parties, and on balance not influence the outcome at all?

Because Wallace derived more than half his votes from the South, and because most Southerners consider themselves Democrats, it is easy to conclude that Wallace hurt Humphrey more than Nixon. But it is doubtful that the third-party voters, in the absence of Wallace, would have rushed headlong into the arms of Hubert Humphrey. More likely, Wallace's main support came from the far less predictable breed of Southern Democrat typified by the former governor himself; certainly many who voted for Wallace had voted for the Republican presidential nominee in 1964.

When the 1968 returns are studied closely, *Wallace does not seem to have influenced the final outcome at all.* This can be demonstrated by comparing the results of the 1968 election with those of 1960. The Republican candidate was the same in both cases, the political complexion of the Democratic ticket was similar—and the outcomes were similar enough to virtually discount the Wallace effect. For example, consider the states that Nixon took in 1960, and those he won in 1968.

For example, consider the relationship between the states that Nixon took in 1960 and those he won in 1968, as displayed in Table 1 on the following page. Note that 35 states (Nixon's 24 plus the 11 Humphrey states Nixon lost in 1960) went to the same party in 1968 as they had eight years earlier. Furthermore, the 8 states Nixon gained in 1968 were those he had narrowly missed taking in 1960. In other words, Richard Nixon's harvest of states in 1968 was ex-

Table 1.

Nixon's Popular Vote, 1960	Nixon States, 1968	Humphrey States, 1968	Wallace States, 1968
50.0% or more	24	2	0
49.0–49.9%	5	2	0
47.5–48.9%	3	3	0
47.4% or less	0	6	5
Total	32	13	5

actly what he would have won in 1960 had he done slightly better—*despite George Wallace.*

The Wallace impact is also minimized when one looks at Nixon's share of the two-party vote in all sections of the nation in 1960 and 1968.

Table 2.

	Nixon's Two-Party Percentage, 1960	Nixon's Two-Party Percentage, 1968
Northeast	47	46
South	48	53
Midwest	53	52
Far West	51	53
Nation	50	50

Except for the South, Nixon's proportion of the two-party vote in 1968 was almost exactly what it was in 1960—*despite George Wallace.*

Nixon's popular vote had the same geographic make-up in 1960 as in 1968.

Table 3.

	1960	1968
Northeast	30.6	29.0
South	15.6	17.5
Midwest	36.8	34.2
Far West	17.0	19.3
Total	100.0	100.0

Furthermore, the geographical breakdown of the Humphrey vote was nearly identical to Kennedy's in 1960.

Table 4.

	Kennedy, 1960	Humphrey, 1968
Northeast	34.1	34.2
South	16.6	16.0
Midwest	33.1	32.2
Far West	16.2	17.6
Total	100.0	100.0

That is to say, each party's 1968 electoral coalition was almost identical, on a geographic basis, to what it had assembled in 1960—*despite George Wallace.*

According to the Gallup poll, only nonwhites, the grade-school educated, farmers, and Catholics shifted their major-party preferences significantly between 1960 and 1968. But most of the major demographic groupings—whites, both sexes, the college- and high-school educated, professionals and businessmen, white-collar and manual workers, all age groups, Protestants, Republicans, Democrats, and independents—came out about the same in both years—*despite George Wallace.*

For the most part, then, Nixon and Humphrey split the nation in 1968 much as Nixon and Kennedy had split it in 1960. This suggests that George Wallace took roughly the same number of voters from each party—although perhaps half those who supported him in the early autumn but deserted him by election day seem to have been Democrats.

This last observation tells a great deal about how the electorate behaved during the final months of the campaign. In mid-August—after the Republican convention, but before the Democratic meeting—Richard Nixon received a 45 percent rating in the Gallup poll, his highest since December

1967 (when he was paired against Lyndon Johnson, without Wallace). Even after the debacle in Chicago, however, Nixon slipped back to 43 percent, his high of the previous spring (against Humphrey and Wallace). From then until election day, he deviated no more than one percentage point from that rating. In the aggregate, all the action was between the Humphrey column, the Wallace column, and those who listed themselves as undecided. Though the Republican campaign may have been successful in its specific appeals to potential Wallace voters, it lost one vote to the Democrats for every one it picked up from Wallace. (This is not too surprising, considering what had to be done to attract Wallace's admirers.) Similarly, for every vote the GOP ticket won from the undecideds, it also lost one of its own to the Humphrey-Muskie team. And for every vote Richard Nixon won directly from Hubert Humphrey, Humphrey won one right back. (See Table 5.)

Table 5.   Gallup Poll Figures for the Last Three Months of the Campaign

Date	Nixon	Humphrey	Wallace	Undecided
August 8–11	45	29	18	8
September 3–7	43	31	19	7
September 20–22	43	28	21	8
September 27–30	44	29	20	7
October 3–12	43	31	20	6
October 17–21	44	36	15	5
October 31–November 2	42	40	14	4
November 5 (actual)	43.4	42.7	13.5	

While the Nixon-Agnew ticket remained paralyzed at the 43 percent level, the Democrats chipped away at the American Independent Party's following, getting almost one third of this vote and all those who were undecided.[1] The old F.D.R. coalition had enough resiliency and tenacity after all to resist attacks by both Richard Nixon and George Wallace. As Richard M. Scammon, former head of the Bureau of the Census and now with the Governmental Affairs Institute, put it:

> The old Democratic coalition was not dead this year, except in the South. The Negroes, the Jews, the intellectuals, and much of labor remained loyal.

Scammon added, "But 1968 could be the coalition's last hurrah." During the 1968 campaign, however, neither Richard Nixon nor Hubert Humphrey had the nerve to roll the corpse into the grave and cover it up. The "old politics" of voting still prevailed in 1968 in the labor force, the suburbs, and even—despite Wallace's strong showing—the South.

Organized labor is perhaps the most obvious example of a group once vitally concerned with economic issues, but now affluent enough to worry about such special questions as the race of the man next door and the deleterious effects of the welfare system on the nation's moral fiber. Therefore, this group was seen as the prime target for Wallace's appeals in the North—the celebrated backlash vote. Nixon assumed that by taking a relatively hard line on social issues, he could share these Democratic defectors with Wallace. What he forgot was the lesson of 1964—that a backlash appeal to the blue-collar vote will fail unless the candidate guar-

[1] Again, this only represents what happened in the aggregate; the Gallup poll reported that "As many as 19 million voters (i.e., one quarter of the total) said they had at some point during the campaign intended to vote for a candidate other than the one they ended up voting for."

antees a continuation of the economic security that made this bloc susceptible to the backlash in the first place. And in 1968, as in most years, the Republicans fell short in this regard. Not always on merit, the Democrats succeeded in identifying themselves with such beneficial programs as Medicare and Social Security, and with a strong pro-labor philosophy.

According to Gallup, the Republicans have taken the following share of the union vote in recent presidential elections. (See Table 6.)

Table 6.

1936–48	less than 30%
1952	39%
1956	43%
1960	35%
1964	27%
1968	29%

Nixon's 1968 share of the union vote dropped six percentage points from 1960, and (because Humphrey won 56 percent of this vote) he even netted less (34 percent) of the two-party union vote in 1968 than eight years before. And significantly, from early October to November 5, Humphrey (according to Gallup) picked up fifteen percentage points with the union vote.

In September 1968, the Gallup poll reported that Nixon and Humphrey were dividing manual laborers about evenly, each getting about one third, with Wallace getting one fourth and the rest undecided. On election day, however, one half of the manual labor vote went Democratic, and only a little more than one third stayed with Nixon. Indeed, Nixon's share of the two-party labor vote was up only one percentage point from 1960, despite the fact that George Wallace was supposed to draw many union members away from the Democratic column. Clearly, a magnificent opportunity to capture a major element of the Democratic coalition had been lost.

Much of the labor-backlash stereotype also includes the Roman Catholics, and a number of commentators have noted Nixon's sharp improvement over the Republican share of this vote in the past two elections. Of this there is no doubt, but when Nixon's 1968 showing is compared to Dwight D. Eisenhower's share of the Catholic vote, it is less impressive. (See Table 7.)

Table 7. GOP Share of Catholic Vote.

1952	44%
1956	49%
1960	22%
1964	24%
1968	33% (36% of two-party vote)

Nixon's percentage falls roughly halfway between the highs of the 1950's and the lows of the 1960's. It is highly misleading to suggest that the Catholic vote is going Republican to any significant extent, especially because the improvement may have been the result of the large numbers of Catholics who are joining the middle class. According to NBC's national precinct samples, even the Italians, the most Republican of all Catholic nationality groups, gave a majority of their vote to Humphrey.

Another economically liberated group with "swing" potential in 1968 was the suburbanites, who held the balance of power in several major states. Suburban voters supplied both Nelson Rockefeller and Eugene McCarthy with preconvention support, and they were willing to cross party lines both ways for an appealing candidate.

By November 1968, these voters apparently realized that

no such candidate remained in the race. Though *Time, Newsweek,* and *U.S. News and World Report* all noted a decline in the Republican share of the suburban two-party vote, it seems clear that the suburbs did not deviate very far from their 1960 performance. Take, for example, Nixon's showing in the counties surrounding New York City. (See Table 8.)

Table 8.

	Nixon %, 1960	Nixon Two-Party %, 1968
Bergen, New Jersey	59	58
Essex, New Jersey	44	43
Fairfield, Connecticut	54	55
Hudson, New Jersey	39	41
Nassau, New York	55	54
Orange, New York	61	62
Rockland, New York	55	53
Suffolk, New York	59	64
Union, New Jersey	51	50
Westchester, New York	57	54

As with so many other groups, it was 1960 all over again for these suburbs.

The South has been a tempting target for Republican strategists for the last twenty years. Over this period, its electoral votes have been divided as shown in Table 9.

Table 9.

	Democratic	Republican	Other
1948	99	0	39 (Thurmond)
1952	81	57	0
1956	60	77	1 (Jones)
1960	81	43	14 (Byrd)
1964	90	47	0
1968	25	66	46 (Wallace)

Generally, Republicans have sought to woo Southern voters with two approaches. One, the Eisenhower-Nixon strategy, was to aim at the more populous states of the so-called peripheral South (Florida, Kentucky, North Carolina, Tennessee, Texas, and Virginia), emphasizing a philosophical conservatism likely to appeal to the new business and professional elite. The other approach, used by Barry Goldwater, was built on opposition to a strong federal civil-rights program and achieved its greatest success in the Deep South. As Goldwater discovered, the Deep South strategy is likely to cost the candidate the peripheral South (because of the rising black vote, overriding economic considerations, and a stubborn Democratic tradition), and the rest of the country as well.

This year, by following the first approach, the GOP candidate was able to increase his share of the major-party vote in the South over his 1960 showing, and his electoral votes as well. This was undoubtedly owing in large part to the absence of a Southerner on the Democratic ticket, and perhaps to Strom Thurmond's maneuverings in the Carolinas. But here again, Nixon gained few converts during the campaign, as shown by the Gallup figures for September and the final result. When the aggregate vote alone is considered,

Table 10.

	Nixon	Humphrey	Wallace	Undecided
September	33	21	38	8
Election	35	31	33	

Humphrey appears to have picked up the bulk of the Wallace waverers and the undecided voters.

Republicans could view Nixon's performance in the South with complacency if it were not for his failure among two key groups within the region—blacks and Latin Americans.

The NBC national-precinct sample indicated that Humphrey won more than 90 percent of both groups in the South (and more than 90 percent of *all* blacks in America). This is particularly significant because more and more members of these groups are being enrolled as voters each year; these groups are unquestionably responsible in large part for the fact that, although the percentage turn-out of voters dropped during the 1960's in the nation as a whole, it rose in the South.

Table 11.

	1960 Turnout	1964 Turnout	1968 Turnout
Alabama	31%	36%	51%
Arkansas	41	50	51
Florida	50	53	56
Georgia	30	43	44
Kentucky	59	53	51
Louisiana	45	47	54
Mississippi	25.5	33	50
North Carolina	53.5	52	54
South Carolina	30.5	38	46
Tennessee	50	51	53
Texas	42	44	49
Virginia	33	41	50

In the South, as in so many other parts of the nation, the Republicans failed to capture many voters who might have made a change. Furthermore, the GOP in 1968 seemed to lose contact with the newest groups in the electorate.

The Republican candidate in 1968 failed to take advantage of the numerous opportunities for party realignment that existed earlier in the year.

Though the GOP has been a minority party since the Depression, it seems unwilling or unable to take the steps necessary to broaden its appeal. And so it has left many disaffected members of the old Democratic coalition to wander, disappointed, back into the fold. A question remains, one that confronted the Republican presidential nominee this year and one that confronts all GOP candidates: What kinds of issues are likely to appeal to such diverse groups as union laborers, suburbanites, and Southerners (and which Southerners, black or white, urban or rural)?

At a minimum, it seems obvious that a Republican candidate must not:

1. *Appear too conservative on economic, bread-and-butter issues.* He must not, in short, fit the usual Republican stereotype of being pro-big business, antilabor, antiminimum wage, and anti-Medicare. This should enable him to get his foot in the door with union labor.

2. *Appear too militant on foreign-policy issues.* The swing vote in the suburbs is sensitive to these issues. With their high educational level, the suburbanites have been the key group to turn against the Vietnam war, and they comprise a highly internationalist segment of society. A return to cold-war clichés is likely to alienate them.

3. *Appear too unsympathetic to equal rights.* The Southerners who voted Republican in 1956 and 1960 obviously remained in the party despite its moderately pro-civil-rights position (for the period). And if this group were combined with enough of the newly enfranchised black and Latin American voters, the Republicans could expect to carry the larger states of the South for many elections to come.

Before a candidate can hope to appeal for a specific bloc's votes, he must prove that he has its members' "gut" interests in mind. Republicans can use sophisticated, collateral approaches to seal the loyalty of a group ready to be persuaded, but if GOP candidates fail to demonstrate sympathy for a bloc's primary concerns, efforts at secondary appeals will not be accepted as having been made in good faith. Nixon's cries for law and order did not captivate union members, because he still looked too much like the candidate of big business—with his Wall Street letter suggesting a lenient approach to securities regulation, and his expressed willingness to keep the oil-depletion allowance (which even Wallace sporadically opposed). His sophisticated radio addresses on such subjects as the nature of the Presidency and new political alignments failed to win many intellectuals and suburbanites because he was coy about the war in Vietnam—to them the paramount issue. Nixon's proposals for black capitalism fell on deaf ears in the black community because he was Strom Thurmond's candidate and because the concept appealed more to worried whites than to poor blacks. Civil rights is one issue that unites all Negroes, but less was said on the subject in this election—by either major party—than in any presidential campaign of this decade.

Richard Nixon's strategy of noncommitment failed, according to practically all available data, to increase the Republican share of the two-party vote over 1960. (The only group with which Nixon did relatively well was the farmers. But they are declining in numbers, and have a notorious tendency to vote against the incumbent party. Orville Freeman probably delivered the farm bloc to Nixon in 1968; in 1972 Orville Freeman will not be around to help.)

But when all is said and done, the question of how to attract the wavering voters is probably not merely a question of issues. Political analysts were struck this year by a number of seemingly illogical phenomena: hawks voting for McCarthy; Robert Kennedy supporters winding up with Wallace; and similar developments. The reason seemed to be a respect for a man's style and courage rather than his position on specific issues.

Perhaps what the voters of 1968 were really seeking was a man of strong personal charisma—regardless of his stands on issues. Richard Nixon, dealing in platitudes, and Hubert Humphrey, beating the Administration's drums, simply did not fill the bill. Humphrey was finally able to lure the disenchanted by raising old specters, showing some spunk, and making a few gestures to the left. The bland campaign of Richard Nixon lured few new voters.

Samuel Lubell, who usually deprecates the importance of issues in American elections, commented in mid-October: "No candidate can hope to create the image of a leader who inspires trust and confidence unless he discusses the critical issues in specific detail." Continuing, Lubell wondered if "Nixon's 'play-it-safe' campaigning may not cause him to muff a historical opportunity . . . to develop and articulate a program of action around which the quiet, moderate majority in the country can rally."

And so it was in 1968, with the triumph of a lost opportunity to assemble a new American majority.

CHAPTER 7. The Working Man

With increasingly less logic but undiminished persistence, organized labor has remained a pillar of Democratic majority. Labor was a principal link in F.D.R.'s coalition, and such labor leaders as George Meany have long been a part of the informal Democratic hierarchy. The organizational talents of the labor movement and its ability to produce for candidates at both the national and local levels have become legend over the past three decades. Originally, the basis for this close cooperation was the economic situation of the individual working man, who saw the GOP as pro-business and directly opposed to his personal needs and security.

As the political prognosticators of 1968 considered the role of labor, they saw many factors ready to intervene between the working man and the party of F.D.R. The average union member no longer had the continually pressing economic problems that had so long determined his political allegiance. In fact, some elements of the labor movement objected to the economic and social treatment accorded another stalwart of the old coalition, the black American. And in view of Lyndon Johnson's cordial relations with many of the country's biggest businessmen (Johnson being no mean capitalist himself), it seemed more difficult for the GOP to be branded as the party of the fat cats. George Wallace was assaulting the labor force for votes, and individual Republicans had been doing well with the working man at the local level. There was an extraordinary opportunity this year for the Republican Party to capture a large segment of the hourly-wage worker's vote—but it was an opportunity which was not grasped by GOP leaders.

There is strong evidence that the votes of union members —and of all hourly-wage employees—were ripe for picking by the Republicans in 1968. In the minds of newly affluent working families, the bread-and-butter labor issues took second place to concern over the Vietnam conflict, inflation, civil rights, law and order, and high taxes. The trade-union member—more likely than not a young suburbanite—was not much impressed with the traditional party of labor, the Democratic Party. This is not to imply that the working man—union or nonunion—was moving to register Republican. He was still a Democrat, but his mind was open to the GOP appeal.

Certainly the old stereotype image of the working man has become obsolete. Forty-six percent of union families currently report incomes between $7,500 and $15,000 a year, according to a poll taken by the Committee on Political Education (COPE) of the AFL-CIO. Twenty-five percent of all union members are less than thirty years of age, and 50 percent are less than forty. Nearly 75 percent of union members under the age of forty live in suburban communities; 50 percent of all union members now live outside the central city.

In August 1967, a COPE poll of union members found that repeal of Section 14b of the Taft-Hartley Act—the so-called right-to-work provision that has long been anathema to the working man—was viewed as the least important of the major issues. The implication of this rating becomes even clearer when it is noted that water- and air-pollution control, truth in lending, and truth in packaging were viewed as most crucial by the union men and women. Nearly a year later, in June 1968, the Communications Workers of America listed Vietnam, civil rights and riots, and inflation and tax increases as the top three national concerns of its membership. What was happening was that the union members were becoming less responsive to labor problems, and were behaving more like the middle class.

Public Opinion Surveys, Inc., of Princeton, New Jersey, conducted a telephone poll of 409 specially selected union members across the country during the period September 20–25, 1968, for *The New York Times.* In reporting 34 percent of the union preference for Hubert Humphrey, 32 percent for Richard Nixon, and 25 percent for George Wallace, the pollsters found that 47 percent of those polled either did not know whom the AFL-CIO had endorsed (Hubert Humphrey) or thought its endorsement had gone to one of the other candidates. The importance of union endorsements was discounted by the *Times* poll. Though 20 percent of the respondents said they "almost always" supported the union-endorsed candidate, 22 percent said they "almost never" did. The bulk, 54 percent, were in the broad "sometimes" field between. Forty-nine percent of those interviewed disapproved of President Johnson's handling of the war in Vietnam, only 36 percent actually approved of the conduct of the war, and 15 percent were unsure. A Machinists Union poll confirms that a sizable minority of union members differ with their leadership over key liberal and Democratic programs. In July 1968, 22 percent of the machinists disapproved of massive federal aid to the cities—a concern rated as the most important national issue by only 1 percent. Tax relief was listed by 55 percent as the most important issue in the election.

The director of COPE, Alexander E. Barkan, summed up the generation-and-issue gap existing within organized labor's ranks in an article in the August 1967 issue of the *American Federationist:*

> Where support appears least strong generally is among younger members, and more and more the trade union movement is becoming a younger movement. While two-thirds of members over 30, for example, said they pay a lot of attention to their union publications, only half of those under 30 do. . . . It is the younger members who are both less informed and less concerned with [the] issues. The tribulations of 30 years ago are remote from a young member's experience. The Depression is a moment of history and the issues it spawned are tangential to his life or unrelated to his problems. To younger members, Franklin D. Roosevelt, who was a live inspiration to many of us, is but a name in the history books and his great achievements a matter for the archives.

While this trend was building, fresh signs of union support for Republicans began to appear in the 1966 elections. Nelson Rockefeller, running for reelection as governor of New York, received more than 25 union endorsements in his battle against Democrat Frank O'Connor. Tacit support for the governor came also from such traditionally Democratic and Liberal Party stalwarts as the New York State Labor Federation and the Amalgamated Clothing Workers. In April 1966, the International Association of Machinists and Aerospace Workers, the fourth largest labor group in the country and third largest affiliate of the AFL-CIO, ran a two-page spread in its official publication, *The Machinist*, telling its 900,000 members what a good job six Republican senators and twelve Republican congressmen were doing. Entitled "For a Grand New Party," the article noted that these eighteen legislators "are Republicans of a new breed, capable of attracting city voters. Their records are worthy of serious consideration." Pictured were Senators Thomas

Kuchel, John S. Cooper, Margaret Chase Smith, Clifford Case, Jacob Javits, and Hugh Scott, and Congressmen Paul Fino, Seymour Halpern, Frank Horton, Ogden Reid, Alexander Pirnie, Robert Corbett, Joseph McDade, John Saylor, Richard Schweiker, William Ayres, and Alvin O'Konski. That was 1966; two years later, the GOP's chances with labor should, if anything, have been even better.

A majority of organized labor's leadership does not have a history of being friendly to Republican candidates or office-holders. This does not mean, however, that the ties that bind the labor hierarchy and Democratic office-seekers are always strong ones. Senator Robert Kennedy found that his early association with the McClellan Committee hearings on labor corruption in 1959 had come back to haunt him in the days just before his tragic death. Eugene McCarthy, referred to as "51 percent liberal" by some labor officials, was opposed by the great majority of union leaders in his bid for the Democratic nomination for President. At one point in his campaign, Senator McCarthy accused labor's officialdom of "selling out for a White House dinner invitation."

But Hubert Humphrey was a man toward whom labor leaders felt warmly, and George Meany, president of the AFL-CIO, wasted no time after Lyndon Johnson's dramatic March 31 withdrawal in shifting labor's support to the Vice-President. It soon became clear that all the apparatus of organized labor would be engaged first in getting Hubert Humphrey nominated and then in securing his election. The question became how much of the rank-and-file support the Republican nominee and George Wallace would be able to attract.

Labor's behind-the-scenes support was crucial to Hubert Humphrey's preconvention maneuvering. The AFL-CIO's Committee on Political Education (COPE) worked quietly for Hubert Humphrey in the days before the convention, and was a vital part of the Humphrey operation at the International Amphitheater in Chicago. COPE director Alexander Barkan, one of the shrewdest political operatives in the country, managed labor's efforts at the convention. Lane Kirkland, Meany's administrative assistant, Andrew Biemiller, AFL-CIO legislative director, and Al Zack, public relations director, joined Barkan in a special office on the amphitheater balcony, where they kept in contact with the 201 labor union officials who were delegates and the 103 who were alternates. The "labor caucus" represented forty-three states and was influential in defeating the anti-Humphrey forces on a series of important floor fights—rules, credentials, and the platform's Vietnam war plank. Some of the more prestigious union officials in attendance at Chicago included Ivan W. Abel, president of the United Steelworkers Union and of the AFL-CIO's Industrial Union Department, a member of the Pennsylvania delegation, and John Lyons, president of the International Association of Bridge, Structural, and Ornamental Ironworkers, from Missouri. Both are AFL-CIO vice-presidents and executive council members. Labor's showing here was in sharp contrast to the handful of union officials at the Republican convention, where the only notable was Lee W. Minton, president of the Glass Blowers Association.

But in the fall, Hubert Humphrey found himself in an uphill battle. Richard Nixon came out of the Republican convention as the leader of a unified party and exemplar of a program bound to appeal to working people—law and order, cures for inflation and the war, and an end to "the mess at home and abroad." George Wallace stepped up his appeal to the white working man's fear of Negro gains, and it soon appeared that the Alabamian would reap great benefits from the nervous state of American society.

A June Gallup poll gave Humphrey 47 percent of the

union members' vote, as against 28 percent for Nixon and 18 percent for Wallace. A poll of the Connecticut membership of the United Automobile Workers conducted in August gave Wallace 30 percent, with Nixon and Humphrey splitting the rest. At the Ford Motor Company's Lincoln and Mercury plant in Middlesex County, New Jersey, a poll of 100 workers found 62 in favor of Governor Wallace. At a General Motors plant in the same state, a sample of 500 union men gave Wallace 73 percent of the vote. Wallace was even able to garner some unsolicited endorsements from union locals. Working men would say Wallace had "guts." He expressed their concern with high taxes, peace marches, the intellectual establishment, and the whole myriad of problems associated with life in an advanced industrial state. He played on the belief that the government had done something for everyone but the working man. Richard Nixon, too, tried to dance to this tune, appealing regularly to the "forgotten man" and the "silent American."

The labor establishment took arms against these threats with a total political budget estimated variously at anywhere from $20 to $50 million. COPE alone set aside $750,000 for registration campaigns (as of August, only 42 percent of the Los Angeles union membership was registered and only 30 percent in Cleveland's Cuyahoga County) and $500,000 for "political education." The AFL-CIO regularly taxes each member one and one-third cents each month for its "Special Purpose Fund," which amounted to $2,229,338 for fiscal 1967 and was spent primarily on "voter registration" and "influencing state legislation." In 1964–1965 COPE gave $942,000 directly to candidates. It is believed that this amount was considerably increased in 1968, even though the departure of the United Automobile Workers from the ranks of the AFL-CIO cost COPE $180,000. Commented one Democratic Party leader in Southern California: "Without labor's guarantees, we couldn't have had even the office and phones we needed, and they put up at least half of the people we had."

Union newspapers delivered the message to the faithful. The October edition of the Brotherhood of Railway and Airline Clerks' monthly magazine contained no fewer than forty-four pictures of Hubert Humphrey in twenty-four pages. A column by the Vice-President began appearing in nearly all union publications in August. Local labor leaders attempting to endorse Nixon or Wallace were threatened with political reprisals by their national officers. (The only prominent labor official to endorse Nixon was David Mac-Donald, a past president of the United Steelworkers Union.) The AFL-CIO even recorded a campaign song, "The Spiro T. Agnew Blues." A sample lyric:

Around my block, we say Polack and have some names
for Italians and Jews,
But that fat Jap taking a nap gave me the Spiro T.
Agnew Blues.

In a more serious vein, the AFL-CIO National Auxiliaries, made up of the wives, mothers, and children of union members, asked the families of union men to give one day a week until election day for "approved" political activity. COPE began a computer system to collect data on the national AFL-CIO membership for political purposes. Data-processing systems were set up in California, Colorado, the District of Columbia, Connecticut, Maryland, New Mexico, Ohio, Pennsylvania, and Texas, and "political profiles" were prepared on approximately 3.5 million union members. Major union emphasis was placed on sixty congressional districts, including all those in which friends of organized labor lost by less than 5 percent in 1966. COPE endorsed candidates in 353 races for the U.S. Congress—326 for the House

(186 of whom were victorious) and 27 for the Senate (15 of whom won).

In at least one instance labor decided that efforts to register its own union men were counterproductive. In Michigan, UAW president Walter Reuther stopped a drive to register voters in normally Democratic white working-class neighborhoods who had been dropped from the lists because of failure to vote. Interestingly, the registration drive was redirected at Detroit's black inner city, where four out of five Negroes who voted were expected to choose Humphrey. In Chicago, where some 100 union staffers worked nearly full-time on politics, the labor emphasis was on delivering half a million "Vote, Baby, Vote" leaflets on the Negro south side. Los Angeles union organizations imported more than 100 farm workers to help get Mexican-Americans to the polls. As labor figured it, the unregistered whites were apt to be for Wallace, whereas the unregistered blacks or browns would be for Humphrey.

The union effort was an extraordinary one in 1968. In part, it was activated by fear of Wallace—not so much because Wallace might win as because he could elect Richard Nixon. Nixon was still poison to labor's officialdom. COPE's Al Barkan put it bluntly: "Don't let anybody kid you that there's a new Nixon. Nixon's the same union-hater he's always been." The national labor leadership had convinced itself that a Nixon victory would mean a drastic change in labor's position in American life. One edition of the Machinists Union newspaper went so far as to claim that legislation already in Congress would "destroy industrywide bargaining, cram a federal open shop down labor's throat, abolish the National Labor Relations Board, outlaw multi-union bargaining, smash traditional collective bargaining, and undermine labor's political efforts." "If a conservative"—read Richard Nixon—"is elected," the editorial said, "he could later alter the whole stance of government from a protector of labor's rights to an oppressor."

The dangers of Wallace were evident, Richard Nixon was a favorite target, and Hubert Humphrey belonged to organized labor out of long loyalty and present need. The stage had been set for a massive effort, and organized labor delivered as promised: the coffers were open, and there were no embarrassing strikes and no slowdowns. Some unions distributed a sixteen-page anti-Wallace booklet to their members. The Southern Committee on Political Ethics, an organization financed by labor, foundations, and individuals, prepared this pamphlet, which described Wallace's anti-union positions, his support of right-to-work laws, and the low level of Alabama's unemployment benefits and workmen's compensation.

Another reason for organized labor's huge campaign effort was the Democratic nominee himself. Labor leaders had worked to get Humphrey the second spot in 1964 and had boosted him for the top of the ticket in 1968—Hubert Humphrey was in debt to these men and in need of their assistance. Here was organized labor's opportunity to give the nation the closest thing it had known to a labor party. Here was an opportunity to ensure that the Rooseveltian liberalism of the 1930's would remain alive for at least four more years. And what better man to fight in this holy crusade than the man who had actively supported Taft-Hartley, whose support for labor's concerns during his terms in Congress was never strong, and who had been quoted after his first election to the House in 1946 as saying, "I was elected to smash the union bosses," Richard Nixon himself!

Election day appeared to vindicate the efforts of organized labor, for the Republicans managed to win only the same two-party percentage they had polled in 1960. Without the active support of big labor, Hubert Humphrey would not have been able to launch a viable campaign, and would not have come as close as he did on November 5. Richard Scammon of the Governmental Affairs Institute, for one, believes that intensive campaigning by labor leaders accounted for the Humphrey-Muskie ticket's carrying Michigan (where 40 percent of the eligible workers belong to unions) and New York and Pennsylvania (with 2.5 million and 1.5 million union members respectively).

There is little doubt that organized labor's massive election drive had an impact. But it is easy to overestimate the size of this impact. Labor provided the Democratic Party with the national campaign machinery that the party lacked because of its state of disarray and disunity. But the polls mentioned earlier rather conclusively indicated that most union men have little respect for their leadership's voting recommendations and that the number of members who actually read the union publications is small. Furthermore, the Republican campaign, too, was well financed, and aimed to a large extent at this same working man. To understand the Republican failure to mount a serious challenge to the Democratic-labor axis, we must look to other factors.

First of all, the union man is a behavioral Democrat in the voting booth. It is not that he is incapable of voting for a Republican, but every Republican has to overcome a suspicion in the mind of the union member that the GOP is against his interests. As the working man becomes less concerned with the bread-and-butter issues, the presumption grows easier to overcome, but it nonetheless remains. Where a Republican can demonstrate the proper concern, he can win even in the heart of union territory, as evidenced by Congressman Donald Riegle's smashing victory in Flint, Michigan. Riegle carried his heavily unionized district with

56 percent of the vote last fall, whereas Nixon ran far behind.

Richard Nixon came across to the average working man as the typical Republican—a man at home with the wealthy interest groups, and not quite attuned to the problem of America's workers. Besides the Wall Street letter and the pledge to retain the oil-depletion allowance, Nixon's assurance in Fort Worth that he would toughen import restrictions on beef and his apparent insensitivity to the plight of the farm workers in California contributed to labor's uneasiness. Whatever the merits—political or otherwise—of these positions, they were ill suited to attracting the labor vote and destroying the Democratic coalition. Commented a truck driver from Union, New Jersey: "I used to be a liberal. Now I'm more conservative, but I wouldn't vote Republican." And in Trenton, Michigan, during the campaign, a supervisor at an auto-frame plant observed, "Nixon talks like he knows everything—just like a Republican."

There was a lesson for Republicans in George Wallace's nearly successful bid for labor's support. When a Republican runs his campaign, as Barry Goldwater did in 1964, so as to appeal exclusively to other Republicans and to those right of center on the political spectrum, he inevitably will alienate union members and their families. A third-party movement emanating from the Democratic Party, however, can run a right-wing campaign and attract sizable rank-and-file support. The Wallace movement was a populist movement, stirring grass-roots support and taking full advantage of racist sentiment. To many working men, Wallace represented firmness and consistency and a feeling for the "little guy," not traditional conservatism. George Wallace's unsolicited endorsement by UAW Chevrolet Local 659, the United Automobile Workers' second largest, would have been an unimaginable feat for Barry Goldwater. Wallace's continuing extremism, his inexperience, the massive campaign against him, his choice of Curtis LeMay as a running mate, and the normal rejection of third-party movements all helped to diminish his appeal to union men by November 5. His campaign proved that it takes more than being right of center to win the heart of labor.

The Democratic-labor coalition is not invincible, and in fact some dents were inflicted on it last fall. Democratic Governor Richard J. Hughes claimed that the Wallace vote reduced normal Democratic margins in urban, and heavily unionized, New Jersey counties, and made it possible for Nixon to carry the state. Furthermore, the Nixon Administration has come into office fully cognizant of labor's antagonism. With the business community strongly opposed to many of labor's pet projects—the foremost being coalition bargaining—it is no time for the unions to be at odds with the Administration. Some movement toward reconciliation is likely.

The Democratic-labor coalition showed evidence of weakness at the congressional and state levels in 1968, as a number of Republican gubernatorial, senatorial, and congressional candidates owed their victories to the support of union members. Indeed, some local unions went so far as to endorse Republicans their membership favored, as was the case with Detroit Congressman Jack H. MacDonald. Republicans now hold the governor's office in nearly all the major industrial states.

There were even surprising signs of latent local-union support for Nixon during the campaign. Patrick Juliano, deputy secretary of the department of labor and industry in Pennsylvania, managed to gather 200 union officials to meet with Nixon in Pittsburgh in late October. Unfortunately, such an appearance violated John Mitchell's concept of the GOP game plan, and Nixon was unable to attend because of "scheduling difficulties."

Organized labor also had a serious problem with those

Democrats who view it as an obstruction to a revival of their party. During the 1968 campaign, COPE rejected those Democratic candidates whose dovish views it found unacceptable. Full support was denied William G. Clark in his attempt to unseat Senator Everett McKinley Dirksen in Illinois; John J. Gilligan, running for the Senate from Ohio, found himself desperately short of funds, his labor support growing slimmer after he defeated labor's main target, Senator Frank Lausche, for the Democratic nomination; Allard K. Lowenstein made a successful bid for Congress from New York's Fifth District despite mild labor opposition; Speaker Jesse Unruh returned to the California Assembly enjoying only partial labor support. John Gilligan summed up his experience with labor's hierarchy:

> They said in effect, "How dare you say anything about Lyndon Johnson and the war after all he's done for the working man?" Isn't that a ridiculous statement? But the point they were making was you just don't attack the guy on the top as long as things are going good for the membership. If you do, you're a quibbler, a fancy Dan. If you attack, you might bring the whole thing down around their heads.

Now young turks of the Democratic Party are sensitive to the treatment accorded them, are determined to create a new coalition—one that does not include George Meany.

So in 1968 rank-and-file labor did not rebel, as many had expected, but the GOP did not give them as much of an excuse to rebel as many had hoped. Nonetheless, Vice-President Humphrey was defeated, and President Nixon began his Administration with no obligations to organized labor. At the same time, there is still reason to believe the working man will continue to be receptive to attractive Republican candidates. As Lawrence O'Brien, former Democratic National Chairman, admits, "The old Cadillac Square syndrome" is dead.

Many of the present and future leaders of the Democratic Party neither need nor particularly want organized labor's political support. Contrary to the gloss labor and the Democratic Party presented during the campaign, there are some serious problems within the Democratic-labor alliance. An aware Nixon Administration, open to the leaders of organized labor and sensitive to the concerns of the rank-and-file, might well be able to make serious inroads into the Democrats' most traditional and useful power base.

CHAPTER 8   America's Blacks

It is a good indication of how much has changed during the past eight years that at one point during the presidential campaign of 1960 the late Dr. Martin Luther King, Jr., was considering a public endorsement of Richard Nixon. (In fact, his father, the Reverend Martin Luther King, Sr., did endorse the Nixon-Lodge ticket.) In 1968, King's successor and closest friend, Ralph Abernathy, traveled the country in the closing weeks of the campaign telling overflow congregations that he didn't think *either* of the candidates was much good, but that everybody had better get out and vote for Hubert Humphrey anyway, because the election of "tricky, slicky Dicky" would be a disaster for black America.

This was sheer demagoguery, of course, and Abernathy knew it. Nevertheless, the election returns in the nation's black communities were something of a disaster for Richard Nixon. In mid-September, Nixon strategists were saying that they hoped for a minimum of 20 percent of the black vote "in order to govern effectively." The GOP national ticket got about half that, and in the process badly hurt black GOP candidates, such as James Farmer, the former executive director of CORE, who ran for Congress in Brooklyn, and others with large black constituencies. In Texas, for example, Joe Kirven, an attractive black candidate for the Texas legislature from Dallas County, could get only 33 percent of the vote in the county's black precincts— though polling 48 percent overall.

Richard Nixon was supported by only 740,000 black Americans last November, whereas 6.6 million voted for Hubert Humphrey. In George Gallup's demographic breakdown of how the electorate voted on November 5, no group gave a greater percentage to the Humphrey-Muskie ticket than the category Gallup listed as "nonwhite." The GOP's 1968 performance in the black community was only marginally better—a few hundred thousand votes—than Barry Goldwater's had been in 1964, and Goldwater's total was almost small enough to be considered the mistake vote. Across the country, the Nixon vote in black communities was so small that the statistics are barely worth analyzing. Yet, if vote returns are not very useful here, a bit of history will be; for in looking at what has happened in this country in the past four decades, it is clear that there were millions of black people who would have voted for Richard Nixon last year, if only he had given them the chance.

It was in the early 1930's that black people began voting Democratic. Because most of them were poor, they were susceptible to the revolution wrought by Franklin D. Roosevelt. More importantly, during those years most of the old Republican machines in the Northern industrial cities began to give way to younger, more vigorous Democratic bosses. These men were quick to forge alliances with leaders in their cities' impoverished Negro districts. In the decades that followed, black Southerners poured into the Northern cities by the thousands in search of better opportunity, and the Democratic organizations took it on themselves to educate them in the ways of their new urban environments. One of the first lessons, not surprisingly, was voting, a custom the blacks had had little experience with in the South. For the first time since Reconstruction, the voter rolls swelled with the names of new black voters—only this time, almost all of them were Democrats.

Blacks remained loyal to Roosevelt and the Democratic Party throughout F.D.R.'s reign. But in the early 1950's, a trend began to develop—slowly but noticeably, the number of blacks voting Republican started to grow. In 1952, 21 percent of the "nonwhite" vote went to the Republican presidential ticket; in the 1956 landslide, it jumped to 39 percent; in 1960, it settled a bit at 32 percent. Evidently, as the American economy expanded, more and more black people were making it from the ranks of the poor into the middle class. Like many others before and since, they were acquiring a degree of allegiance to the Republican Party in the course of their upward movement. Throughout the 1950's, the vote returns from the lowest-income black communities—mostly the Northern inner-city slums—remained fairly constant at 10 to 15 percent Republican. But new and relatively prosperous black communities were beginning to emerge in and around the big cities of the North and South. In 1952, only 7 percent of nonwhite American families had incomes of more than $7,000 (measured in constant dollars), but by 1960 the figure had grown to 19 percent. Probably a near-majority of these people voted for Richard Nixon in the 1960 election.

Since 1960, our economy has boomed as never before, and a large part of that growth has been in the "service sector," where more and more companies have found it in their interests to hire and promote black people. As a result, the black middle class has grown at an accelerating rate. On November 5, 1968, about 40 percent of all black American families had incomes over $7,000—admittedly a shamefully small percentage, yet a startling jump from 1960. In fact, this was the first presidential election for which political statisticians had to take special samples in middle-class black precincts.

But the middle-class black Republican vote—which had reached 50 percent in some communities in 1960 before vanishing in the Goldwater debacle of 1964—did not re-appear in 1968. Some of the more prosperous black neigh-borhoods in Chicago gave Richard Nixon nearly half their vote in 1960; in 1968, they gave him 10 percent or less. The same could be said for Philadelphia, San Francisco, St. Louis, and New York City. In the black Fourth Ward in suburban Rahway, New Jersey, President Eisenhower won 63 percent of the vote in 1956 and Nixon over 40 percent four years later. Yet in 1968 the 19 percent polled by Nixon was far closer to Barry Goldwater's 12 percent showing than to his own 1960 mark.

In fact, one is hard put to find *any* black districts, no matter how well off, that gave the Nixon-Agnew ticket more than a quarter of their vote. One of the few is Baldwin Hills in Los Angeles, where the vote for Nixon was 31.6 percent; Max Rafferty got 30.6 percent the same day. But in nearby Watts, Nixon polled a trifling 6.6 percent.

What happened to this black middle-class vote? Though Nixon may have wanted it, he didn't want to do anything conspicuous to get it. The strategy of overtly seeking the Wallace vote meant that large black crowds had to be avoided and the issue of school desegregation fudged. Un-happily and avoidably, Spiro Agnew's knack for the in-discreet phrase confirmed the post-1964 impression of the Republican Party as antiblack and antipoor. Nixon's de-mands for law and order and his only temporary use of the tag "with justice" were not likely to win votes in a black community that needed to be convinced of Republican good will. As with the labor vote, the Republicans were faced with the task of overcoming a presumption of untrustworthi-ness.

Meanwhile, the Democratic ticket had a great deal going for it in the black community. Even with his admirable civil-rights record, Humphrey may not have had the appeal of a Robert Kennedy, but the domestic achievements of the past eight years were not lost on Negro voters. President Johnson had declared war on poverty and had passed more civil-rights legislation than any other President; though many white liberals forgot all this in the bitterness over Vietnam, blacks did not. And the power of the Kennedy legacy could hardly be overestimated. J.F.K. samplers and photographs are to this day as common on the south side of Chicago as in the south end of Boston.

If a charismatic figure such as Robert Kennedy had headed the Democratic ticket in 1968, Nixon might really have been in trouble. Though the percentage of nonwhites voting in the South was up from 44 percent in 1964 to 51.4 percent in 1968, elsewhere in the country the opposite was true. In the North and West, Bureau of the Census figures indicated that the percentage of eligible whites going to the polls dropped from 74.7 in 1964 to 71.8 in 1968. But the drop-off among registered blacks was more substantial— from 72 percent in 1964 to only 61.4 percent in 1968. Though Wallace (and Nixon) may have driven some blacks to the polls to protect their own interests, political analysts are now arguing that others, at least the poorer ones, turn out to vote only for a charismatic leader. Thus, though Humphrey did extremely well among those who voted, Robert Kennedy would probably have attracted a greater proportion of blacks to the polls—possibly enough to erode Nixon's slim margin in such close, vital states as Illinois.

It was not that Nixon completely failed to address himself to the black community. Reportedly, he spent nearly one-third of a million dollars on advertising and promotion aimed specifically at black districts—a figure that was surely far above the Democratic expenditure. And what he said was perhaps as candid and intelligent as any campaign oratory on the subject has ever been. But under the circumstances, it was also embarrassingly inappropriate. Blacks, especially middle-class blacks, did not vote for Richard Nixon because they did not trust him. And they did not trust him because, in terms of what they wanted to hear from him, he put last things first. He spoke of the need for individual self-respect and dignity. Though it may be true that a black person is moved by these new impulses, the one thing he does *not* want is to be patted on the head for them by a white man. Similarly the need for widespread managerial and professional skills, the need for greater access to capital, the need for greater control over future economic and political development, all of these needs are keenly recognized within the black community. But these, too, are sensitive points for whites to be lecturing blacks about, because blacks have a very firm idea about who has been denying them these skills and opportunities.

At this point in history, black people are, in the phrase of one writer, "the most untogether people," torn by controversy over their role and future in America. But there is one thing, with regard to their relations with whites, that they all agree on, and that is civil rights. They want a firm, unequivocal commitment, and they did not get one from Richard Nixon in 1968. "We must move beyond the old civil rights," he said in speaking of the need for black business development. But blacks are more sensitive about their civil rights than any other group in America; to them, these rights are not "old," but new and precious. In their relations with the white community (and particularly in their relations with the government and with white Republican politicians), what they want first of all is an absolute guarantee of racial justice. If Richard Nixon had made emphatically clear his commitment to civil rights—in the streets, in the courts, in the schools, in the voting booth, and in the real estate office —black people would have been far more disposed to listen to his ideas about dignity, economic development, and black capitalism. (Of course, it could be argued that for every black vote Nixon gained on civil rights, he would have lost a white vote and that many blacks would not have believed him, no matter what he said or did. In this area, however, the Republicans could have taken advantage of the presumption of conservatism and disinterest that has dogged them since 1964. They had a certain amount of leeway before the general public began to suspect them of racial liberalism; and they could have pointed to the Supreme Court decisions and congressional enactments that would have bound any victorious administration to continued efforts in the field of civil rights.) But until the Republican ticket could remove all doubt about its stand on the primary issue of civil rights, its efforts on the secondary concerns were useless.

As it was, Richard Nixon was rather like an inexperienced young man making a too-hasty proposition to a girl he really didn't know very well. Never confident of ultimate success, he tried to *talk* his way into an affair, tried to use cold reason, so as to retain the greatest poise if and when he was rejected. But in such delicate matters as getting black voters into the Republican column, it takes more than logic. It takes trust and warmth—and it takes time, which brings us to the question of 1972.

Many concerned Republicans despair of making any inroads into the black community in the next four years. Especially in the event of another Kennedy candidacy, the chances of President Nixon's improving on his poor 1968 showing are said to be particularly bleak. But this is not necessarily so. Many Republicans do run very well in black communities. "The Democrats have done more for Negroes," explained one black housewife in Philadelphia last fall. "But I'll vote for a Republican if he's for us . . . I would have voted for Rockefeller."

In 1965, John Lindsay's black support (45 percent of the

Negro vote) was crucial in electing him New York's first Republican mayor in decades, and one year later, Nelson Rockefeller polled slightly less while winning his third term as governor. In 1968, Jacob Javits, running for reelection as New York's senior senator, far outpaced the GOP presidential ticket in the black community. A sampling of several black voting districts tells the story: Buffalo's Thirteenth Ward—Nixon-Agnew 7 percent, Javits 28 percent; the Seventy-second Assembly District in Central Harlem—Nixon-Agnew 10 percent, Javits 29 percent; the Twenty-sixth Assembly District in Springfield Gardens, Queens—Nixon-Agnew 12 percent, Javits 42 percent. NBC's sample precincts showed Javits getting 23.4 percent of the black vote, three times the 7.3 percent polled by the GOP presidential ticket. And on the predominantly Negro south side of Yonkers, Nixon polled 2,982, Javits 4,306, and Republican Congressman Ogden Reid—who had been active in local slum-improvement efforts—5,240.

Nor is New York the only state where the black vote has been helpful to Republican candidates. In Oklahoma, former Governor Henry Bellmon ran 25 percent ahead of Nixon-Agnew in the Negro wards of Tulsa and Oklahoma City in his successful race for the U.S. Senate—and Bellmon's opponent, incumbent A. S. (Mike) Monroney, was not without a strong civil-rights record. In Arkansas, black voters gave a huge majority to Winthrop Rockefeller for governor, though they rejected Nixon by equivalent percentages. And in Maryland, Congressman (now Senator) Charles Mathias demonstrated that the efforts of the Nixon-Agnew ticket to win blue-collar votes did not have to jeopardize a strong showing in the black precincts.

Mathias was challenging Democratic incumbent Daniel Brewster. The race was a microcosm of the three-way presidential contest, for on the right lurked a third candidate,

George Mahoney. (Mahoney had run as a Democrat for governor of Maryland in 1966 on the backlash theme "Your home is your castle." It had been a golden opportunity for the GOP, and Spiro Agnew, projecting a substantially more moderate image, had defeated Mahoney.) In 1968, Mathias was able to pull a stunning coup, winning Brewster's Senate seat with 47 percent, whereas the Nixon-Agnew ticket lost the vice-presidential nominee's home state with 43 percent of the vote. And whereas Nixon barely won 4 percent of the black vote in Baltimore—Agnew certainly didn't have much of an appeal there—Mathias took between 14 and 20 percent in black precincts. But Mathias also ran ahead of the national ticket in labor districts; in the United Auto Workers stronghold of Washington County, Mathias captured a 59 percent majority, whereas Nixon polled only 47 percent. Mathias had paid attention to labor's bread-and-butter concerns, but had also worked for open-housing legislation in the Congress, thus winning the informal endorsement of the state's NAACP.

Very soon a majority of black Americans will be relatively middle class. These people can be expected to watch the Nixon Administration closely, but with an open mind, and to reward four years' work well done with their votes. Nothing could be more condescending—racist, if you will—than to suppose that if a voter is black and the Democratic candidate is named Kennedy, the Republican ticket has no chance at all. It wasn't true in 1960, and it doesn't have to be true in 1972.

It should be understood, however, that there is probably little that can be done to win many votes in the poorest black communities. Those of the lower economic classes, no matter what their skin color, are less likely to be interested in political issues that rarely touch their daily lives.

One must have a fairly full belly and a reasonably secure existence in order to spend much time worrying about the progress of the Paris peace talks or the meaning of an ambiguous phrase at a presidential news conference. The voting habits of lower-class people are more likely to be dependent on the local political structure—who has the power in the immediate community, who is able to get them a job, who is able to help out with personal problems. And in most of the poorest black communities—that is, in the Northern slums—this power resides in the Democratic Party. Much of the money spent by the antipoverty program, especially the funds channeled through the Community Action agencies, has in fact been used to bolster local Democratic organizations, and to the extent that the more flagrantly political programs are cut, the local Democrats will lose an important source of patronage. But besides this, there is little imminent relief.

Of course, the poor-black vote diminishes as the middle class grows, and this trend can accelerate only if the new Administration's antipoverty and human development policies are successful. And many of these new middle-class blacks will support Richard Nixon in 1972, if he heeds the lessons of the past election. There is no reason why Nixon cannot win these votes while at the same time discharging the mandate of those who supported him in 1968.

First and foremost, his support of civil rights must be strong and unequivocal; in many cases this will simply be a matter of enforcing the law. Many believe this is a settled issue in America, but it is not. If President Nixon is not resolute, blacks in the South will soon be suffering for the progress they have made in the last few years. For many thousands of Wallace supporters in the South believe that, though Nixon is not one of their own, his heart is with them. They would like to undo such progress as has been made in school desegregation and voter registration in recent years, and the Nixon Administration can facilitate this simply by remaining passive. In the next few months, these people will be testing the new Administration's intentions; they must be disabused, firmly and immediately. If not, the Republican Party will deserve and receive very few black votes in 1972.

Second, it must be made clear that anticrime does not mean antiblack. It is a painful fact that blacks account for a disproportionate share of America's criminal population, but so too are they disproportionately the *victims* of crime. In particular, middle-class blacks are prime candidates for a law-and-order campaign, for they suffer doubly from the nation's unhappy crime rate—both personally, as victims, and socially, because of guilt by association. Black middle-class citizens will be attracted by an administration that does something about their immediate and acute crime problem—but not by one that continues to trumpet the "code words" of law and order. During the fall, a Negro leader in Cleveland commented:

> We know what they [the Republicans] mean by law and order. They mean when people get out in the streets to express their grievances, not law and order when it comes to peddling dope to people, killing them in their homes and warping their lives in other ways.

And a responsible definition of law and order ought to include obedience to Supreme Court mandates and compliance with nondiscrimination clauses in federal contracts. This nation needs a campaign against crime, but the matter must be carefully put. It would be extremely beneficial to emphasize that in reducing crime, and especially in reducing the influence of organized crime, the Administration is attempting to alleviate one of the most oppressing problems of the black community.

In general, President Nixon must emphasize that Americans are one people, with common stakes and common goals. Black people want it known that they are black and proud, but this does not mean they have lost interest in being part of American society. Special programs will help and will be appreciated, but not if they only lead to gilded ghettos; rather, they must result in a fuller and more equal partnership in the common undertakings of our society. A few more blacks in high-level, visible government jobs would help demonstrate the Administration's commitment, especially if these officials—as has rarely been the case in the past—have some real power to affect the lives of black people.

There is every reason to expect that in the next four years President Nixon will go a long way toward building a bridge of trust and good will to a group of people who are presently very skeptical. This would be a giant step forward in fulfilling the President's pledge to "bring us together," whereas failure to attempt it will almost surely tear us apart.

CHAPTER 9   SUBurbia And Its Young

America's middle class, now geographically centered in suburbia, has long formed the base of support for the Republican Party. Even before the Depression shifted the country's political alignments, the middle class was the backbone of the GOP, though F.D.R. stripped away much of the flesh, leaving the party in a distinctly minority status. Republicans, however, have come to take their chief constituents for granted, and in 1968 much of the passion of the middle class—if not its vote on election day—found its expression in the Democratic Party.

The war in Vietnam had been going well enough, from a public-opinion point of view, until draft calls were expanded to the point that the sons of suburbia were no longer automatically excluded from the fighting. Students had found they could avoid the draft merely by continuing their education beyond the undergraduate degree. But in February 1968, most deferments for graduate students were eliminated, and the class of 1968 spent several traumatic months wondering if September would find them in a Vietnamese rice paddy.

So the war came home to suburbia. These people had never had an opportunity to express an opinion on the American involvement, and in fact, Congress had never been asked to declare war; so the suddenly concerned citizen was not even able to hold his representatives or senators accountable. Nor had the rationale for sending 500,000 men across the Pacific Ocean been explained to the satisfaction of the middle class, whose members, considering themselves well educated, felt they ought to be able to understand. The war had just happened, almost independently of the democratic process, and now the middle class looked desperately for a way out.

The GOP offered no candidate to speak to the anxiety of its traditional constituency. In this atmosphere, therefore, Eugene McCarthy was able to capture the heart of the suburbs, and of the college young. The youth provided the commandos for his unprecedented campaign. (It is unlikely that the nation will soon again witness the outpouring of support furnished by students in the New Hampshire and Wisconsin primaries.) But it was the elders back home in suburbia who provided the money and votes.

Certainly this support centered around the main issue of the Vietnam war. But it must also be noted that many admired McCarthy's integrity and his views on the limited nature of the Presidency, which promised the individual greater control of his own destiny and environment. Richard Goodwin recognized the needs of the suburbanite when he wrote in *The New Yorker*:

> It is the middle class whose discontent and uneasiness lack aim, and some of whose members found through McCarthy a hope that purpose and value could be restored. . . . They were looking for some way in which they could regain control of and play a real part in the enterprises of society.

Many of these McCarthy supporters were registered Republicans.

Polls in early July showed the Minnesota senator winning

between 12 and 20 percent of this group's vote against either Nixon or Rockefeller. In Oregon, where the Democratic registration lists are heavy with middle-class voters, McCarthy was able to defeat Robert Kennedy, whose personal appeal found more acceptance with blacks and in lower-middle-class working communities. The August conventions, however, eliminated the possibility that a paladin for suburbia would joust in the fall campaign.

In the wake of McCarthy's exhilarating campaign, and predictable defeat, the middle class was emotionally exhausted. After a year of violence and unrest, marked by the assassination of two American folk heroes and the debacle at Chicago, the white-collar and professional people of suburbia decided to support Richard Nixon. The hope was to return to peace and normalcy, for all greater expectations had been dashed. Thus, an enlarged middle-class vote returned to the GOP—its desertion in 1964 having forewarned the Republican disaster of that year—and though hardly consumed by enthusiasm, this vote formed the basis of Richard Nixon's presidential victory.

The theory behind this vote was that a new administration could not be worse than the old, and, as Walter Lippmann wrote, that a Republican President would be in a better position to end the war. But this was not a victory for principles or programs. Nixon was a familiar face who did not generate strong emotions, save negative ones among the small group of diehard liberals who still clung to the memory of his 1950 Senate campaign against Helen Gahagan Douglas in California. In 1968, Nixon gave the suburbanites a chance to vote against the Administration that had presided over chaos at home and abroad, without forcing them to make the bewildering choice of what to do next. James J. Kirkpatrick put it succinctly in an article in the

National Review: "[This is] no return to principled conservatism. . . . [People] just want to sit down for awhile."

The 1968 results should not be misread, for the campaign illustrated how shaky is the Republican hold on suburbia. After all, the GOP's principal appeal was to the physically comfortable American, concerned with law and order, inflation, and the general drift at home and abroad. In White Plains, New York, on September 10, 1968, Nixon sounded the theme of "the forgotten American" before his suburban audience. "The people of the suburbs," he said, "don't need orders from Washington telling them what they must do. The people of the suburbs need men in Washington who will ask them how Washington can cooperate in what they're doing already." His radio speeches in late October touched directly on the problems of taxation, revenue-sharing, and inflation, which are the main material preoccupations of the residents of the suburbs.

But in spite of this appeal and the total disenchantment with the Johnson Administration, the results on election day were distinctly mixed. Though a great recovery was made from the Goldwater disaster of 1964, Nixon's plurality in middle-class areas was no greater than it had been in 1960 against the charming and articulate John F. Kennedy.

The Nixon-Agnew showing did not match the predictions of the pollsters or of GOP professionals. According to the CBS survey, Nixon won 51 percent of the suburban vote, to Humphrey's 40 percent. The post-election Gallup poll gave Nixon a 47 percent share of the white-collar vote (to Humphrey's 41 percent), 56 percent of the vote cast by professionals (to Humphrey's 34 percent), and 54 percent of the college-educated vote (to Humphrey's 42 percent). Especially dismaying was the Republican failure to win over the large group of initially uncommitted voters. Only among the professional personnel did the Nixon-Agnew percentage rise during the campaign, from 51 percent at the beginning of October to 56 percent on election day. But even here, the Humphrey-Muskie ticket made a gain of twice the size— from 24 percent to 34 percent. Meanwhile, Nixon's percentage of the vote declined over this same period in the white-collar and college-educated categories. Among the white-collar workers, Nixon slipped from 50 percent to 47 percent, whereas Humphrey rose from 27 percent to 41 percent. Among the college-educated voters, Nixon dropped from 57 percent to 54 percent, whereas Humphrey soared from 24 percent to 42 percent.

Alarming, too, was the fact that the Nixon vote from the middle class often did not even achieve its 1960 level. Nixon won 61 percent of the college-educated vote against Kennedy in 1960, but he slipped to 54 percent in 1968 (56 percent of the two-party vote). Meanwhile, the Humphrey-Muskie ticket polled 42 percent of the college-educated, a gain of 3 percent despite the presence of George Wallace. Nixon's share of the white-collar vote declined from 52 percent in 1960 to 47 percent in a three-man race in 1968 (but Humphrey fell even more, and Nixon's slice of the two-party vote actually rose one point). Once again, only the professionals really returned in force to the Republican column. They had cast 58 percent of their vote for Nixon in 1960; in 1968, 56 percent went for the GOP ticket, whereas 34 percent voted Democratic, giving Nixon a 4-percentage-point boost in his two-party rating. Though these categories are crude approximations for the middle class, they are sufficient to demonstrate some weak spots in the once-solid Republican bloc. The decline is even more apparent when we note that even in 1960 Nixon failed to match General Eisenhower's 1952 or 1956 showings in any of these categories.

The full scope of the lost opportunity can be better appreciated by looking at the results in specific suburban areas, traditionally considered Republican bastions, where there were high hopes of riding the Nixon coat tails to congressional and state victories. Though there were a few exceptions, notably in the Chicago suburbs and in Nixon's home state of California, generally the President's pluralities were down from their 1960 levels. In one area there was a congressional gain (Lawrence J. Hogan in the Maryland suburbs of Washington, D.C.), and in that instance the GOP House candidate ran way ahead of Nixon. Nor were many advances recorded in suburban races for the state legislatures.

The greatest disappointments came in the East, where local professionals had hoped to return Republicans from congressional districts that had gone Democratic in 1964. In the New York metropolitan area, Nixon ran behind his 1960 pluralities in two of the three largest suburban counties, though he made a dramatic increase in the third. His plurality in Nassau County shrank from 61,000 to 50,000; in Westchester County, where he made his "forgotten Americans" appeal, his margin plunged from 53,000 to 39,000. Only in Suffolk County did he increase his plurality, from 53,000 to 91,000. More discouraging was the fact that the congressional delegation from the over-all area remained at four Democrats and three Republicans, though there had been predictions that one and perhaps two seats would change hands. Across the river in the Republican stronghold of Bergen County, New Jersey, the results were similar. Nixon's plurality shrank from 69,000 in 1960 to 63,000 in 1968, despite GOP County Chairman Nelson Gross's prediction of a 100,000-vote victory. The flaccid showing in Bergen County probably cost New Jersey Republicans an additional seat on the state's congressional delegation—in a district that had been especially redesigned by a Republican legislature. (The Democratic incumbent did get a great deal of help from former McCarthy supporters.)

In Pennsylvania, NBC's precinct sample showed Nixon with an edge of less than one percentage point over Humphrey (45.6 to 45 percent) in the middle-income urban category,[1] though senatorial candidate Richard Schweiker rated a big majority of 58 percent with this group. In this traditionally Republican category, estimated by NBC to include slightly less than 40 percent of the state's electorate, the difference between Nixon's and Schweiker's performances was the major demographic factor that resulted in a new Republican senator from Pennsylvania, even while the state's 29 electoral votes went for Humphrey. Nixon's poor performance probably forfeited the twelve-percentage-point gap between the senatorial and presidential candidates.

In the Boston suburbs and the Maryland suburbs near Washington, Nixon ran behind Humphrey—and far behind his own vote in 1960. In Massachusetts, he lost by a greater margin to Humphrey than he had to Kennedy in 1960. This was largely due to his failure to repeat his successes in the wealthy towns of Winchester, Newton, Belmont, Concord, Lexington, Lincoln, Weston, and Wellesley. Despite the penchant of the Maryland suburbs for voting for the incumbent Administration, to which many of the local electorate owe their jobs, it is noteworthy that Nixon lost the combined vote of Montgomery and St. George's Counties by 3,000, whereas Republican senatorial candidate Charles Mathias won the counties by 50,500 and congressional candidates Gilbert Gude and Lawrence Hogan rolled up majorities of 71,000 votes.

Outside the East, the results were not so bleak, though the mixed trends were rarely satisfying, given the Republican tradition in the middle class and the hopes of using this constituency as a base for building a governing majority. The most significant gain came in the Cook County suburbs

[1] NBC's breakdowns included four categories: high-income urban, middle-income urban, low-income urban, and rural.

outside Chicago. Here, Nixon increased his plurality from 19,000 in 1960 to a whopping 220,000 in 1968. In St. Louis County, Missouri, the Nixon vote showed a relative gain of 24,000 votes, from a 9,000-vote deficit to a 15,000-vote plurality. Such gains in the Midwest, however, were offset by losses in the metropolitan areas surrounding Minneapolis, Minnesota, and Madison, Wisconsin, and in the smaller middle-class cities of Michigan. In Washtenew County, i.e., Ann Arbor, Michigan, where Congressman Marvin Esch won with 56 percent of the vote, leading Nixon by nine percentage points, Nixon dropped 4,000 votes from his 1960 showing, while Humphrey polled 7,000 more than Kennedy had.

In the South, it was difficult to assess the GOP ticket's true strength because of the great vote-getting power of Wallace. In Shelby County (Memphis), Tennessee, Wallace apparently delivered a plurality to Humphrey, but Nixon ran well in middle-class and suburban areas. In North Carolina, Nixon ran better than he had in 1960. NBC's breakdown showed him carrying nearly 50 percent of the middle-income urban vote, whereas Humphrey and Wallace split the remainder.

In the large states of Florida and Texas, the results again were mixed. Nixon lost strength in the conservative Republican fortress of St. Petersburg, but gained in the Miami and Fort Lauderdale areas. He retained a plurality of 61,000 in the Dallas area, despite a large vote for George Wallace, and ran up a plurality of 20,000 in Houston. Yet he lost ground absolutely in Fort Worth, dropping from a 13,500-vote plurality eight years ago to a mere 2,000-vote edge in 1968.

In the Far West, California stood out from its neighbors. Nixon improved on his 1960 standing in Los Angeles and San Diego and their suburbs, going from a deficit of 79,000 to a plurality of 43,000 in Los Angeles County and increasing his plurality in San Diego County from 52,000 to 94,000. However, these gains were partially offset by losses in the San Francisco and Oakland areas, where his deficit jumped from 89,000 in 1960 to 132,000 in 1968. Except for Salt Lake City, he showed declining pluralities in all the other Far Western metropolitan areas. He lost both Multnomah County (Portland), Oregon, and King County (Seattle), Washington, which he had won in 1960. In NBC's mostly suburban Puget Sound district of Washington,[2] Nixon trailed Humphrey with less than 45 percent of the vote, whereas Governor Daniel Evans polled a majority. In the Denver area, Nixon's deficit climbed from 200 votes in 1960 to 14,000 in 1968.

If the Republican presidential ticket did poorly with America's blacks, failed to make significant inroads into the Democratic majorities among the working man, and polled either the same or slightly worse among the middle class, what accounted for Richard Nixon's plurality in 1968? Certainly his relative gain with the farm vote was insufficient to make the difference between a loss in 1960 and victory in 1968. Significantly, the answer cannot be found by examining only voting habits. An analysis of the dynamics of America's demographic patterns reveals that the reason for the Republican Party's gain in 1968 is quite simple. The middle class got bigger.

In 1948, when Harry Truman narrowly defeated Thomas Dewey, only 3 percent of the American families earned over $10,000, and only an additional 5 percent were in the $7,000 to $9,999 bracket. In 1960, when Richard Nixon lost a close contest to John Kennedy, the figures had risen and 14 percent were earning over $10,000, with 20 percent between $7,000 and $9,999. But in 1968 when Richard

[2] NBC divided the state of Washington into four regions: Seattle, Puget Sound, the eastern end of the state, and the remainder.

Nixon triumphed, one third of the families living in the United States had incomes over $10,000 and another quarter earned between $7,000 and $9,999. In the twenty years from Dewey's defeat to Nixon's victory, the median income of America's families (in constant dollars) almost doubled.

As Lawrence O'Brien recognized, "the Democrats are moving to the suburbs and becoming independents or Republicans." From 1950 to 1968, the suburban population rose from 37 to 68 million, whereas the numbers of those living in the central cities, small towns, and rural areas increased only slightly. In the city of Chicago, for example, the total vote dropped by 240,898 between 1960 and 1968. At the same time, the drop in all of Cook County was only 49,065, meaning that the suburban communities had an increased vote of nearly 200,000. And in these suburbs (i.e., Cook County exclusive of the city) Nixon increased his plurality by 200,000 from 1960 to 1968—an important factor in winning Illinois's twenty-six electoral votes for the Republican column.

The Vietnam war, the cleverness of Richard Nixon's campaign strategy, the liabilities of Hubert Humphrey, and the voters' desire for a change may all have contributed to the Republican presidential victory. Yet these factors were all dependent on the public's ephemeral moods, and certainly none was capable of conclusively rendering F.D.R.'s coalition impotent. Rather it was the slow and steady growth of the American economy—freeing the voters from the economic concerns tying them to the Democratic Party— that contributed the most permanent component to Richard Nixon's marginal gains with the American people in 1968.

Though Republicans may attempt to draw satisfaction from the fact that their constituency finally came into its own, the outcome of the election does not warrant complacency. Certainly it is difficult to draw striking conclusions or discern new trends from the 1968 election results in middle-class America. The GOP ticket was not a great success among the materially satisfied, stable suburban voters, even though much of the Nixon campaign was aimed at them. After the election, Seymour M. Lipset, professor of social relations at Harvard University, commented:

> Humphrey did comparatively well in the suburbs. What seems to be happening is that the younger, well educated middle-class Republicans are more liberal than they used to be.

These voters are what the Ripon Society calls "the frontlash." Highly independent, well informed, mostly middle and upper middle class, largely suburbanite, and often leaning Republican, this is a group that went overwhelmingly for Johnson in 1964 and preferred McCarthy or Rockefeller in summer 1968. It is increasing rapidly as more of the populace completes college. The unexploited potential stands out in particularly bold relief when the Nixon figures are compared with those Republicans who made strong frontlash appeals. Mathias, Schweiker, and Evans are obvious examples. In addition to Esch, Gude, and Hogan, two other Republican congressional candidates stand out. In a suburban area of San Francisco, Paul McCloskey won 79 percent of the vote in a district that was carried by both Humphrey and Democratic Senate candidate Alan Cranston. Charles Whalen won Dayton, Ohio, and its environs with 78 percent of the vote, carrying local Republicans into offices Democrats had held for over half a century. Again this happened in an area where Humphrey and the Democratic Senate candidate, John Gilligan, also won.

These are exceptionally dramatic cases, but they are

clearly not exceptional in illustrating how the frontlash phenomenon might have helped the Republicans. It was a vote the GOP's presidential ticket should have had this year, would have had in September, but did not get on November 5. It is the vote that Theodore Roosevelt took with him when he left the Republican Party in 1912, and it has yet to return permanently at the presidential level.

Part of the Republicans' problem was undoubtedly Spiro Agnew, who failed to inspire the confidence of even his home-state voters. A *New York Times* poll of 1,269 top executives found that whereas 85 percent favored Nixon, 57 percent were negative toward Agnew. Certainly this attitude toward the vice-presidential nominee must have hurt the GOP ticket.

The reactions to Nixon and to the campaign strategy he chose to follow were also critical. In a year when Senator Eugene McCarthy had stirred many suburbanites with his issue-oriented approach the Nixon campaign gave the appearance of a highly polished machine, concentrating entirely on the process of getting elected. After McCarthy's frank analysis of the war and its effect on the nation, Nixon's moratorium on discussion of Vietnam had a hollow ring. As he did with labor and the blacks, Nixon based his appeal to the suburbs on secondary issues, such as inflation and revenue-sharing. These were valid concerns, but they could not replace the principal emotional issue of the war.

And it was not just Vietnam. Nixon appeared to hedge on several other issues. He was for integration but he felt the federal government should not withhold money from schools that fail to correct racial imbalance. He was for aid to ghetto areas, but only if it would be noninflationary. Despite the tremendous odds in his favor, owing to middle-class worries over civil unrest, inflation, and the war, Nixon failed to cash in with this important Republican constituency because he did not present a positive program with at least some appeal to the humanitarian aspects of the affluent—and particularly of the affluent young. Rather than invoking lofty ideals, Nixon deliberately pitched himself as a lesser evil—neither a racist such as Wallace nor a puppet such as Humphrey. Because Nixon was free (unlike Humphrey) to articulate his own proposals, he was expected to do so; failing, he led many hero-hungry suburbanites to conclude that Hubert Humphrey's babblings were noble by comparison.

This is not to say that Nixon lost all of his liberal and moderate Republican support, or that independents and Democrats did not vote for him. It appears that about one fourth of his vote (8 to 10 million) came from people who voted for Johnson in 1964. He was supported by at least 7 percent of the Cranston voters in California, mostly Kuchel Republicans who could not take Rafferty. He shared larger numbers of voters with other Democratic senatorial candidates, such as Wayne Morse in Oregon, Harold Hughes in Iowa, Gaylord Nelson in Wisconsin, mostly in swing areas of these states. These are not voters that Nixon can take for granted in 1972. Their support would almost certainly dwindle, for example, if the new President made a strong effort to compete for Wallace's vote.

President Nixon must now carefully contemplate why he failed to gain significant majorities in much of suburbia, for the Democratic Party is setting its sights on this segment of the electorate. In his farewell speech, retiring Democratic National Chairman Lawrence O'Brien told his party: "My advice is: Look to the suburbs. That's where many of our Democrats have gone." O'Brien's successor, Senator Fred Harris, has echoed this theme: "One of our problems is to win back the voters in the suburbs." The battle for the suburban vote has not been won; it has only begun. In these troubled times, a Hamletian attitude may not be successful.

The children of affluence will be even more difficult to win. Though only a small minority are members of such New Left organizations as SDS, a large percentage have the feeling that there is something wrong with the present political and social structure of the United States. Many accept the thesis of the post-industrial society posited by Daniel Bell and popularized by John Kenneth Galbraith, in which public service and the universities will play an increasingly prominent role. They want to be on the leading edge of these emergent forces. Though physical maturity comes earlier to this generation, economic maturity arrives later, and thus—even more than their parents—today's youth are frustrated over their inability to control their own lives.

The 1968 campaign was the first in which great numbers of students played an important part. Senator Eugene McCarthy was able to turn a base of students into a nationwide constituency. None of the presidential nominees, however, was able to elicit much enthusiasm from youth, though small groups of Young Republicans and Young Democrats did some effective work for Nixon and Humphrey. Most young Americans simply did not participate in the general election, probably because of the let-down that affected suburbanites of all ages after the death of Robert Kennedy and the defeat of Eugene McCarthy.

Gallup estimated that half the registered voters between the ages of twenty-one and twenty-five did not vote, though this group composed 10 percent of the potential electorate. Of those, a majority voted for Humphrey. According to Gallup, Humphrey picked up seventeen percentage points between September and November among voters under thirty years of age, whereas Nixon lost substantial ground, from a nine-point lead to a nine-point deficit. These are the voters and the leaders of the future and, though they were ready to vote Republican, they went 5 to 4 for Humphrey on election day.

The Nixon campaign did not entirely neglect the students and recent graduates. Both the Republican platform and Nixon's acceptance speech stressed that youth should be given a piece of the action. One of the first announcements of the campaign, on September 9, 1968, was the formation of a Student Coalition under the direction of Sam Williams and John Campbell, former leaders of the Rockefeller New Majority. The group was to serve as a clearinghouse for ideas. "The spirit of this new generation," the announcement read, "is essential if we are to translate into action the fresh and bold ideas that the burgeoning social problems of our era demand." The concept of the Youth Service Agency was introduced as a concrete example of the role that youth might play in government. Student groups were reminded, too, of Nixon's support for a volunteer army, the 18-year-old vote, and community development corporations to aid the ghetto.

But the hope that these youth groups would play a meaningful role in the campaign and serve as partners in a continuing dialogue with the new Administration was soon dispelled by the lack of response to their ideas on the part of the Nixon campaign team. Governor Agnew's public statements on student protesters and the role of the young in society did little to encourage youthful support. In New York City, Agnew denounced student protesters as followers of persons "associated with the Communist cause," seemingly ignoring the possibility that there might be some legitimate grievances against the educational system. In his paternalistic speech of October 15 in Indianapolis, he suggested that neither the youth nor the poor should help to solve their own problems, but should leave such matters to the establishment. Finally, Agnew's denunciation of his opposite number, Edmund Muskie, for failing to stop a youth who claimed to be burning his draft card, invited a classic and predictable response: At a later appearance, a young man in the back of the auditorium loudly announced he was burning *his* draft card, while Agnew stood helpless on the stage.

Such statements and incidents only served to strengthen the view, already held by a large proportion of the college-age population, that Nixon was unwilling to take action on the nation's critical issues. Nixon's equivocal statement about the role of HEW in school desegregation seemed to mean he was turning his back on the entire civil-rights struggle of the 1960's, and it cast doubt on the sincerity of his suggestions for investment in the ghetto and improved job-training for the unemployed.

In this McLuhanesque age, when substance often gives way to appearance, Nixon seemed unwilling or unable to "tell it like it is." A generation that felt the nation was in crisis did not respond to a candidate who would not comment on the Vietnam war. Unlike Muskie, neither Republican candidate squarely faced the question of protest against the draft. Nixon often seemed to project multiple and divergent positions; worse, he presented the image of an emotionless man more concerned with people as statistics and votes than as human beings. Perhaps 1968 was just not a good year for interesting the young in Republican candidates. Only a few, such as John Sears in his race for sheriff of Suffolk County (Boston), gubernatorial candidate Paul Eggers in Texas, and Congressman McCloskey in California, were able to generate large-scale support among the young. Most of the student enthusiasm that survived the conventions went to Democratic peace candidates, such as Harold E. Hughes in Iowa, John J. Gilligan in Ohio, and Allard K. Lowenstein in New York. Both Hughes and Lowenstein won in traditionally Republican areas. Nixon hardly needed to do anything to appear the most peaceable of the three presidential candidates because Humphrey was stuck with Johnson's war and Wallace was Wallace. But, nonetheless, he couldn't do it.

The Republican President still has an opportunity to win some support among the affluent young, but it will take evidence of a real social concern and the ability to translate that concern into an effective mixture of public and private initiative. A *Fortune* magazine survey in January 1969 found Nixon more popular than Humphrey among the young, though the President trailed Senators Edward Kennedy and Gene McCarthy. Also, Nixon was disliked by fewer members of this group than either Johnson or Humphrey. With an end to the Vietnam war, he could begin to build some strength among these important voters of the future.

The first step will be to convince the youth of America that the Republican Administration really cares about solving the nation's problems. This will not be easy, despite the popularity among young people of the Lindsays, Percys, and Hatfields. Mrs. Sharon Percy Rockefeller voiced the skepticism of many young people who might have been Republicans when she told her wedding guests she found it difficult to imagine why any young person would join the GOP. A determined attempt to enlist college students and young professionals in the work of government would provide new reasons. And after all, the Democratic Party has not been a place where young men can get ahead quickly. However, such efforts will have to provide meaningful participation in which youth has some say in the projects. It cannot be as hamstrung as the Peace Corps and VISTA have been, for returning volunteers have already warned the college-age population of the inflexibility of entrenched officialdom.

But time is not with the Republicans in this effort, for the memory of 1968 hangs heavy. More idealistic than their elders, young Americans found it difficult to stomach Nixon's campaign equivocation, following so closely on the strong honesty of McCarthy. Lyndon Johnson, the GOP's chief asset among the young, has gone into retirement, leaving Nixon and the memories of the autumn at center stage, where the President is a convenient scapegoat for everything that goes wrong. Senator Ted Kennedy, a likely presidential candidate in 1972, has a great hold on Americans of all ages, but especially the young, as the last remaining link to the Camelot era.

Shortly after the election, columnist Roscoe Drummond wrote:

> The most significant political reality today is that a new voting majority is coming into being in the next few years. It will be made up predominantly of politically conscious young voters who are going to insist upon more participation and more authority in party decisions, plus the steadily expanding affluent, suburban middle class—labor and white collar—of the $10,000-plus income.

This new majority could be strongly Republican. But in 1968, many of its members, both present and potential, found the party wanting. If the opportunity to capture this group is lost it will not come again for a long time.

Part III. The Election Results in Perspective

In America, the Presidency is the pinnacle of political success and consequently a way of describing it. Yet, the political war for the American electorate's heart (and for power to implement a party's ideas) is not decided solely by the presidential battle, for there are many other battles, fights, and skirmishes that dot the political landscape. For a party truly to prosper, it must win at all levels. Behind the Republicans' minority status of the 1960's lay the failure in the 1950's to extend presidential successes to the Congress, the state houses, and the courthouses. Similarly, Richard Nixon won the top political battle of 1968, but from the standpoint of a stronger Republican Party, there may be reason to fear a repetition of the 1950's.

In Part II we tried to show that despite signal opportunity for major realignment of political voting patterns in 1968, the Republican Party at the presidential level was unable to broaden its base of support significantly. Opting for a national strategy that in the end had only shallow effect, the GOP gave the Democratic Party, then in desperate trouble, the chance to regroup for 1970 and 1972. The GOP victory that could have precipitated a progressive coalition under the Republican standard, and the chance to relegate the Democrats to minority-party status for years to come slipped away.

In Part III we examine this battle-vs.-war question from another perspective, measuring the Republican successes around the country in the Congress, the state houses, and at local levels.

CHAPTER 10. How Large a Victory?

Once more, let us recall the original script. Following the GOP success of 1966, political experts from both parties predicted that 1968 would bring a resounding Republican return to power. In 1967, the party gave substance to these forecasts by producing two significant campaign wins with a strategy based solely on dissatisfaction with the Democratic Party. In Kentucky, Louie B. Nunn won the governorship for the GOP for the first time in twenty-four years and added several Republican seats in the legislature. His campaign slogan—"Tired of the War? Vote Nunn!"—caught the public fancy, though Nunn never explained how he would influence foreign policy from the state house in Frankfort. At the same time, New Jersey Republicans replaced a 2 to 1 deficit in both houses of the legislature with 3 to 1 majorities after a campaign on the elusory platform of "Why Wait Till '68?"

Until the middle of October, in fact, there was little doubt that the GOP strategy would win the Presidency by a smashing margin. The Democratic campaign was an object of ridicule, seemingly as badly divided after an angry, embarrassing national convention as the Republicans had been in 1964. Early reports showed Vice-President Humphrey carrying only Rhode Island and the District of Columbia. Some predicted he would run third in the electoral college.

With overwhelming success at the top of the ticket, it was

said, Republicans would make sweeping gains in the Senate and the House of Representatives. The only question, in fact, was whether they would control the House or fall just short. Gains in governorships and state legislatures and local offices also were predicted.

But that was not what happened on November 5. By a margin so narrow as to keep Americans glued to the television screens for twelve hours after the polls closed, the nation elected a Republican President. In the House of Representatives and at the state level, the electorate made only the slightest changes. Almost nothing was clearly decided by the election, no policies rejected, no mandate given. No coalitions were created or broken. The balance of political power was not decisively changed. That one of the closest national elections in American history could occur when circumstances so heavily favored a decisive Republican renascence raises the question: Will the fact that the GOP realized only slight gains stemming from the presidential victory, in effect give the Democratic coalition time to adjust for a new period.

"Mandates" are taken more seriously by political commentators than by officeholders, but Richard Nixon undoubtedly recognizes that almost no new President in our history has entered office with such an indecisive one. Others have had low popular and electoral votes, low margins over their opponents, low congressional support. But never have all these factors combined to confront one chief executive. In 1912 Woodrow Wilson received a lower percentage of the popular vote than Nixon did in 1968 (41.9 percent compared to 43.4 percent), but Wilson won 435 electoral votes to 96 for his combined opponents (both former Presidents), running a full seven percentage points ahead of Theodore Roosevelt, his strongest rival. And Wilson also carried the Congress, whereas Nixon is the first new President since Zachary Taylor not to bring at least one house of the legislature into office with him.

Mr. Nixon actually received 2.3 million fewer votes than he did in 1960. Indeed, there were six more states (Maine, Michigan, New York, Pennsylvania, Washington, and West Virginia) with a total of 113 electoral votes that Nixon could have carried in 1968 if he had just polled the number of votes he received in each of them in 1960. To millions of Americans restless for change, the GOP ticket offered too little improvement to make a trip to the polls worthwhile. (One British cartoonist summed it all up when he had one recently-invaded Czech say to another, "Well, Comrade, at least we don't have to choose between Richard Nixon and Hubert Humphrey.")

In seventeen states, the number of votes polled in 1968 was lower than that registered in 1964; and in nineteen states there was a drop in the number of votes cast from 1960 to 1968. Just one fourth of the voting-age citizens cast their ballots for Nixon-Agnew in 1968. As one Republican observer put it, "This is the closest thing to a minority government the American political system can produce."

Starting with the twenty-six states he carried in 1960, with 229 electoral votes, Nixon lost two, Maine and Washington, to the Humphrey-Muskie ticket, and with them thirteen electoral votes. From this base, the GOP nominee added Delaware, Illinois (which he lost only by fraud in 1960), Missouri, Nevada, New Mexico, New Jersey, North Carolina, and South Carolina, with eighty-six electoral votes, to give him the total of 301 [1] votes in the electoral college. Without Illinois and South Carolina, or without New Jersey, North Carolina, and Delaware, Nixon wouldn't have reached the magic number of 270. It was that close.

---

[1] He should have received 302 votes, but though one Republican elector possibly obeyed the eleventh commandment and didn't "speak ill" of the GOP ticket, he decided he wouldn't vote for it.

But it didn't look close following the August conventions. Early in the fall, some of the nation's leading news publications conducted surveys of the fifty states and concluded that the Nixon-Agnew ticket would win well over 300 electoral votes, with the Democrats trailing far behind.

Table 12.   Early Electoral-Count Surveys.

Date	Publication	Nixon	Humphrey	Wallace	Toss-up
Sept. 6	Christian Science Monitor	372	85	52	29
Sept. 15	The New York Times	346	42	77	73
Sept. 16	Time	328	121	39	50
Sept. 16	Newsweek	329	54	89	66
Oct. 6	The Washington Post	346	46	53	93
Nov. 5	Electoral vote won	302	191	45	

But on election day, Nixon's electoral total did not match any of these predictions, while Humphrey far exceeded his early allocations.

On an individual state basis, the story was similar. (In Table 13, nineteen states, including six of the seven with more than twenty electoral votes, are listed. For each of the three candidates, the results of a poll by a major newspaper in the state and the election-day percentages are given along with the net change. Whereas Humphrey improved his showing over his poll rating in *every* state and Wallace did in none, Nixon's performance was mixed. His rating with the public improved in some states, deteriorated in others. Yet only rarely did he pick up more than half of the undecided vote, and his improvement was *never* as good as Humphrey's.

Part of the Humphrey finale can be attributed to change

of heart during the last five days caused by President Johnson's bombing-halt notice on the Thursday preceding the election. Certainly the pace quickened following the President's television appearance; GOP polls in Texas show that the voters were switching to Humphrey even as they went to the voting booth. "The bombing halt almost did us in," an important Nixon staffer noted. "We thought for twenty-four hours we had lost the whole thing." But though the Nixon camp certainly must have realized this possibility, it appears there was no planning for this contingency, an almost incredible oversight.

Nixon and his advisers recognized early in the campaign that the initiative on Vietnam lay with their opponents. They reasoned that if the Republican nominee became a dove the Administration might be able to manipulate events so as to make his position look foolish. If he became a super-hawk, the argument continued, peace overtures by the President could isolate him from an electorate that was tired of the war. Thus, the result of this reasoning led Nixon to stake out a position calculated to offend no one: The Republican Party was, of course, for an "honorable peace."

But in his attempt at ideological balance, Nixon left himself open. For those in the electorate who continued to be mystified by the war, who had thought they had found a savior in McCarthy or Robert Kennedy, the fall campaign offered no hope. In such a mood, the obviously political maneuver of a bombing halt, forced on Saigon before the election date, came as a straw to be seized in desperation. Nixon's refusal to take an identifiable position permitted the Democrats to make political mileage out of *any act* that appeared to be progress in Vietnam.

It was argued in Chapter 6 that Wallace drew votes about equally from the Democratic-leaning and the Republican-leaning segments of the electorate. As far as the coalitions

Table 13. Newspaper Opinion Polls and Election Results for Nineteen States.

Figures in Percentages *

Date Poll Released	State and Polling Organization	Nixon			Humphrey			Wallace			Undecided
		Poll	Vote	Change	Poll	Vote	Change	Poll	Vote	Change	
Sept. 22	Arizona Arizona Republic	45	55	+10	19	35	+16	12	10	− 2	24
Sept. 15	California California State Poll	43	48	+ 5	34	45	+11	7	7	0	16
Sept. 23	California California Poll	47	48	+ 1	30	45	+15	8	7	− 1	15
Sept. 29	Colorado Denver Post	51	51	0	28	41	+13	11	8	− 3	10
Oct. 27	Connecticut Hartford Times	44	44	0	31	50	+19	12	6	− 6	6
Nov. 1	Illinois Chicago Sun-Times	47	47	0	39	44	+ 5	14	8	− 6	—
Sept. 28	Indiana Indianapolis News	44	50	+ 6	20	38	+18	21	11	−10	15
Oct. 13	Iowa Des Moines Register & Tribune	56	53	− 3	27	41	+14	11	6	− 5	6
Oct. 10	Massachusetts Boston Globe	31	33	+ 2	44	63	+19	8	4	− 4	17
Oct. 20	Michigan Detroit News	40	41	+ 1	39	48	+ 9	16	10	− 6	5

Figures in Percentages *

Date Poll Released	State and Polling Organization	Nixon			Humphrey			Wallace			Undecided
		Poll	Vote	Change	Poll	Vote	Change	Poll	Vote	Change	
Sept. 22	Minnesota *Minneapolis Star & Tribune*	44	41	− 3	45	54	+ 9	9	4	− 5	2
Oct. 6	Nebraska *Omaha World Herald*	52	58	+ 6	19	32	+13	12	8	− 4	17
Oct. 13	New Hampshire *Boston Globe*	59	52	− 7	28	44	+16	6	4	− 2	7
Oct. 28	New York *The Daily News*	42	44	+ 2	46	50	+ 4	8	5	− 3	4
Oct. 23	Ohio *Cleveland Plain Dealer*	44	45	+ 1	33	43	+10	12	12	0	11
Oct. 24	Oregon *Portland Oregonian*	50	50	0	32	44	+12	9	6	− 3	9
Sept. 19	South Dakota *Sioux Falls Argus-Leader*	58	53	− 5	17	42	+25	9	5	− 4	16
Sept. 20	Texas *Dallas Morning News*	30	40	+10	30	41	+11	25	19	− 6	15
Oct. 13	Utah *Salt Lake Tribune*	61	57	− 4	27	37	+10	8	6	− 2	4
Oct. 13	Wyoming *Denver Post*	50	56	+ 6	26	36	+10	15	9	− 6	9

*Voting percentages may not add up to 100 percent because of rounding-off and minor candidates.

that make up the Republican and Democratic parties, Wallace had little effect. However, there were a number of states in 1968 in which the election was close and where the margin of victory (whether Nixon or Humphrey won) was appreciably smaller than the Wallace vote. In such states, had Wallace been out of the race, his absence might have made a difference in the result.

There is little doubt, for instance, that Wallace on the ballot cost Nixon Texas. Humphrey's margin of victory was only 39,000 votes compared to the 584,000 cast for George Wallace. In Texas it seems likely that the people who cast their votes for Wallace, generally rural dwellers, probably would have preferred Nixon over Humphrey in a two-man contest. And in fact, in the absence of Wallace, only 53.5 percent of his supporters would have had to cast their vote for Nixon to give Texas' twenty-five electoral votes to the Republicans.

Elsewhere in the nation, however, the working man who voted for Wallace probably would have had a slightly higher propensity to cast a Democratic rather than Republican ballot in the absence of the American Independent Party. In New Jersey, where Nixon's victory margin was 61,000, Humphrey would have required only 61.5 percent of the Wallace vote to win a two-man race. In Illinois, Humphrey would have needed slightly over two thirds of Wallace's votes, in Ohio less than 60 percent. These three states are significant because over one third of the electorate in each comes from the work force (New Jersey 38 percent, Illinois 38 percent, and Ohio 36 percent [2]), and in each of these states, labor gave Wallace a larger percentage of its vote than did the electorate as a whole. In New Jersey, Wallace polled 11 percent of the labor vote; in Illinois the figure was 16 percent, and in Ohio 15 percent.[3]

[2] These figures are from NBC's sample precincts.
[3] *Ibid.*

Humphrey also could have taken Delaware and Missouri in two-way contests by picking up 63 percent and 55 percent of the Wallace vote respectively. Nixon, on the other hand, would have carried Maryland in a two-way contest if 55.7 percent of the Wallace voters had selected him. Of the states which went to either Humphrey or Nixon, but not by a clear majority, the Wallace vote could have been important in thirteen; that is, in thirteen states the losing candidate could have won by picking up Wallace's votes at the rate of two for each one that went to his opponent. Three of these (Texas, Washington, and Maryland) were won by the Democratic ticket. Of the ten that went for Nixon, four are in the South (Florida, Kentucky, South Carolina, and Tennessee), but despite the former Democratic omnipotence there, it is doubtful that Nixon would have lost them to Humphrey in the absence of Wallace.

However, in the other six (Alaska, Delaware, Illinois, Missouri, New Jersey, Ohio) it is a distinct possibility that the Wallace candidacy hurt Humphrey and assisted Nixon in adding their total of eighty-seven votes to the GOP electoral count. As for the forty-five electoral votes Wallace won for himself, all were from the Deep South and probably would have gone to Nixon had Wallace not run. When these are added to the electoral count in Texas (which, as has been said, Nixon surely would have won in Wallace's absence), it is possible to conclude that Wallace cost Nixon seventy electoral votes (eighty if Maryland is included).

In short, it seems that the gains and losses occasioned by Wallace canceled each other out. Certainly it is very difficult to see how the Nixon-Agnew ticket would have done appreciably better if George Wallace had not been on the ballot on November 5.

Though many had predicted that redistricting would help the Republicans in the House of Representatives, the GOP added only four seats, far short of the thirty needed to win control. Though the Republicans lost two seats in the West, they picked up two in the South and another in the Midwest. But in the Northeast, the base of Gerald Ford's dream of occupying the speaker's chair, the Republicans managed to gain one solitary seat. Only thirty-nine freshmen congressmen were elected, about half the average for the last several decades, and only nine incumbents were defeated; only fourteen seats changed partisan loyalties. For Nixon, the congressional showing was worse than in 1960, when even in defeat he had brought in twenty new House seats.

But in the Senate, the Republicans scored a big gain; the addition of five GOP seats was the biggest since 1950, when they had increased their membership in the "World's Most Exclusive Club" by the same number. Still it must be recognized that the Republican percentage of the total Senate vote was down slightly from 1966. More important, it is generally conceded that at the senatorial and gubernatorial levels the voters appear to make a distinction between the candidates and their party labels; Republican candidates for these offices in 1968 rarely were hurt or helped by the top of the ticket. In the Northeast, Nixon did poorly, but his party ran progressive candidates and won all but one Senate race. In the West, Nixon did well, but the GOP tended to nominate candidates to his right and won only four of ten seats.

In Wisconsin, South Dakota, and Idaho, a trio of Democratic liberals—Gaylord Nelson, George McGovern, and Frank Church—were all considered to be in deep trouble. Yet clear victories by Nixon in their states could not prevent these embattled doves from winning reelection over conservative Republican nominees Jerris Leonard, Archie Gubbrud, and George Hansen.

In contrast, progressive Republicans were able to win

three Senate seats in states carried also by the Humphrey-Muskie ticket. In Maryland and Pennsylvania, Congressmen Charles Mathias and Richard Schweiker defeated incumbents Daniel Brewster and Joseph Clark, in each case despite the fact that the Nixon-Agnew ticket polled less than 45 percent. And in New York, Senator Jacob Javits won a stunning third-term mandate of over a million votes, double the Nixon national plurality, whereas Nixon-Agnew lost the state by 370,000.

In the front offices of the state houses, the Republicans won a net increase of four governorships, taking into account the resignation of Spiro Agnew and the consequent loss of Maryland. They now control thirty of the fifty states. Though the GOP lost two governorships, it gained seven others, marking a significant comeback from a low after the 1964 elections when the GOP governors numbered only seventeen. The Republican Party now governs six of the seven largest states, and it even made a good run in the seventh, Texas. A full 85 percent of the population outside the South now live in a Republican-governed state.

But the Democrats still control more state legislatures than do Republicans, and GOP legislative gains in California, New York, Indiana, and Iowa (in each they added control of one house) were partially offset by loss of the lower houses in Michigan and Pennsylvania. The Republican Party now controls both branches of nineteen legislatures; half of the GOP governors have the fortune of working with a legislative branch controlled by their own party. The Republican gains were strategically placed this year, and after the high increase of 503 legislative seats in 1966 (owing primarily to the natural revival after the Goldwater disaster, in which almost 500 legislative seats were lost), thirty-eight new seats hardly represent a Republican tide. It would appear that the mere forty-three percent of the legislative seats held by Republicans reflects the level of the public's confidence in the GOP, for at this level voters seldom identify with individual candidates and the winner is usually determined by party labels.

All in all, if 1968 represents the peak of Republican fortunes, as many were saying it would, in October, then the Republican Party is in serious trouble. It is not that the American electorate lost its appetite for change between August and November 1968. Rather they lost, in large measure, their confidence that a Republican President would produce the kind of change they desired.

Unlike 1964, Republicans cannot find a scapegoat for a disappointing performance by looking to "disloyal" elements in their own party. As Mr. Nixon said over and over again all fall, the GOP has rarely been so well united. But as has also been said over and over again, a unified minority is still a minority.

CHAPTER 11   The Northeast

The Northeast was a self-contradiction in 1968. Nixon and Agnew were overwhelmingly rejected, while Republican candidates in senatorial and gubernatorial races won convincing victories. State GOP organizations in the Northeast have produced local structures that stage effective campaigns at all levels despite the posture of the national party and a substantial Democratic registration margin. In the five gubernatorial contests in 1968, Republican candidates won four away from Democratic control, losing the fifth, and Republicans now control six of the region's twelve chief executive posts, including those in the major industrial states of Pennsylvania, New York, and Massachusetts. The GOP success story is repeated at the U.S. Senate level, where Republicans won five of six contests in 1968 to give them a 13 to 11 edge over the Democrats.

Candidates for U.S. Congress and for the state legislatures find party affiliation a controlling element in voter behavior, particularly in a presidential year. It is at this level that the effect of the national Republican Party on local candidates becomes most evident. For instance, the GOP in the Northeast won only 49 out of 122 seats in the U.S. House of Representatives, about 41 percent. Some of the best chances for picking up enough seats to give the GOP control of the House were contests in this region, yet the campaign waged by the national ticket eliminated the possibility that these opportunities would materialize.

To be sure, a strong, progressive, and well-organized state Republican organization can offset the effect of the national ticket at these levels—New York, for instance, was able to regain control of both houses of the state legislature in 1968 —but the local party often finds such an upstream swim too much. In Pennsylvania, the GOP lost control of the lower house in 1968, while Nixon was losing the state by over 100,000 votes. And in New Jersey, site of a dramatic GOP state-legislature comeback in 1967, the Republicans failed to pick up the expected two to four U.S. representative seats, although Nixon eked out a narrow 62,000-vote victory.

In contrast to the convincing regional-party resurgence in contests for those offices where national-party identification is not a controlling factor, Richard Nixon and Spiro Agnew suffered conclusive losses. The GOP presidential ticket won only twenty-seven of the region's 149 electoral votes, polling 43 percent of the popular vote compared to the clear majority won by Humphrey and Muskie.

A closer look at this region, and the reasons for success by state and local Republican candidates, may explain the poor showing of the national ticket and provide some further lessons for the future of the GOP. The Northeast is characterized by a megalopolis—Herman Kahn calls it BosWash —that encompasses the District of Columbia and all the states in the region, except those on the periphery (West Virginia, Vermont, New Hampshire, and Maine). Indeed, the Nixon-Agnew showing in the District of Columbia and the eight states that compose this Northeastern urban-suburban corridor is even more revealing, for the Republican presidential ticket received only twenty out of a possible 131 electoral votes. In the two states where Nixon polled

best—Delaware (45 percent) and New Jersey (46 percent)
—the sizable Wallace vote in normally Democratic working-
class districts may have been responsible for his victory.

In 1960, Richard Nixon won only Maine, Vermont, and
New Hampshire in the Northeast. Although he added Delaware and New Jersey in 1968 (while dropping Maine), the
reason for his poor showing was basically the same: Nixon
lost the Northeast in the cities. Yet much had changed in the
intervening eight years, and no longer does the Republican
label automatically mean defeat in the urban centers. The
Democrats still have overwhelming registration advantages,
but Republican candidates in New York, Boston, and elsewhere have proven that the cities are no longer the exclusive
domain of the Democrats. A different Nixon might have
carried the cities and thus the Northeast, but the GOP
nominee decided not to try and ran substantially behind
local candidates in almost every major urban center. His
campaign of noncommitment threw away the opportunity
to unify his party in the Northeast and vault it into a majority position; instead, the party was left fragmented.
Nixon consistently trailed state and local Republican candidates, providing little but a drag on the lower elements of
the ticket.

The reasons for what might appear as political schizo-
phrenia in the voting behavior of the region's residents are
to be found in the election strategies employed by the Republican candidates. The voters were consistent; the Republicans were not. GOP candidates who campaigned on
progressive platforms and who openly and positively sought
the big-city vote were elected to office. The Nixon-Agnew
strategy of going after the normal Republican vote and
slyly courting Democratic voters intrigued with Wallace
was conspicuous in its failure. In these opposing strategies
lies the 1968 Republican story in the Northeast.

A survey of the nation's major urban centers gives a vivid picture of the GOP presidential ticket's weakness. In an analysis based on sample precinct data, CBS discovered that the larger the city, the lower the vote for the Republican standard-bearer.

Table 14.

Community Size	Nixon	Humphrey	Wallace
Cities 500,000+	34%	59%	7%
Cities 50,000–500,000	40%	51%	9%
Small cities	45%	46%	8%
Rural-small town	51%	40%	9%
Suburbs	48%	37%	16%

In the compact Northeast, with its numerous major metropolitan areas, the inverse relation between community size and Nixon's percentage of the vote was telling. In Pennsylvania, for example, the Nixon-Agnew ticket's lopsided loss of Philadelphia couldn't be offset by Republican pluralities in suburban and rural areas.

An examination of how the presidential ticket ran with respect to other GOP candidates is also revealing. In Baltimore, Congressman Charles Mathias, running for the Senate on a progressive urban-oriented platform, ran 50,000 votes ahead of the national ticket. In Wilmington, Delaware, Republican National Committeeman Harry Haskel knocked out an incumbent Democrat in the mayoralty race, carrying the city with a margin of 5,000 votes; Nixon lost it by 10,000. In Philadelphia, Republican senatorial candidate Richard Schweiker ran 50,000 votes ahead of the presidential ticket; Nixon lost by better than 250,000 votes. The Allegheny County (Pittsburgh) results are similar, Nixon losing by 6.5 percent, while Schweiker eked out a razor-thin 8,000-vote win.

In New York City, where Republican John Lindsay is the

mayor, Senator Jacob Javits carried the city, running some 500,000 votes ahead of Nixon, who lost by worse than 2 to 1. Upstate in Erie County (Buffalo), Nixon lost by 74,500, though Javits was winning by 40,000. In Boston, the Democrats have an 8 to 1 registration advantage, but John Sears, narrowly losing his race for sheriff of Suffolk County—a contest not guaranteed to attract much public attention—ran 70,000 votes ahead of Nixon-Agnew. In a city dominated by Irish and Italian ethnic politics, Yankee Sears missed carrying Boston by only 14,553 votes.

Of the major cities of the Northeast, only in Washington, D.C. (which has no partisan elections), Hartford, Connecticut (where Republican Ann Ucello was elected mayor in 1967), and Newark, New Jersey, did Nixon-Agnew not run behind local GOP candidates. Everywhere else, the national ticket trailed local Republicans by considerable margins.

In some respects, these election results represent a schism within the GOP ranks in the Northeast. Many Republican candidates found it beneficial not to associate their campaign too closely with the national ticket; at best, Nixon's strategy would have a neutral appeal to their constituents. By and large, these were moderates who had supported Nelson Rockefeller's bid for the party's presidential nomination, and the requirements for winning election at home were not always consistent with the postconvention goal of uniting with the party's national leader.

The question is whether the emotions of disunity will linger. Probably not, for both the moderates facing local contests and the regulars working on the Nixon campaign won. Yet, local candidates remember how difficult Nixon's strategy made their own campaign efforts, and those who actively supported the presidential ticket recall how uncooperative were some local Republicans. In New York State, some tried to blame Rockefeller and Senators Jacob Javits (who was up for reelection) and Charles Goodell for "footdragging" in their support of Nixon. Yet, Rockefeller was both explicit in his repeated statements of support and active during the campaign. Both senators made campaign appearances upstate for Nixon in the last days before the election. Indeed, if anyone can be faulted for failure to support GOP candidates, it must be vice-presidential nominee Spiro Agnew, who appeared at a dinner of the New York Conservative Party, an organization whose major purpose is the destruction of progressive Republicans, particularly Rockefeller, Javits, and Lindsay.

Compared to the Democrats, particularly in New York State, the GOP leaders were enthusiastic in their support for the national ticket. Nixon and Agnew, and their strategy of ignoring the cities, must bear the blame for defeat.

CONNECTICUT

Nineteen sixty-eight was supposed to be a Republican year in Connecticut. Everybody said so. The Republicans said so; the Democrats did, too. Political analysts predicted it; pollsters concurred. What factory workers told GOP senatorial aspirant Edwin H. May raised his hopes. The Nixon-Agnew ticket was given a good chance of carrying the state, and the GOP had reason to hope that May would defeat Senator Abraham Ribicoff. Four Republican candidates were expected to be elected to the U.S. House of Representatives. There was even hope that the GOP could eliminate the 2 to 1 Democratic margin and capture control of the lower house of the state legislature.

Instead, Nixon-Agnew lost by 60,000 votes; May lost by over 100,000. Only two Republicans were elected to the U.S. House, and the GOP only picked up a net of seven seats in the state house of representatives and one seat in the state senate.

What happened? The Connecticut Democrats, never

overly enthusiastic about Humphrey—and less so after he dumped State Chairman John Bailey as national chairman—returned from the Chicago convention divided and unhappy. Senator Abe Ribicoff, a party maverick with an uncanny ability for taking publicly controversial stands, had broken with the national leadership in Chicago over the Vietnam war and had openly scorned the actions of Mayor Daley's police by pointing his finger at Daley and denouncing the latter's "Gestapo tactics" on national television. This break extended into the state Democratic Party. The Democratic dissidents, who had stolen the headlines and a quarter of the delegates before Chicago, rallied defiantly behind Ribicoff, but not behind Humphrey. This split delighted the Connecticut GOP. But Ribicoff's long career in public life had not been forgotten by the voters. Having served in the legislature, as governor, in the Kennedy cabinet, and in the U.S. Senate, he was known statewide. His billboards simply proclaimed, "Send Abe Back to Washington." His Republican opponent, Ed May, Jr., was little known outside his former Hartford congressional district. With zealous McCarthy troops working the precincts and with strong support from Governor Dempsey, his former lieutenant governor, Ribicoff gained strength rapidly. Sensing the security of his own prospects, he moved toward more open support of Humphrey. In an interview with *The New York Times,* he commented candidly on his relationship with the regular Democratic organization: "If the party's mad at me, well, that's just too bad. They need me more than I need them." Although the statement raised considerable controversy, its audacity was matched only by its accuracy.

The Democratic schism almost disappeared as Ribicoff seized the leadership of both factions. Party unity, successful appearances by Humphrey and Muskie, and the dramatic national shift in voter sentiment combined to bring the Democrats from far behind to a convincing victory.

Democratic pluralities in the urban areas could not be offset by comfortable Nixon margins in the suburbs and rural areas. The Wallace vote was significantly lower than predicted, and it seemed to hurt Nixon more than Humphrey, with Wallace's percentages larger in rural Republican areas than in blue-collar, urban Democratic areas. Furthermore, Wallace voters apparently only voted for their candidate and then left the booth, ignoring the other contests.

May aimed his campaign at wooing the blue-collar vote away from its traditional Democratic home and tried to exploit the ideological split between the liberal Ribicoff and the conservative Democratic Senator Thomas Dodd. His imitation of the Nixon strategy—at one point he even showed some factory workers how to split their ticket for himself and Wallace—in the face of Ribicoff's great popularity, resulted in his running well behind the losing Nixon effort and would seem to eliminate him from serious consideration as the 1970 challenger to Senator Dodd.

Only two Republicans won election to important offices. In the Fourth Congressional District, encompassing suburban Fairfield County, the heartland of Connecticut Republicans, Lowell Weicker, Jr., the protégé of Republican National Treasurer William Middendorf, ran an elaborate campaign, complete with visits from Ronald Reagan and Nelson Rockefeller. Despite this, the heir to the Squibb pharmaceutical and Bigelow carpet fortunes ran 7,000 votes behind Nixon. A supporter of a bombing halt, Weicker still defeated incumbent Donald Irwin, a Great Society liberal and Vietnam hawk, by 9,000 votes.

The real Republican success story, however, was that of Congressman Thomas Meskill, former mayor of New Britain, who carried every one of the forty-seven cities and towns in his Sixth Congressional District, which covers most of the Northwest quadrant of the state. Running a relatively con-

servative campaign, he forged his support in urban areas on
the strength of two years of superb constituent service and
was helped by having a political unknown as his Democratic
opponent. Because of his well-balanced victory, he bears
watching for one of the 1970 statewide races.

One important GOP casualty was Nicholas Lenge, the
young, attractive House minority leader, who was defeated
for reelection when his normally Republican, but heavily
Jewish, West Hartford constituency went solidly for Humphrey and the rest of the Democratic ticket. Lenge was being
groomed for the 1970 gubernatorial contest, but it is questionable whether he can stage a comeback in time. On election night, the words "Poor Nick, Poor Nick" echoed like
a funeral dirge through Republican state headquarters.

Though Connecticut has comparatively little ticket-splitting, owing to the party lever, two groups of Connecticut
residents split their tickets extensively in 1968: those in the
Sixth Congressional District and those in hard-core Republican communities. Residents of Democratic communities,
especially urban centers, did very little splitting, in spite of
the fact that many of these communities—such as Hartford,
New Britain, Stamford, Waterbury, and Meriden—have
elected Republican mayors in recent years. Urban residents
appear willing to vote for Republican personalities, but not
for an unproven Republican slate. Republicans need ticket-
splitting to win when their ticket is headed by a weak personality, but it is the GOP voter, not the opposition, who is
more inclined to abandon the party standard.

DELAWARE

As Ralph Moyed of the *Wilmington Evening Journal* put
it on November 6, 1968: "Republicans yesterday finished a
job they started two years ago; they made Delaware a Re-

publican state." Building quickly on decisive 1966 victories, the GOP ran well-organized, well-financed campaigns in 1968. Republicans won contests for U.S. representative, governor, lieutenant governor, auditor, and treasurer (the latter two by better than 10 percent pluralities). They secured a 2 to 1 margin in both houses of the state legislature, and GOP candidates broke the Democratic monopoly in Wilmington by electing a mayor and taking 3 of 12 city council seats. Republicans also gained control of a majority of county offices.

Nixon's cautious and uninspiring approach to issues was well suited to the mood of the electorate, especially his emphasis on law and order. He received a 7,500-vote plurality, but his candidacy had little effect on local races.

In fact, it appears that Nixon and the rest of the GOP ticket may have been helped by William V. Roth, Jr.'s 35,000-vote victory—the largest plurality in the history of Delaware's lone congressional seat. Having run an energetic campaign, mixing new progressive ideas like home ownership for low-income families with more conservative stands on fiscal responsibility and law and order, his response to his overwhelming mandate was encouraging. The day after his victory, Roth retraced his campaign trail to thank voters for their support. First elected in 1966, the forty-seven-year-old congressman was at the Chrysler and General Motors plants in Newark on the morning of November 6 wearing a new button saying, "I thank you, Bill Roth." He may be the first Delawarean in some time to build up a modicum of seniority in the U.S. House of Representatives, having already gained considerable recognition in his first term by his efforts to produce a comprehensive catalogue of federal programs.

The gubernatorial race was significantly influenced by the law-and-order theme. GOP candidate Russell Peterson, a du Pont executive who had started campaigning in May 1967, edged incumbent Democrat Charles L. Terry by 2,100 votes. Peterson campaigned as a progressive and took a more moderate position on the continued presence of the National Guard in Wilmington than did Terry. Terry had called out the troops in the aftermath of Martin Luther King, Jr.'s assassination, but had refused to withdraw them even after six months, when their presence was no longer needed. Most other major GOP candidates, however, tended to take positions embarrassingly close to Terry's, and Peterson himself wavered slightly. His victory resulted from the combination of a strong, well-financed organization, an emphasis on his own general support of law and order, and extensive person-to-person campaigning.

The other major GOP victory was produced by National Committeeman and former Congressman Harry G. Haskell in the Wilmington mayoral contest. The key issue in Wilmington (as well as around the state) was the continued presence of the National Guard. The Wilmington black community, 30 percent of the electorate, was bitterly insulted. Haskell's liberal reputation, his policy of backing the original use of the Guard while calling for an end to those conditions that had produced the fears and tensions that pervaded the city, an appearance by his old friend Nelson Rockefeller, and a well-organized, well-financed campaign in which he spent over $100,000—all these overcame a 2 to 1 Democratic registration to unseat incumbent John Barbiaz by over 5,000 votes of the 35,000 cast (while Nixon was losing Wilmington by 10,000 votes). Barbiaz suffered from a poorly organized and inadequately financed campaign and from disharmony with Terry on the Guard issue, twice reversing his position.

The keys to Republican success at the polls were money, organization, and publicity. Removing the Guard from Wilmington was almost the first official act of Peterson and Haskell, a good beginning for building a successful Republican government. Fiscal problems, racial tensions, and conservative inertia in the state pose short-term temptations for the GOP to assume a more backsliding posture. The demise, however, of Terry's conservative influence on the Democratic Party—and the room this opens up for young and progressive Democrats—together with the gradual urbanization and industrialization of rural areas of the state, place longer-term pressures on the GOP to seize the present opportunity and build a strong, "problem-solving" image to assure its continued dominance.

THE DISTRICT OF COLUMBIA

The District of Columbia is the only 100 percent urban electoral area in the nation and has one of the largest black populations of any city. That the Nixon-Agnew ticket, in receiving only 18 percent of the vote, suffered its worst defeat in the nation's capital is symptomatic of the party's major weaknesses.

The GOP did not expect to win the District balloting for the Presidency, the only partisan political office for which District residents can vote. Efforts were made, however, to improve the party image and to build grass-roots support and trust through personal contacts between Republican workers and voters. To increase party visibility and demonstrate concern for local affairs, the District GOP endorsed candidates, regardless of party affiliation or philosophical orientation, for the nonpartisan school-board contests, the first such election in nearly a century. Now that President Nixon has appointed D.C. GOP Chairman Gilbert Hahn to head the city council, the local party has the opportunity to demonstrate the quality of its municipal leadership.

But the future of the GOP in the District will not be determined locally except by action of the White House. The arrival of the new Administration is important both in highlighting the contrast and the opportunity. The national Republicans now have the chance to try their hand at solving the problems of the capital. The postinaugural anti-crime programs and the announcement of a community-rebuilding program during President Nixon's tour of the rubble-strewn riot area are two immediate demonstrations of the tremendous power of the national government over the District. Of course, if Nixon's strong advocacy of home rule is successful, the election of Republicans will depend crucially on his success in dealing with the needs of this 100 percent urban constituency. But beyond this narrow objective, his success here may foreshadow the Northeast reaction to a reelection campaign in 1972.

MAINE

The story in traditionally Republican Maine in 1968 was Senator Edmund Muskie, and he, unfortunately, is a Democrat. Muskie is responsible for the existence of a functioning Democratic Party in Maine and he won the distinction in 1954 of becoming both the first Catholic and the first Democratic governor in Maine's history. After Nelson Rockefeller (who was born in Maine, has a summer home in Seal Harbor, and for whom there was considerable grass-roots enthusiasm in the state) was unsuccessful in Miami Beach, interest in Maine turned to Edmund Muskie. On November 5, the Muskie-Humphrey ticket, as many Democratic politicians referred to their standard-bearers, won 55 percent of the vote, though Nixon had carried the state with 57 percent only eight years before. Both Democratic congressmen were returned to office. Moreover, although Muskie's appearance on the ticket has to be considered an asset for other Democrats, both congressional candidates equaled the vote of their presidential ticket. Republicans remained in control of both houses of the state legislature, despite the Democratic gains of four seats in the Senate and ten in the House. Democrats also made further inroads into county offices.

Muskie is far and away the dominant political figure in the state. He will be heading the Democratic ticket in 1970, running for another term in the U.S. Senate, and the ironic challenge for GOP leaders is to convince voters to split their tickets, for no one thinks Muskie can be seriously threatened. Ticket-splitting in Maine is discouraged by the presence of a large "party box" above each slate. Efforts of the Republicans to eliminate this box have been unsuccessful, and party officials face a tough task in promoting ticket-splitting.

The Maine Republican Party still carries an image of negative conservatism with the younger voters. Elden H. Shute, the losing GOP candidate in the Second Congressional District, ran a vigorous campaign, but took a traditionally conservative Republican approach to state, national, and world problems. In the First District contest, however, Horace Hildreth, although losing, succeeded in making inroads with the young.

Basic Republican strength, both in the way of superior candidates and in voter allegiance, is shown by the party's continued dominance on the lower portions of the ticket, but the 1968 returns, notwithstanding Muskie's appearance on the top of the ballot, indicate a continuing deterioration of Republican strength. Though many sections of the state remain solidly Republican, the GOP support in the cities, larger towns, and areas of economic and population growth is slipping. U.S. Senator Margaret Chase Smith is the leading Republican in the state and has life tenure if she chooses, but she, unlike Muskie, has shown little interest in party affairs and organization. And though there are a few prominent GOP figures, such as Attorney General James Erwin, a possible gubernatorial candidate in 1970, and a group of promising young state legislators, the state party's leadership is still largely composed of aging and rather conservative Republicans who have traditionally resisted new ideas.

MARYLAND

The Nixon-Agnew ticket was narrowly defeated in Maryland (by 12,290 votes) but its national victory elevated a Democrat to replace Agnew as governor. However, of equal importance locally and perhaps even of more importance for the Republican Party nationally was the election to the Senate of Charles "Mac" Mathias.

Mathias, progressive and aggressive, had to struggle for most of his votes in a traditionally Democratic state. When the AFL-CIO endorsed his opponent, Senator Daniel Brewster, without granting Mathias a hearing, Mathias requested permission to discuss the issues in Steelworker's Hall at Dundalk. His request refused, he appeared outside to distribute his own campaign literature. There he encountered Dominic Fornaro, president of the state AFL-CIO's Committee on Political Education (COPE). Mathias asked why labor had endorsed him in his congressional race in 1966 if it was so upset about his voting record. Fornaro conceded that COPE would probably have repeated the endorsement if Mathias had run again for the House—a statement that Mathias made sure all nearby reporters heard.

With a background of legislative activity in civil rights and as a member of the House committee on the District of Columbia, Mathias also sought support in black communities—one third of the electorate in Baltimore City. On October 16, the same day he confronted Fornaro, Mathias went to a Washington, D.C., neighborhood center to discuss, with the residents, the cause of disturbances in the area the previous few nights. He skillfully survived some interruptions by Rufus Mayfield, a local black leader, and participated in an extended discussion. The next day, Mathias followed up the meeting by proposing "community service teams" to counteract the efforts of agitators.

In a race that mirrored the national contest because of the presence of ultra-conservative George P. Mahoney running as an independent, Mathias' strategy of aggressively seeking the votes of both the alienated blacks and the alienated working men, rather than merely projecting his Democratic opponent as the associate of the Johnson-Humphrey Administration and himself as the lesser evil, gave him a 100,000-vote victory compared to the 20,000-vote loss recorded by the Nixon-Agnew ticket.

In congressional races, the Republicans picked up one more seat to give them half the U.S. House delegation. Larry Hogan, running in the heavily Democratic Fifth District, which covers suburban Prince Georges County, defeated the incumbent Democrat, to whom he narrowly lost in 1966, by mixing a strong law-and-order stand, a progressive civil-rights position, and a relatively liberal Vietnam platform with two years of acting as the district's unofficial ombudsman. In Mathias' old Sixth District, Republican J. Glenn Beall, Jr., son of a former U.S. senator from the state, retained the seat for the GOP. In the Eighth District, which covers suburban Montgomery County, Republican incumbent Gilbert Gude ran well ahead of Nixon-Agnew (who ran up a four-percentage-point deficit) and was returned to office with 61 percent of the vote. And finally, on the conservative "eastern shore," Rogers C. B. Morton again overcame a 2 to 1 registration deficit to breeze to his fourth term. In the other four districts, heavily favored Democrats easily retained control.

MASSACHUSETTS

In 1968, Massachusetts Governor John A. Volpe became one of the few politicians ever to campaign actively for the Republican vice-presidential nomination. Though the Bay State's rank and file preferred Nelson Rockefeller as the party's standard-bearer—"Rocky" was expected to have considerably longer coat tails than Richard Nixon—Volpe recognized that a balanced ticket would preclude his sharing the national campaign chores with Rockefeller and accordingly cast his lot early with Nixon. The move disturbed many Republicans, for it looked as if naked ambition had superseded the state party's best interests. Thus, while the Democrats were voting for McCarthy in the Bay State primary, the GOP rejected favorite son Volpe for Rockefeller on a write-in. Miffed, Volpe blamed the press for giving so much coverage to the potential Rockefeller candidacy, and bitter feelings soon developed within the convention delegation as Volpe attempted to win second-ballot support for his candidate.

Though Volpe's dream was never realized at Miami Beach, he returned to the state only long enough to repack for the fall campaign trail. The local press made a game of reporting the number of days the governor spent out of the state, and, with the subsequent drop of Volpe's popularity, the prospects for some attractive legislative candidates, lured into active politics by the state chairman, disappeared. On November 5, all congressional incumbents were reelected. In the Seventh Congressional District, young GOP challenger William S. Abbott garnered 42 percent of the vote—16 percentage points higher than the GOP candidate in

1966—against seventh-term incumbent, and former J.F.K. roommate, Torbert McDonald, a vulnerable candidate who was saved only by the reaction against Nixon-Agnew in Massachusetts. The GOP ranks in the state legislature dropped so low that Republicans were no longer able even to sustain the governor's veto. Arriving back from the Nixon victory party in New York, Volpe confided to the public at an airport news conference that though he certainly was disappointed that the Nixon-Agnew ticket had failed to carry Massachusetts, the President-elect himself had thanked the Bay State governor for helping the GOP ticket carry New Jersey.

Nixon lost Massachusetts with a plurality that was 200,000 votes larger than the margin of defeat he sustained at the hands of the state's own John Kennedy in 1960. But Volpe was victorious, even though he was forced to accept a cabinet post that he had publicly belittled during the fall as presenting an insufficient "challenge" for a man of his talents. In a parting gesture of good will, Volpe announced a pay increase for state employees, though leaving the problem of raising the necessary revenue to his successor, Lt. Governor Francis Sargent. What had looked like a promising rebirth of the Massachusetts Republican Party only two years before—when Volpe, Brooke, Richardson, and Sargent had won the top four statewide contests—now had become a joke.

Recent political history has demonstrated that Republicans can win in Massachusetts as long as their candidates are sensitive to the important fact that independent voters outnumber both Democrats and Republicans—1,100,000 to 900,000 and 550,000, respectively. Nixon-Agnew, running a campaign that centered on traditional Republican appeal, were completely out of touch with the Massachusetts political scene. In fact, it is evident that the Nixon camp wrote

off Massachusetts early. The only real organized activity was
a fund-raising dinner in Boston that raised large sums, all
of which were taken out of state. With Democrats already
jousting for their party's gubernatorial nomination, it will
be tough for the GOP to bounce back.

NEW HAMPSHIRE

Nixon-Agnew carried this northern New England state
by 52 percent, but the 155,000-vote total was not impressive, given the Republican orientation of the state or Nixon's
primary victory of 79 percent. Nixon trailed Senator Norris
Cotton, who was elected overwhelmingly against the challenge of popular Governor John W. King, and the two GOP
congressmen, Louis Wyman and James Cleveland, who won
reelection by still greater margins of roughly 2 to 1. Republicans swept the election, and now hold every statewide
office except that of Senator Thomas McIntyre. They hold
better than a two-thirds majority in the state senate and
should do as well in the contest for assembly seats in 1969.

In the primary contests for governor, a moderate, Walter
R. Peterson, Jr., won the GOP nomination when several
conservative candidates divided the right-wing vote. The
opposite happened on the Democratic side, and Peterson
faced a conservative candidate, Emile R. Bussiere. In a
basically conservative state, Peterson had a tough battle,
but still managed to win by 14,524 votes.

NEW JERSEY

Nixon made three visits to New Jersey and Hubert Humphrey made two as both tried hard to woo the nation's
eighth largest state. The Nixon loss to Kennedy in 1960 by

only 22,000 votes was changed to a 62,000 victory in 1968, although the state GOP had predicted a 200,000-vote margin. There was considerable tension among the state's Republicans during the fall campaign, however, as a result of efforts by Senator Clifford Case and others on behalf of an open, presumably Rockefeller, convention.

In 1960, Nixon toured the Negro areas of Newark with Jackie Robinson. In 1968, he stayed in the suburbs, and Robinson toured the ghetto with Humphrey. Although the Nixon committee decorated eighteen storefront headquarters in black areas, a widely used newspaper advertisement perhaps was more indicative of the campaign's tenor. A white man was depicted with his head bandaged, over the caption: "He doesn't complain. He doesn't demonstrate. He doesn't march. He doesn't riot. He just doesn't want to get mugged again, that's all. Do something about it. Vote Republican."

This was not a watershed election in New Jersey. The GOP was coasting on two years of success, beginning with Case's 464,000-vote margin in 1966 and continuing with the 1967 legislative landslide. Nixon's 62,000-vote plurality and the 57,000-vote plurality of the GOP congressional candidates in 1968 were a further continuation of this trend. Yet Republicans haven't held the governor's chair since 1954 and, lacking the unifying influence of statewide patronage and control by a strong governor, they are split into many local fiefdoms. Based either in congressional districts or in strong county organizations, these GOP factions operate independently and range in philosophy from very conservative to quite liberal. This fragmentation has produced local personal allegiances rather than a general spirit of party loyalty, thus hindering the construction of a strong statewide party. In fact, Democrats have no trouble selling fund-raising tickets, whereas Republicans still have debts outstanding from 1961. It may be that the recent Republican successes are more attributable to desire for change than to any inherent GOP strength.

For example, the 263,000 ballots cast for George Wallace —although fewer than predicted—represented a protest vote that could have altered significantly the outcome of a close two-party race. Although some Wallace ballots probably were cast by voters who registered only to be able to vote for him, the Wallace campaign attracted members of both major parties. In normally Democratic urban ethnic and blue-collar areas, Wallace obtained significant support and Nixon ran slightly better (at least in some) than he had in 1960, but Humphrey still carried every such district. Wallace also did well in southern rural counties, eating more heavily into Republican pluralities there. And in several traditionally Republican counties in northern New Jersey, both Nixon and Humphrey ran behind the 1960 percentages for Nixon and Kennedy respectively.

Though the GOP had expected to pick up a minimum of two more congressional seats, the line-up remained the same—nine Democrats and six Republicans. The Republican-dominated legislature had gerrymandered—over the veto of Democratic Governor Richard Hughes—the district of Democratic incumbent Henry Helstoski so as almost to ensure a GOP victory. Depending largely on his 100 percent ADA voting record and on precinct work from McCarthy supporters, Helstoski upset able Assembly Majority Leader Peter Moriates, who, like Nixon, made no inroads into the black and Jewish communities. In the other major House race, incumbent Democrat James J. Howard won reelection in his traditionally Republican district on the strength of four years of careful constituent service.

New Jersey Democrats are making overtures to the McCarthy elements, and generally trying to adapt to new developments. Neither party, however, has made concerted efforts to mobilize the young or the black vote. Over 100,000 of those who have become eligible to vote since 1964 did not register for the 1968 elections, and the turnout of black voters was substantially below that of 1964 in several areas. (Humphrey took about 90 percent of the votes of those casting ballots.) Much of the political outcome in New Jersey in the next few years will depend on which party can develop these sources as well as attract the support of the one third of the electorate listed as independent. (Republicans and Democrats split the remaining two thirds of the electorate almost evenly.) Conservative GOP Congressman Charles W. Sandman, whose rural, southern New Jersey district is below the Mason-Dixon line, but who supported Rockefeller at Miami, has already declared his candidacy for the 1969 gubernatorial contest. Liberal GOP Congressman William Cahill has also declared, and several other potential candidates are expected to enter. The race should be strongly competitive and it looks as if a Republican—the right Republican—could win the job for the first time in fifteen years. This race, and the accompanying state legislative elections, the first major contests in a Northern urban state carried by Nixon in 1968, will be watched closely as the first important tests of strength for Nixon and the GOP.

NEW YORK

It can be argued on the basis of present officeholders that New York is a Republican state: The governor, lieutenant governor, secretary of state, attorney general, two senators, the mayor of New York City, and both houses of the legislature are Republican. Only the congressional delegation is controlled by the Democrats. But rather than serving merely as a measure of the state's partisan preferences, these successes illustrate how Republicans can nominate winning candidates in a highly urbanized state (45 percent of the votes cast in the 1968 presidential election came from New York City).

Nixon aimed his campaign at the suburbs, the small towns, and the white middle-income city-dweller living in neighborhoods bordering the black communities that were themselves completely ignored. Though this strategy worked moderately well in upstate suburbs and towns—although even here Nixon's plurality decreased by some 150,000 votes from his 1960 margin over John Kennedy—it backfired in the state's major cities and in the New York City suburbs where Republican candidates in statewide contests must score well to win. Here Nixon misjudged the attitudes of the voters and failed to recognize their increasing identification with the city and their sharing of its problems. Only in the more rural Suffolk County did Nixon do as well as expected, and even there he only equaled his 1960 percentage. In Westchester and Nassau counties, however, he fell short not only of his 1960 showing but also of the performances of other such recent GOP candidates as Eisenhower, Rockefeller, and former Senator Kenneth Keating. He also failed to equal his 1960 vote in New York City. Altogether, Nixon lost the state by 400,000 votes—a drop of about 3.5 percent from 1960.

It is important to note that about half a million liberal voters—primarily in New York City and its suburbs—stayed home, apparently dissatisfied with both Nixon and Humphrey. This was New York State's lowest turnout for a presidential election since 1948.

In the state's U.S. Senate contest, incumbent Republican Jacob Javits faced not only the uncompromising dove Paul O'Dwyer but also the suave and persuasive Conservative Party candidate, James L. Buckley. He still won and by his biggest margin ever, 1.1 million votes. His statewide edge of almost 300,000 votes over the Nixon-Agnew ticket cannot be attributed merely to the senator's drawing power in New York City. Upstate, Javits led the national ticket by 42,000 votes, and his plurality of 600,000 far exceeded the 120,000 margin for Nixon-Agnew.

Javits' campaign and the successful efforts by local GOP leaders to regain the state assembly and strengthen GOP control in the state senate absorbed most of the energy, enthusiasm, and dedication of GOP workers. Especially in the upstate areas, there was strong apathy among the rank and file for the national ticket, in spite of solid support from the state GOP leaders.

Although the balance of the state's voters remain ideologically just to the left of the nation's center, as indicated by totaling the Javits, O'Dwyer, and liberal stay-at-home vote in 1968, the Conservative Party—whose 1968 candidate for the U.S. Senate received over a million votes—is now the third major party in the state (supplanting the older Liberal Party) and a force to be reckoned with. The Republican Party, however, cannot win consistently in the state by running conservatively inclined candidates. This will be even more true in the future as pockets of Democratic strength increasingly appear in traditionally Republican upstate areas. With the Conservative Party out to control New York State politics through the state GOP, the Conservative strategy for 1970 bears close watching.

Already, at the state assembly level, several new Republicans were elected with Conservative Party help. The dilemma for the assembly majority leader, Perry Duryea, is to continue to present progressive programs in the face of Conservative Party insistence that its help in returning control of the assembly to the GOP be rewarded.

On the congressional level, the Republicans lost two seats in New York City, but added two upstate, leaving the delegation split 26 to 15 for the Democrats. In a nationally watched race in suburban Nassau County, Allard Lowenstein, nationwide leader of the McCarthy campaign, nosed out his Conservative-Republican opponent Mason Hampton. Conservative support backfired in this race by pushing many moderate Jewish Republicans into Lowenstein's camp.

Mayor Lindsay must stand for reelection in 1969, and Senator Charles Goodell faces the voters one year later, along with Nelson Rockefeller and the rest of the statewide officers. The New York Republican Party is in a precarious situation; it will be hard-put to retain all it has today in the face of what will be a more sophisticated, more unified approach to statewide elections by New York Democrats. The votes the GOP candidates will have to go after in 1970 are those half million stay-at-homes of 1968. Many of these are middle-class suburban and urban Catholics with traditional Democratic ties who voted for McCarthy in the New York 1968 primary. In the last several elections, they have been supporting liberal Republicans, as have, to a lesser degree, their Jewish neighbors. As long as the GOP continues to nominate moderate to liberal candidates and as long as such candidates make every effort to keep strong organizational and patronage ties with traditional upstate Republicans who are loyal to the GOP, as Senator Javits has done, the party will have a good chance of remaining the most relevant, responsive, and successful of the parties in New York State.

PENNSYLVANIA

During spring 1968, Governor Raymond Shafer was fond of reminding people that no Republican presidential candidate had ever been elected without carrying Pennsylvania. That indicator joins "As Maine Goes, So Goes the Nation" and similar myths in political oblivion. The victorious Nixon lost Pennsylvania by 117,000 votes.

With the national ticket's defeat, the GOP lost every state office contested this year, although every losing candidate received more votes than Nixon. One of the losing statewide GOP candidates was quoted as saying: "Once again we move with a loser, Nixon. When the head of a ticket loses, we lose." The only victorious Republican was Richard Schweiker, who downed liberal Senator Joseph Clark by a 259,888 margin. Among the many factors contributing to Clark's loss was a rift with the Italian Democrats and, indeed, the entire regular party apparatus. Schweiker capitalized on this and other anti-Clark sentiment, overcoming his lack of name-identification with an extensive speaking campaign and a series of four half-hour television debates. The interest generated in this race was high, and 56,000 more ballots were cast for the U.S. Senate than for President.

Nixon sought support where Republicans traditionally go —the rural areas and the suburbs. He stayed away from black neighborhoods and even, to some extent, middle-class Jewish communities and passed up opportunities to appeal to the labor vote. Interestingly, Nixon ran much less strongly than he had anticipated in suburban areas. The Philadelphia suburbs (Bucks, Montgomery, Delaware, and Chester counties) gave Schweiker a 180,000-vote margin over Clark, twice the Nixon lead over Humphrey. Schweiker also ran ahead of Nixon with various ethnic groups across the state.

Republicans retained control of the state senate (27 to 23), but lost the state house to the Democrats (95 to 108). The congressional delegation remained the same (14 Democrats, 13 Republicans) in races that related little to the national contest. Looking to the future, former Philadelphia District Attorney Arlen Specter is still a potential GOP figure, despite his upset loss to Philadelphia Mayor Tate in 1967, and the Shafer-Scott-Scranton moderates hold control of the state party, ensuring that successful statewide candidates be of their stripe.

RHODE ISLAND

The Republican Party of Rhode Island, which had flourished under the progressive leadership of Governor John Chafee, was buried under the Humphrey landslide in 1968. In the GOP's worst showing in the fifty states, the Democrats outpolled the Nixon-Agnew ticket by 2 to 1, a margin that exceeded John Kennedy's victory in 1960. John Chafee ran more than 60,000 votes ahead of the national ticket in his bid for reelection (even though advocating a state income tax). It was not enough. Chafee lost the state by 12,000 votes, Nixon by 120,000. Only Attorney General Herbert DeSimone, elected for his first term in 1966, survived on the strength of his progressive activist record.

Such a prospect had seemed unbelievable in the spring, when the Rhode Island Democrats were searching for a fall guy to challenge the popular Chafee. They settled for Judge Frank Litch, while the Republicans argued over who would challenge the two incumbent Democratic congressmen, both of whom were considered vulnerable.

Chafee had been able to overcome large deficits in the national ticket before. In 1964, when Goldwater was losing the state 3 to 1, Chafee won by 90,000 votes, but this time his tax position did not sit well with the voters, especially because his opponent steadfastly asserted that additional taxes were not needed.

Another factor in the Republican loss seems to have been inadequate organization and too great a dependency on the personal appeal and coat tails of Chafee. On election day, for instance, the wife of one of the holders of a patronage job, rather than working at her volunteer center, was having her hair done so that she would look nice at the governor's victory celebration. Another worker, protesting the criticism of poor organization in the party, said he believed that all organizational problems would be solved in 1970 when Lt. Governor O'Donnell would be elected governor. Such pre-election dreams contributed to the Republican defeat. By contrast, in areas where local organization was strong, such as Portsmouth, there was a near Republican sweep, and both the tax issue and the Nixon candidacy were overcome. The GOP will have to face up to its organizational problems if it is to take advantage of any opportunities for a comeback in 1970.

The Democrats do not have an easy future, either. They are completely responsible for the state's government and may find that the fiscal restrictions that they campaigned on are indeed too tight. If the Republicans play their cards right, they may be back in power in two years.

VERMONT

In 1962, in this traditionally Republican state, the GOP was thrown out of the governor's mansion for the first time in a century by Philip Hoff. Hoff rode the Johnson landslide to reelection in 1964 and won again in 1966 by opposing a sales tax. But in 1968 Hoff decided not to seek reelection.

The combination of Hoff's departure and the return of Richard Nixon to the GOP ticket created a glowing opportunity for the Vermont GOP—one they did not let get away. Behind the party's first full-time paid chairman, Elbert Moulton, appointed in 1967, all six statewide candidates campaigned as a team—"The Team for the Times." Finances, scheduling, and advertising were all handled by Moulton's office; all candidates used the same group literature piece. And all won handily.

Senator George D. Aiken and U.S. Representative Stafford led the GOP ticket unopposed, and Nixon won a straight majority of the vote. Republicans added to their strength in the state legislature, giving them a two-thirds majority in each house.

WEST VIRGINIA

Richard Nixon never came to West Virginia in 1968, and Governor Agnew only managed to arrive the day before the election. George Wallace made two appearances, and both Humphrey and Muskie visited the state. Humphrey also had the advantage of the exposure from his intensive, though unsuccessful, primary bid there in 1960. He tied the package together with campaign oratory that recalled all that Presidents Kennedy and Johnson had done for West Virginia, particularly against unemployment and on behalf of anti-poverty programs. Humphrey won by 70,000 votes and received 50 percent of the vote without much apparent Nixon opposition, even though West Virginia's location should have made it a prime target for Nixon's border state appeal.

The Republican gubernatorial candidate, six-term Congressman Arch Moore, Jr., had done little for the state's party organization outside his own district. In his fall campaign against Democratic State Chairman James M. Sprouse, Moore was the only Republican candidate with adequate finances, and this allowed him to separate himself sharply from the other candidates and the national ticket. The contest was tainted by conflict-of-interest charges on both sides, though Sprouse was the hardest hit. He was linked to the "state house gang," some of whose members had been convicted for conspiracy in connection with alleged kickbacks. Moore squeaked through with less than a 15,000-vote margin.

The newest political light in the state is young John D. (Jay) Rockefeller, IV, who campaigned on a platform of clean elections and who led the Democratic ticket with his election as secretary of state. Rockefeller arrived in the state in 1964 as a poverty worker and Republican; in 1966 he became a Democrat; in 1968, secretary of state. In 1972, he is expected to seek the governor's office, which the GOP won in 1968 for only the second time in thirty-two years.

One bright spot for the GOP was its showing in races for the house of delegates. Before 1966, there were only nine Republicans in the house of delegates. That year a group of progressive GOP candidates waged an aggressive campaign and boosted the GOP total to thirty-five. This new blood was instrumental in getting much progressive legislation passed, and the voters, apparently pleased with their performance, reelected nearly all the incumbents and sent two additional members to the house and two more to the senate.

Besides Moore, other GOP personalities to watch include former Governor Underwood, Charles H. Haden, a Morgantown attorney who ran unsuccessfully for attorney general in 1968, and John S. Callebs, a Marshall University professor who ran unsuccessfully for secretary of state against Jay Rockefeller in 1968 after almost winning the same race in 1966.

The stigma of Republicanism in Democratic areas of the Northeast seems to have been overcome by individual GOP candidates in the Northeast. Although many urban citizens in these states still vote a fairly straight Democratic ticket, greater sophistication among the electorate has allowed individual Republican personalities to run largely on their own merits. In Massachusetts, a candidate merely has to establish his own identity to assure himself of independent consideration.

The examples of Lindsay in New York, Mathias in Maryland, Sears in Boston, and Peterson in Delaware indicate that the party is moving in a more progressive direction. The important question is whether this turn is sharp enough to capture an increasingly fast-moving electorate. It is clear by this time that the party cannot grow in the East by campaigning strictly to its own members. The GOP has found its new success by turning attention to the young as well as the old, the worker as well as the manager, and this trend should become more pronounced as natural selection narrows down the "old guard."

But a party must be strong at all levels, and until the whole party, on the national as well as on the state levels, gains a reputation for concerned regard for urban problems, the Northeast GOP will remain vulnerable, particularly in the state legislatures and county offices. In fact, if the Republican Party should attempt to resurrect a modern version of the mid-nineteenth-century Whigs, with a coalition of Midwestern and Western conservatives and Southern Bourbons, irreparable political harm would be done to Republican interests in the Northeast, and, in the long run, across the nation. For example, one immediate Republican goal is the securing of enough seats to give the GOP control of the U.S. House of Representatives by 1970, with the party's best opportunities lying in congressional contests in the Northeast. A moderate, progressive, urban-oriented stance by the national Republican Party could secure these victories without alienating Republican support in the Midwest, the Far West, or the New South.

The most important immediate elections for the party in the Northeast are the 1969 mayoral in New York City, the 1969 gubernatorial in New Jersey, and the 1970 Goodell Senate race in New York. New York City is a showcase for Republican city government, and if Lindsay fails, Democrats in the nation's cities will point to his failure, to try to repel Republican challenges. With the vast media exposure of the New York contest, the national impact of the results will be substantial. The New Jersey contest, being the first important statewide race in a Northern industrial state carried by Nixon in 1968, will provide an important indication of the reaction of metropolitan America to Nixon's first ten months in office.

Should the GOP continue to steal the traditional Democratic big-city vote and to maintain its strength among other metropolitan voters by nominating salable candidates, the party's future in the Northeast will certainly brighten. Should these efforts fail, the GOP future may be darkened considerably by a Kennedy shadow. In Massachusetts, the Kennedy presence on the 1970 ballot already is generating conflict between the tactical choices of the state GOP and those of the national party. It would be of immense assistance to local Republican candidates in Massachusetts in 1970 if Kennedy were unopposed and spent most of his time campaigning for others outside of the commonwealth. Of course, such a dry run for 1972 by Kennedy would be frowned on by the Republican in the White House.

CHAPTER 12. The South

The South, once a Democratic preserve, has become the region most actively cultivated by the Republican Party. Since 1952, when what was called a "genuine, breathing Republican" was still a curiosity in the South, the party has conducted a determined drive to mine the region's political riches. This fascination with the South, which reached fantasy proportions in 1964, was important again to the Republican campaign of 1968.

The sight of former Dixiecrat Strom Thurmond standing shoulder-to-shoulder with Richard Nixon as he received the presidential nomination symbolized the power of the Republicans' Southern thrust. Thurmond's endorsement and the pledges to the Dixie delegations would constitute Nixon's Southern credentials.

The blood-red Wallace stickers that had flooded the South were a measure of the region's general mood. It was the issue of the former Alabama governor that would set the tone of the campaign. Voters from the Mason-Dixon line to the Rio Grande were ready to protest the seemingly endless Vietnam war, the briefcase-toting HEW officials, the "guideline business," and the breakdown of law and order. Wallace's "Stand Up for America" campaign had blended old-fashioned racism and distrust of the federal government into an appeal to the common man that tapped the wide stream of Southern discontent.

The Republican response, as we indicated in Chapter 4, was to give the South a choice by appearing to offer an echo. Nixon's Southern campaign avoided a direct attack on Wallace's stands and, instead, centered on the plea to "make your (protest) vote count" and the warning that "a vote for Wallace is a vote for Humphrey." The message was aired over North Carolina country and western stations with a commercial saying, "That little white rabbit [Wallace] can outrun anything in the cotton field, but this United States, it's a lot bigger than a cotton field." In Mississippi, the theme was embellished by State Chairman Clarke Reed, who charged that some Wallace supporters were acting in collusion with the national Democrats to elect an "ultra-liberal" President. The issues were not disputed in the South; it was the Wallace electoral arithmetic that was challenged directly.

Nixon's stands were presented unemotionally. The Republicans publicized the responses given by Nixon before the closed delegate meetings in Miami, assuring voters that the Republican nominee favored "freedom-of-choice" school desegregation, appointment of "strict constructionists" to the Supreme Court, and greater state and local flexibility in the enforcement of open housing. Also discussed were Nixon's firm stance on law and order and his views on such locally important issues as the protection of domestic textiles from foreign competition. Only with Nixon in the White House, it was argued, could the South regain the national influence of which it has been deprived by the Democrats.

The sustaining principle of the Southern Republicans' catechism had been that only through one of the two *major* parties could the South elect a President who would restore "constitutional government," "states' rights," and "economic conservatism." Its corollary was that the conservatism of the Republican Party made it the natural partner of the South. The Republican Party had based its revival on the belief that such tactics as the formation of third-party movements and independent elector slates failed to satisfy the national political aspirations of the South. Wallace's candidacy was viewed as a regional protest that could only return the government to "the party of ultra-liberals who have consistently treated the South with disrespect."

The most dramatic support of the Nixon ticket came from his Dixie disciple, Strom Thurmond. Returning to South Carolina as a king-maker, the locally revered senator mobilized the state's Republican organization for Nixon. Beginning in early September, the "Thurmond Speaks Committee" ran spot television commercials almost nightly with endorsements of Nixon by such heroes as Thurmond, and former baseball player Bobby Richardson. The senator's prestige also was invoked in the slogan "Help Strom, Elect Nixon," which was adopted for the campaign. It was a personal referendum, and in South Carolina, at least, Nixon was carried to victory on Thurmond's shoulders.

Republicans who were seeking election were less eager than Thurmond to associate themselves openly with the Nixon candidacy. The three-man presidential race made it unlikely that Nixon would achieve a majority in any Southern state, and promised a heavy undertow for candidates who closely linked their campaigns with his. Most candidates were relying on the Wallace voters to continue their protest by moving to the Republican column after casting their presidential ballots. Indeed, it can be said that support for the top of the ticket by Southern candidates—in a region that frequently lectures others about party orthodoxy—was much weaker than in the Northeast.

In North Carolina, GOP Congressman James Gardner aimed his gubernatorial campaign at the rural eastern section of the state, where a heavy Wallace vote was expected, rather than at the more populous and Republican Piedmont and west. Against the advice of the party regulars, he openly sought Wallacite support, telling voters, "I don't disagree in substance with George Wallace over anything." The Gardner attempt to straddle the protest vote became awkwardly apparent on the two occasions he shared the speaker's platform with Nixon and both times failed to mention the presidential nominee's name. After his opponent, Lt. Governor Robert Scott, endorsed the Humphrey slate, Gardner went as far as to say that "Scott has only one presidential candidate while I have two."

Gardner's stridently conservative campaign apparently soured many of the state's urban Republicans and moderately conservative Democrats and is credited with losing him the election. The Wallace vote on which Gardner was depending fell far below expectations, whereas Gardner lost by substantial margins in such urban and pro-Nixon counties as Mecklenburg (Charlotte).

In the two other Southern gubernatorial contests, GOP candidates avoided involvement with the presidential race. Arkansas Governor Winthrop Rockefeller relied on a coalition of support drawn from the followers of all three presidential contenders. Although not shedding the party label for the campaign, Rockefeller informed Nixon staffers that neither visits by Spiro Agnew nor Strom Thurmond would be welcome in the state. It was feared that appearances by either could jeopardize the solid Negro support enjoyed by Rockefeller, whereas any active effort for Nixon might spur a Wallacite backlash.

In Texas, a political unknown, Paul Eggers, waged an independent campaign for the governorship, winning the support of the Mexican-American political leadership and of many white liberals by shading his position on law and order and other issues to the left of his Democratic opponent. As Eggers gained momentum, conservative Democrats (who were contributing to Nixon) began to fear a possible upset over the establishment's choice for the governorship, Lt. Governor Preston Smith. They let it be known that unless Eggers' campaign funds were cut back, their own bankrolls would switch to the Wallace camp. Under pressure, the Republican leadership stripped the Eggers campaign to hold Texas' electoral votes for Nixon. But the GOP gubernatorial candidate was vindicated by the election results. Spending approximately one third as much as his opponent, Eggers tallied the highest vote ever received by a Republican in Texas and exceeded the Nixon total by 27,000. With greater financing, Eggers might have pulled Nixon to victory.

In two of the three Senate races where Republicans made a major, realistic effort to win—in all, eight Senate seats were up for election in the South—the Democrats had nominated candidates whose liberal posture and identification with the Johnson Administration made them particularly vulnerable. Conservative Republican Congressman Ed Gurney was challenging former Florida Governor LeRoy Collins for the Senate seat vacated by George Smathers, and Kentucky Republican Marlowe Cook was opposing former State Commerce Commissioner Katherine Peden. In both contests the Republicans ran conservative and won. Congressman Gurney, who had established a record on Capitol Hill as one of the most consistent critics of the poverty program and civil-rights legislation, called his opponent "Liberal LeRoy," and sought to make the election a referendum of conservatism versus liberalism. The inability of Collins to shake off the liberal label earned during his years as governor and as a civil-rights trouble-shooter for the Johnson Administration was politically fatal in a state that for some years had shown a marked preference for staunch conservatism.

In Kentucky, Jefferson County (Louisville) Judge Marlowe Cook swung to the right in his race for the seat vacated by Republican Senator Thruston Morton. Previously considered a liberal by Kentucky standards, Cook struck hard on the issue of law and order, citing his record of law enforcement in Louisville. Miss Peden's defense of the controversial Kerner Commission report, which she had helped to prepare, and her support for the Administration's Vietnam policy gave the Republicans a solid win.

The third Republican Senate victory was in Oklahoma, where former Governor Henry Bellmon, after a two-year absence from public office, defeated Democratic Senator A. S. (Mike) Monroney. The campaign was based primarily on personal attractiveness, and the former governor enjoyed the benefit of the strongest Nixon showing in the South.

In summary, the GOP added no new governorships in the thirteen Southern states, but did increase its share of U.S. senators to seven of the region's twenty-six. In addition, the Republicans won two more congressional seats, one each in North Carolina and Virginia, which still left them thirty-one representatives to the Democrats' eighty-eight.

In the presidential contest, the Republicans made further inroads with the Nixon-Agnew ticket, receiving a plurality of the region's electoral votes, by carrying South Carolina and all of the peripheral Southern states except Texas. The electoral vote won by the GOP was sixty-seven, whereas the American Independent Party tallied forty-five and the Democrats only twenty-five. The threatened Wallace sweep of the South was confined to Arkansas and the black-belt states of Alabama, Mississippi, Louisiana, and Georgia, though he did place second in South Carolina, North Carolina, and Tennessee. The popular vote for the South as a whole was close between the three candidates, however, with Nixon receiving a bare plurality of slightly more than one third of the vote: Nixon got 36 percent of the 17 million votes cast, Wallace 33 percent, and Humphrey 31 percent.

The fear that Nixon's strength in the New South (Virginia, Kentucky, Tennessee, North Carolina, Oklahoma, Texas, and Florida) would be badly eroded by Wallace was not confirmed. Despite a three-man race, Nixon showed a decline here of less than 2 percent from Barry Goldwater's showing in 1964. In contrast, the Democratic decline of 24 percent was nearly matched by the Wallace tally.

In the Deep South, the Republicans tallied 24 percent of the vote, trailing both Humphrey's 25 percent and Wallace's crushing 50 percent. The Nixon total was less than half that received by Goldwater in 1964, and the Republican nominee failed to carry a single county or parish in the states of Alabama, Mississippi, and Louisiana. (These were also the only states in the nation in which Nixon ran third.)

Although Hubert Humphrey and the Democratic Party carried only Texas in the South on November 5, this does not mean that a conservative GOP has risen to dominance in Dixie. With the exception of North and South Carolina, the Republican presidential ticket won the same Southern states in 1968 that it carried in 1960 when the Nixon campaign did not have such conservative overtones. The South still sends fewer Republicans to Congress than does any other region of the country. And it must be remembered that only in the South does the Republican Party not have a majority of the governors, and, indeed, it holds only a tiny minority of legislative seats. The GOP has broken the Solid South— Richard Scammon believes that "the great anomaly has been the South's remaining Democratic so long"—and the national party can rely on it for assistance in winning the Presidency. But in direct contrast with the Northeast, the Republican Party has yet to produce a local structure that can stage effective campaign challenges at all levels, let alone win.

ALABAMA

In Alabama, local Republicans withstood the Wallace tidal wave by ducking under it. Although Wallace carried a massive two thirds of the vote, the three incumbent Republican congressmen (William Dickinson of Montgomery, Jack Edwards of Mobile, and John Buchanan of Birmingham) survived thanks to the party's exclusive effort in their behalf. As GOP Finance Chairman Tandy Little explained, "There was no Nixon campaign in the state. We couldn't afford it. When I say we couldn't afford it, we couldn't afford it because of the incumbents in the state."

The three congressional victories were not party victories, however. Each man had built up a strong personal following, and none tied himself to the Nixon candidacy; in fact, all said that if Wallace threw the presidential election into the House, they would vote the way their districts did— i.e., for Wallace. (One strains to remember any comparable pledge by a Northern state party in 1964, when Senator Goldwater blamed the "liberals" for defeating him.)

In the campaign for the Senate seat vacated by Lester Hill, the victory of the Democratic candidate James B. Allen was never in doubt. Citing his service as Wallace's lieutenant governor, Allen succeeded in establishing himself in the public mind as Wallace's choice. In fact, he had the advantage of running on Wallace's ticket—under the rooster emblem of the regular Alabama Democratic Party. Nonetheless, Montgomery County Probate Judge Perry Hooper (like Jim Martin in his 1966 race against Lurleen Wallace) was afraid to do anything but offer an echo of his opponent's conservative platitudes. Hooper lost by greater than 3 to 1.

The appointment of Alabama Republican Winton "Red"

Blount as postmaster general should make identification with
the GOP more respectable in Wallace country, but it is
unlikely that the Republican Party will be able to mount a
major statewide campaign until the Wallace fever subsides.
In the meantime, Republican success will be measured by
its ability to retain the slender congressional beachhead that
remained when the Goldwater tide receded in 1966.

ARKANSAS

Arkansas is the only state in the union that gave winning
margins at the top of the ticket to candidates from three
different parties. Wallace of the American Independent
Party took the presidential sweepstakes, Republican Winthrop Rockefeller the governorship, and Democratic Senator William J. Fulbright won a fifth term. The GOP
senatorial nominee, Charles T. Bernard, hired the same
public-relations firm that handled Max Rafferty in California,
and he accumulated a bad record for distorting Fulbright's
record. Bernard's strategy was to attract the hawks, by com-
plaining that the foreign relations committee chairman was
soft on communism, and the blacks (who had long been
estranged from Fulbright), by speaking out for equal opportunity. Fulbright traveled the state extensively emphasizing
his long record of service, while not ducking his reputation
as a dissenter, and emerged with an impressive 60 percent
mandate.

The objectives of the Arkansas GOP in 1968 were to
obtain a mandate for the Rockefeller administration and to
create the foundation for a two-party system in the state.
Though Rockefeller and his running mate, Lt. Governor
Maurice "Footsie" Britt, were reelected, they were unable
to carry into office any of the five other Republican candidates for constitutional office. The Rockefeller hope of
winning a substantial number of legislative seats also was

denied. Instead of the thirty seats that Rockefeller predicted the GOP would win, the Republicans were held to an increase of just one seat in each house.

If Winthrop Rockefeller stands by his promise not to seek reelection to a third term in 1970, the Republicans will be in a precarious position. The defeat of the Democrats for the second time by Rockefeller has been followed by efforts to make the party more attractive to Negroes and to the state's reform element, both of which had supported Rockefeller. Without Rockefeller heading the ticket, it seems doubtful whether the GOP could defeat a gubernatorial opponent from the progressive wing of the state Democratic Party.

FLORIDA

At the top of the ticket, the Florida Republican Party is in exemplary condition. The 1966 election of Republican Governor Claude R. Kirk, a classic conservative versus liberal contest, was duplicated this year by the victory of the state's second post-Reconstruction GOP congressman, Ed Gurney, over popular ex-Governor LeRoy Collins in the Senate race. Gurney successfully linked Collins with the unpopular Johnson-Humphrey Administration, and both he and Nixon carried the state by 200,000 votes. The only real surprise was that Wallace placed third.

These victories would seem to promise a bright future for the GOP in the Sunshine State; however, though the party had expected to add three more Republican seats to its congressional delegation, they were lucky in the end to hold the three they had. Nor did Nixon-Agnew or Gurney give any lift to candidates for the state legislature, where the GOP is in a 2 to 1 minority; losing four seats in the state senate, they gained two in the house. And behind the campaign façade of party unity, the Florida GOP has been wracked by a personal feud between state chairman William Murfin and Governor Kirk. Murfin was seeking to expand the powers of the party chairmanship, whereas Kirk was attempting to extend the control of the elected officials over party affairs. The consequent disrepair of the party machinery, together with Kirk's declining popularity among voters—he campaigned for four of the five GOP state senatorial candidates in Duval County; those four lost, whereas the fifth won—will make it difficult for the Republicans to retain the governorship in 1970 when they are unlikely to face an opponent they can taint as liberal.

GEORGIA

The largest, and only, Republican gains in Georgia came not on election day, but on September 19, when five high-ranking Democratic state officials switched their partisan affiliations to the GOP in protest over the seats given Julian Bond's insurgent delegation at the Democratic National Convention. The state agricultural commissioner, state treasurer, state comptroller general, and two public service commissioners were involved in the "big switch," which seemed to have little effect on Georgia's voters, who showered Wallace with 43 percent of the vote and the state's twelve electoral ballots. Nixon and Humphrey split the remainder of the vote, with Nixon placing second, but only three percentage points ahead of Humphrey. The latter did well in urban areas, especially among blacks. Humphrey polled 44 percent in Atlanta, receiving 98 percent of the vote in some black precincts compared to only 21 to 25 percent in white neighborhoods.

The GOP fielded, for the first time since Reconstruction, a serious candidate for the U.S. Senate. Unfortunately, the challenge of Atlanta businessman E. Earl Patton, Jr., was not serious enough to force Senator Herman Talmadge to return from his Potomac home to campaign. Aiding Talmadge were the refusal of the five crossover Democrats to endorse Patton and an election ballot that listed Humphrey's name on a separate column from other Democratic candidates. Talmadge defeated a young Democrat in his party's primary by a convincing 3 to 1 margin, and he did the same to the Republican candidate on November 5.

On the congressional level, the Republicans offered candidates in only three of Georgia's ten districts. The two incumbents, Benjamin Blackburn and Fletcher Thompson, were both returned, but the third candidate found himself in a squeeze that troubled most Republicans running in local races. The Wallace voters returned to their traditional Democratic loyalties below the presidential level, whereas the blacks supporting Hubert Humphrey also voted for other Democrats. The pattern repeated itself in many contests for the state legislature—even when GOP candidates seriously sought the black vote—and the Republicans presently have less than 15 percent of the members of either chamber.

The appointment by President Nixon of state Agricultural Commissioner J. Phil Campbell, Jr., as Under Secretary of Agriculture affirms the GOP's willingness to welcome crossovers, but it remains uncertain whether bitterness toward the national Democratic Party will produce more defections.

KENTUCKY

Nixon's reasonably good 44 percent of the vote in the Bluegrass State was his second highest showing in the South, though Wallace's poor third-place finish (18 percent) probably meant that Humphrey should not have written off the state so early in the fall. In October, Wallace was considered by many to be leading, with Nixon second and Humphrey a very poor third. However, in the end, Humphrey's second place 38 percent was also his best record in the South after Texas.

Marlowe Cook retained the seat of retiring Senator Thruston Morton for the GOP and the congressional line-up remained four Democrats and three Republicans. The scars of Cook's bitter defeat at the hands of Governor Louis B. Nunn in 1967's gubernatorial primary were healed, at least superficially, during the fall campaign, but many Republicans are worried that the rivalry may resurface.

One major concern of the state's Republicans is whether the party's majority in Louisville is disintegrating. In 1967 the Republicans won only one of twelve aldermanic contests in the city, and the 1968 elections seem to confirm that the Negro vote has been lost from the Republican coalition that has dominated the city's politics since 1961. The departure of Marlowe Cook removes the city's most powerful GOP figure and may cause party in-fighting as Republicans maneuver to fill the vacuum.

LOUISIANA

The Louisiana Republican Party, with no important officeholders at any level, remains the weakest if not the most humble state party in the country. The entire GOP election effort in 1968 was directed to the congressional campaign in the Second District between Republican challenger David C. Treen and House Majority Whip Hale Boggs. In Treen's third attempt to defeat Boggs, the chief issues were Boggs's votes for the 1965 Voting Rights Act and the 1968 Civil Rights Act, especially the open-housing provisions. In defense of his record, Boggs emphasized the favors he had done for his constituents and congressional district. Despite Treen's backing by Leander Perez, the head of the state's

Wallace campaign, he was narrowly defeated by an overwhelming Negro vote for Boggs.

In other races, Senator Russell Long was elected without opposition and the Democrats, as usual, swept the remaining seven congressional contests, facing formal opposition in only two, and won *all* the seats in the state legislature.

MISSISSIPPI

In Mississippi, the Republicans made no serious attempts to seek office in 1968. The state had no gubernatorial, senatorial, or state legislative contests, and only one of the state's five Democratic congressmen faced opposition. The lone challenger was former Congressman Prentiss Walker, a product of the 1964 Goldwater phenomenon who later gave up his seat to oppose Senator James Eastland in 1966. Lacking the comfort of Goldwater's proximate presence, Walker was defeated by a margin of 2 to 1.

However, the anger of Mississippi Democrats toward their national party over the seating of the entire insurgent biracial delegation in Chicago already has resulted in the defection of two officeholders to the Republicans. In November, state Senator James Branett of Clinton, a cousin of former Governor Ross Barnett, made the jump. Since the election, the Republicans have won a second convert, state Representative Malcolm Mabry of Coahoma County.

The possibility still exists that there will be a transfer of allegiance by Governor John Bell Williams, who was stripped of his congressional seniority by the Democrats in 1964 for supporting Barry Goldwater. Commenting on the future of the regular Democrats, who were refused seats at the convention, Williams said, "The door is open to everything except a return to the national Democratic Party as presently constituted or to the Communist Party." The major obstacle to a shift to the GOP would be a loss of seniority privileges for any members of the congressional delegation who joined in such a transfer.

NORTH CAROLINA

The Nixon-Agnew ticket carried North Carolina by a comfortable margin and picked up a new House seat, but Democrats won the governorship, retained the contested seat in the U.S. Senate, and captured all other statewide offices. The Democrats also regained control of Mecklenburg County, the state's largest, but lost control of the next two in the ranking, Guilford and Forsyth. The GOP did make gains in the state's general assembly, but it still holds less than one quarter of the seats in either house.

Early betting either gave North Carolina to Wallace or indicated a close finish. John F. Kraft's poll in mid-September found Nixon 29 percent, Humphrey 26 percent, Wallace 27 percent, and 12 percent undecided. Many Republican candidates attempted to ingratiate themselves with the Wallace supporters. However, the three congressional candidates who won their contests (the fourth, Republican veteran Congressman Charles R. Jonas, was unopposed) assumed a more moderate course—avoiding Wallace, while condemning Humphrey and mildly endorsing Nixon. Yet even the more progressive candidates found it almost impossible to break the Democratic Party's hold on the black vote.

The losing gubernatorial bid of Representative James Gardner, and the similarly bankrupt approach of his confederate, Robert Sommers, who ran and lost for U.S. senator, were bitter pills for the state party. At campaign's end, even Gardner admitted that his support for Reagan at the GOP convention, his underestimation of the black vote, and his bad relations with the press had cost him his chance at election. Whether Gardner fades, becomes more moderate, or is replaced in his leadership role may determine the immediate future of the party fortunes in North Carolina.

OKLAHOMA

Former Republican Governor Henry Bellmon, after a two-year absence from the public view, defeated Democratic Senator A. S. (Mike) Monroney, the chairman of the post office and civil services committee. Monroney campaigned largely on the basis of his experience and seniority in the Senate and on the projects he had been able to procure for his state, whereas Bellmon charged that Monroney was ineffective. The only break in what was basically a popularity contest came when Republican State Chairman Bud Stewart charged that Monroney might be in violation of federal law as a result of funds received at an Air Force Association awards dinner.

The election of Bellmon, Oklahoma's first Republican governor, to the Senate gives the GOP control of two of the state's top three elective offices. But in the congressional and state legislative positions, the Democrats remain in the majority. Though Oklahoma gave Nixon his strongest Southern support (47 percent), the hoped-for coat tails did not materialize. In the congressional races the 4 to 2 balance was retained, and in the state legislative contests the Democrats maintained their greater than two-thirds control of both houses.

SOUTH CAROLINA

In the Palmetto State, 1968 was a good year for Nixon, but otherwise a bad one for the Republican Party. Senator J. Strom Thurmond and the state organization worked almost exclusively for Nixon, allowing the rest of the Republican ticket to pursue victory on its own. In contrast, Democratic Governor Robert McNair, Lt. Governor John C. West, and Congressman L. Mendel Rivers all conducted vigorous efforts on behalf of state and local candidates, ignoring the Democratic presidential nominee. A second factor that hurt local Republicans was that the Wallace voters retaliated against them for Thurmond's refusal to support the former Alabama governor.

In the state legislative races, the Republicans were pruned from 17 to 5 representatives and from 8 to 3 senators. A likely congressional win in the Fourth District (Greenville-Spartanburg) failed to develop as the Wallace voters cut the Republicans from top to bottom. Of the Republican congressional candidates, only militant rightist Albert Watson, opposed by a former OEO regional director, was elected.

The most severe defeat was in the rematch between Democratic Senator Ernest "Fritz" Hollings and Republican Marshall Parker. In the 1966 special election to complete the term of the late Senator Olin Johnston, Parker came within 11,000 votes of defeating Hollings. In 1968, without Thurmond's active assistance or name on the ticket, Parker was defeated by 150,000 votes and failed to carry a single county. Throughout the state, Parker's vote closely mirrored that of Nixon, with Hollings receiving the solid support of both the Negroes and the white segregationists.

TENNESSEE

The congressional line-up in Tennessee remained at four Republicans and five Democrats in 1968. In traditionally Republican East Tennessee, the GOP retained its three seats, winning by margins of over 80 percent in two. The fourth victory was in Memphis, where freshman Congressman Dan Kuykendall won reelection with 60 percent of the vote.

In the state legislative races the Republicans gained five

senate seats and eight seats in the house of representatives. The Republican house wins increased their membership to forty-nine of the ninety-nine members, and touched off a marathon bargaining session over the selection of the house speaker in January, culminating when the lone independent helped the GOP organize the leadership.

TEXAS

In 1960, with Lyndon Johnson on the Democratic ticket, Richard Nixon tallied 48.5 percent of the vote in Texas. In 1968, the state's GOP leadership expected to take the South's largest electoral prize for Nixon. They didn't for several reasons: because the old feud between conservative Democrat Governor John Connally and liberal Democrat Senator Ralph Yarborough was put aside for the duration of the campaign; because the Wallace appeal stole votes from the Republicans in the rural areas; and because the Republican pluralities in the urban areas decreased from the 1960 margins.

Most importantly the Republican percentage of the black vote dropped from the 30 percent Nixon received in 1960 to a mere 5 percent in 1968. In the past four years, 165,000 new black voters had been added to the rolls in Texas; it can be said that they, more than anyone, defeated Nixon. If just among them Nixon had been able to achieve the 30 percent share of the black vote he won in 1960, he could have defeated Humphrey. Instead, Humphrey carried by 40,000 votes the only state in the South where the black registration percentage was higher than the white.

The gubernatorial candidate, Eggers, ran approximately twenty percentage points better among black voters. A political neophyte and clumsy campaigner at first, Eggers developed into an aggressive and suave Republican spokesman, and as the more liberal of the two gubernatorial candidates, was popular among college students. The University of Texas at Austin provided the backbone of his staff, and Eggers won most campus mock elections, often with 80 percent of the vote.

VIRGINIA

Nixon carried this state by a wide margin with both opponents polling less than one third of the vote each. While local Democrats ignored the national ticket, the GOP was a picture of unity. However, Nixon had virtually no support from Negro voters, who prior to 1964 had lent considerable support to national GOP tickets—as much as 50 percent—compared to less than 3 percent this year. The same was true for local Republican candidates. For example, blacks helped return David E. Satterfield to Congress from the Third District (which includes Richmond) in spite of efforts of the black Crusade for Voters, which supported Republican John Hansen, and in spite of significant support for Hansen in the Afro-American press.

The Republicans in Virginia increased their congressional representation from four to five seats, preventing a Democratic majority in the delegation for the first time since 1884. The newly-elected congressman, G. William Whitehurst, a television personality and dean of students at Old Dominion College, carried the district of retiring Democratic Congressman Porter Hardy.

Despite the departure of the segregationist white vote to Wallace and the failure of the Republicans to recover any substantial part of the black vote they lost in 1964, the GOP was able to carry the South. The future of presidential Republicanism in the South, consequently, appears to lie with moderate-conservative candidates. As Goldwater showed, if the GOP takes the extremely conservative position necessary to present a positive attraction to the Deep South, it will alienate the entire remainder of the nation, including the rest of the South. The Republican Party now has a core that is located near the center of the Southern political spectrum; it can be expanded by attracting either the more temperate of the Wallace followers or a larger share of the Negro vote.

The GOP likely will be moving in both directions as it seeks to build the majorities that will bring victory in each state. Yet, even in the Deep South, Republicans realize that they must get a share of the Negro vote if they are to win elections. Between 1964 and 1968, the number of registered Negro voters in the South increased from 2,174,000 to 3,112,000—nearly 1 million new voters. Estimates of the Nixon share of the Negro vote range from 5 percent to less. He could have carried Texas and two or three additional states had he received the once-traditional Republican share of the black vote.

Although the Republicans may be able to win selectively in the South on a white-only basis, the cost will be great. At a time when racial turmoil in the cities is the greatest domestic issue, the Republican Administration cannot carry the burden of having encouraged the development of a lily-white GOP in the South. Nor can they afford to isolate the growing number of black voters solely within the Democratic Party. In five Deep Southern states (Alabama, Georgia, Louisiana, Mississippi, and South Carolina) the voting age population is more than one-quarter black. As federal laws become truly effective and more of these voters become registered, the Democratic Party will be able to win a majority in the states with only one third of the white vote. The dynamics of the Southern political population mean that if the GOP ignores the black constituency it may find that it is once again faced with a solid Democratic South.

CHAPTER 13   The Midwest

The Midwest, traditionally the most fertile ground for the Grand Old Party, was expected under the Nixon sun of 1968 to grow a bumper crop of Republican votes, helping to produce a GOP President and improving the political standard of living for party hopefuls at the congressional and state levels. As it turned out, Mr. Nixon reaped what he sowed: the standard commodity, salable but hardly vintage.

To be sure, ten of the twelve heartland states gave their electoral votes to the Republican standard-bearer, an improvement over Nixon's 1960 performance. The two new prizes were Illinois and Missouri. Each lost narrowly in 1960; each won narrowly in 1968. Both were necessary for Nixon's presidential victory.

But in the popular vote, the Nixon-Agnew ticket actually dropped a million votes below the Nixon-Lodge showing of 1960. Forty-seven percent of voting Midwesterners supported Nixon; Humphrey was close behind with 44 percent; and George Wallace trailed with 9 percent. The 4.6 percent lead over Kennedy in 1960 slipped to 3.1 over the allegedly weaker Humphrey.

In five states—Illinois, Indiana, Missouri, Nebraska, and North Dakota—the Democratic ticket slipped further below its 1960 share than did the GOP slate. In Illinois and Missouri, slippage, for which Wallace may be partially accountable, was enough to shift the states into the Republican column.

In seven states (Iowa, Kansas, Michigan, Minnesota, Ohio, South Dakota, and Wisconsin), the Republican ticket lost more ground than did the Democratic ticket, but importantly the slippage did not cost Nixon any electoral votes. In Minnesota and Michigan, the effect was simply to increase the magnitude of the Democratic wins in states generally conceded to Humphrey. In Iowa, Kansas, and South Dakota the Republican strength was so great that the slippage was no threat to the Nixon-Agnew ticket. In Wisconsin, where the drop in both parties' votes was virtually identical, the narrow Nixon win of 1960 was repeated. In Ohio, the Republicans came the closest to being really hurt. The GOP share of the 1968 vote was down 8.1 percentage points from 1960, whereas the Democratic portion declined less than half as much, 3.8 points.

With only a few exceptions, both parties were dropping below their 1960 share of the vote, for the Wallace total in the Midwest was the highest outside the South; in fact, the region accounted for 47 percent of the vote he received outside Dixie. Wallace did poorly in the sparsely populated farm belt, substantially below his national average: Kansas, 10 percent; Minnesota, 4 percent; Nebraska, 8 percent; North Dakota, 6 percent; South Dakota, 5 percent. It was the easternmost, industrialized Midwest that gave him his biggest boost. Five Midwestern states (Illinois, Indiana, Michigan, Missouri, and Ohio) recorded 1.64 million for Wallace, more than one third his non-Southern total.

The Democrats' success in retrieving some of their usual partisans in the working class seems attributable to skillful use of advertising media, to a reawakening party identification in the defectors, and to efforts by the labor unions to undermine Wallace support on the basis of class arguments.

Still another group was brought over by Humphrey's increasing dovishness on Vietnam late in the campaign, coupled with the President's last-minute bombing halt and announcement that peace talks might begin soon. These eleventh-hour developments undoubtedly made it easier for disgruntled Kennedy and McCarthy supporters in particular to move in Humphrey's direction.

Below the presidential level, the biggest Republican gains in the Midwest were in governorships. In the November election, eight gubernatorial chairs were contested, and in all eight states the Nixon-Agnew ticket was victorious. Prior to the election, the two parties split the governors' mansions evenly, but the Democrats were in the unfortunate position of having all six of their seats up for contention in 1968. Of the two contested gubernatorial posts held by the GOP, both were retained: Attorney General Frank Farrar moved up to the governor's office in South Dakota, succeeding retiring Republican Nils Boe, while in Wisconsin the incumbent Republican Warren P. Knowles won a third term.

Among the six Democratic-held governorships, the Republicans picked up three, in Illinois, Indiana, and Iowa. Cook County Board President Richard B. Ogilvie defeated the Democratic incumbent in Illinois by about the same margin that Nixon carried the state. In Indiana and Iowa, the incumbent Democrats retired from their office and Republicans Edgar Whitcomb and Robert Ray were victorious, again running about even with the Nixon-Agnew ticket. The four governorships uncontested in the Midwest this year were all held by Republicans, giving the GOP control of the state houses in nine of the twelve states.

Nine Senate seats were up in the Midwest, and though the Republicans retained the four they already held, they failed to improve on the figure, even though Nixon carried each of the nine states with Senate races. Successfully bucking the Nixon pull were George McGovern in South Dakota, Gaylord Nelson in Wisconsin, and Birch Bayh in Indiana. In the latter instance, the moderate Republican William Ruckelshaus almost pulled through. The GOP did manage to pick up a seat in Ohio, but sustained a compensating loss in Iowa. In both contests, the two parties put forward attractive candidates.

The congressional delegation often represents best the purely partisan views of the electorate, and it is here that the Republican bias of Midwesterners is best exemplified. The region is the only one that sends more Republicans to the House of Representatives than Democrats. The GOP picked up an additional seat in Indiana, but lost two, one each in Missouri and Ohio. Still, the region has a solidly Republican congressional delegation, with over two thirds of the seats held by the GOP.

In state legislatures little changed. The GOP won control of state senates in Iowa and Indiana, but lost control of the lower house in Michigan. Of the twelve states, seven now have Republican governors and Republican majorities in both houses of their legislature. Two states have GOP governors and nonpartisan legislatures. One has a Republican governor and a legislature with split control. One state has a Democratic governor and a Republican legislature. Only in Missouri are there a Democratic governor and Democratic control of the legislature.

In the Midwest 1968 was a year of missed opportunities. Republicans had real prospects of winning the gubernatorial races in North Dakota and Kansas. The Senate contests in Indiana, Iowa, and Missouri were likewise winnable. Several marginal congressional districts with Democratic incumbents might have been taken by the GOP. The words of the disheartened campaign manager of one defeated Republican Senate aspirant tell much of the story quite succinctly: "Nixon didn't give us any coat tails at all."

ILLINOIS

The electorate demonstrated a marked lack of enthusiasm for the choices offered them for President in 1968; 138,000 fewer votes were cast in Illinois than in 1960, despite the population growth. The big drop from 1960 came from the Democratic wards of Chicago. In both elections, Richard Nixon won just over 970,000 votes in Cook County, though he improved his percentage of the total vote there in 1968. The Democrats, who had come out of the county with a better than 437,000-vote plurality in 1960, this time were held to just under a 211,000-vote edge.

Republicans were confident that a ticket topped by Nixon, Senator Everett McKinley Dirksen, and gubernatorial aspirant Richard Ogilvie would generate ample energy to push lesser Republicans over too. Nixon's margin was only 135,000—47 percent of the total. Of the big three, Dirksen fared the best, gaining a better than 273,000-vote plurality, but the predictions had indicated a win of three-quarters of a million votes. The congressional line-up remained unchanged at twelve Republicans and twelve Democrats. Moreover, Democrats took three of four statewide races below governor, winning the lieutenant governorship, secretary of state, and auditor contests. The one Republican advance came in the person of William Scott, elected attorney general. The GOP kept control of the legislature, but lost four seats in the lower house.

In sum, the GOP underestimated the advantages possessed by the Democrats and overrated its own strength. Despite the bad national publicity, the Daley machine is still a potent force in Illinois politics, though the mayor failed fully to marshal that force for the Democratic presidential nominee. However, the Republican senatorial and gubernatorial nominees found that the Democrats were able to muster surprisingly large support for their candidates for several reasons.

First, Governor Shapiro put Ogilvie on the defensive by attempting to link him with alleged corruption in the Cook County sheriff's office during the period Ogilvie held the post. Second, Democratic Attorney General William G. Clark gained some ground on Dirksen because of GOP over-confidence, the senator's advanced age, and the emergence of Clark as an anti-Daley, antiwar Democrat with concomitant appeal to the young, liberal, and reform-minded.

Governor Ogilvie says he will dismantle the corrupt Democratic machine in Chicago, but Republican resources for such an endeavor are not overwhelming. The GOP failure to win the three statewide positions mentioned above will impede Ogilvie's efforts to control the state government. Moreover, the GOP will lose the patronage that Ogilvie was able to dispense as president of the Cook County board, and loss of Republican strength in the legislature won't help either.

INDIANA

Wallace's aides genuinely believed he would outdraw H.H.H. among the Hoosiers. That he didn't was owing to the desertion of his summer fans among the blue-collar workers in the populous Lake County (Gary). However, even though Humphrey staged a major comeback here by winning back Wallace defectors, cutting down the Southerner from 20 to 11 percent, the Wallace movement in Indiana almost certainly was more damaging to the Democratic ticket than to the Republicans. In Lake County, for example, the Republican share of the vote for President was almost the same in 1968 as in 1960; the Democratic vote fell sixteen percentage points, which was about equal to Wallace's total.

The GOP picked up the governorship, as Secretary of

State Edgar Whitcomb defeated Democratic Lt. Governor Bob Rock. Rock made the error of suggesting the possibility that the state's budget might require a tax increase, whereas Whitcomb hit hard in favor of economy in government and new leadership (the state had a Democratic administration) as the answers to the fiscal problems.

In the Senate race, William Ruckelshaus, the thirty-six-year-old majority leader of the lower house of the state legislature and a moderate Republican, strongly challenged popular incumbent Democratic Senator Birch Bayh. Bayh won a narrow victory, scoring just 52 percent.

The Republican strategy in Indiana, as in Illinois, was to key the campaign to the Nixon effort and in so doing to produce a top-to-the-bottom-of-the-ticket sweep. Billboards featured Nixon with other Republican candidates, and literature claimed that "Dick Nixon, Bill Ruckelshaus, and Ed Whitcomb will give us new leadership with new ideas." With the exception of Ruckelshaus all statewide candidates on the Republican ticket were elected.

IOWA

The Democrats of Iowa, remembering 1960, feared an elephant stampede in 1968. They were lucky merely to be run over; they even managed to save the career of local folk hero Harold Hughes by winning a Senate seat for him. To enjoy a sweep, Republicans figured they needed an edge slightly more than the 171,000 votes by which Nixon won in 1960. Early polls by the *Des Moines Register* indicated a margin of 200,000; just before the Democratic convention, Nixon was ahead by 26 percentage points, and his rating went up to 29 in early October. Then the lead slipped to 19 points, and on election day the voters gave Nixon a margin that would have been a huge landslide elsewhere:

12 percentage points (Nixon 53, Humphrey 41, Wallace 6). But the 142,000 plurality could not put over the whole ticket. Hughes beat progressive State Senator David Stanley, who ran the most intensive campaign in recent Iowa history, by half a percent. Another result of the "limited landslide" was the failure of progressive State Senator Tom Riley to oust U.S. Representative John Culver, a Kennedy Democrat brought into office in the 1964 sweep.

But Republicans did make important gains in Iowa in 1968. Robert D. Ray, former GOP state chairman and the state's most important moderate Republican leader, was elected governor. This victory was especially sweet to Iowa Republicans, for of the preceding six gubernatorial contests the GOP had lost five. Republicans also won control of the state senate and now control both houses of the legislature. All statewide contests for state officeholders went Republican, and for the first time since 1963 the GOP will control the complete state government. It has taken two elections to engineer the recovery from 1964.

KANSAS

Kansas was no surprise: Nixon, 55 percent; Humphrey, 35 percent; Wallace, 10 percent. The seat of retiring U.S. Senator Frank Carlson was retained for the GOP by Congressman Robert Dole from the state's rural western district. Dole defeated the moderate former Republican governor, William Avery, in the August 6 primary, and went on to an easy victory over Democrat William Robinson. In the process of winning the nomination and election, Dole, a Goldwaterite in 1964, moved to a more centrist position on some issues.

Republicans retained control of all five Kansas congressional seats and increased their hold on the state legislature, winning additional seats in both houses. They now have sufficient strength to override a gubernatorial veto, and the governor whose veto they must override is Robert Docking. His return was the biggest GOP disappointment of the campaign. Docking overcame the strong challenge of a young and articulate Republican, Rick Harman, who spoke earnestly and bluntly about the need to increase state aid for education, improve civil-rights laws, and pass liquor-by-the-drink legislation. His message was realistic and progressive, and Rockefeller and Lindsay journeyed from New York to campaign on his behalf. He won the liberals, the young, and the bulk of the editorial writers, but not the election.

The reason is Robert Docking, one of a remarkable political breed. Both he and his father, George Docking (a two-term Democratic governor from 1957–1961), are strong fiscal conservatives and have a large personal following in normally Republican areas of Kansas, though as Democrats they have maintained their party's traditional urban support. This combination of conservative Republicans with urban Democrats wins elections for the Dockings.

The financial realities are already beginning to impinge on the conservative Docking administration, and the governor may not be able much longer to satisfy the service demands of the state without alienating many of his conservative backers. In contrast, the GOP in Kansas is strong, healthy, and moderate. William Avery's failure to achieve his long-time ambition to win a Senate seat and the consequent ascension of Dole, coupled with the defeat of Harmon, were blows to the party's progressive wing. But there are many moderates still around: Senator James Pearson, a Rockefeller backer in 1968; Congressman Chester Mize, a member of the Wednesday Club; Attorney General Kent Frizzell, a moderate who aspires to the governorship. And Rick Harman and his 1968 running mate, John Conrad, the former house speaker in the Kansas legislature, may emerge from retirement in 1970 or 1972. As for Dole himself, some observers expect him to grow more moderate with seniority.

MICHIGAN

Throughout most of the late summer and fall, the race in Michigan between Nixon and Humphrey remained extremely close. But on election day, Humphrey achieved a victory margin of over 222,000 votes, significantly better than the 67,000-vote win earned by J.F.K. in 1960.

The impact of the Humphrey victory on other races was considerable. Republican hopes of increasing their two-vote margin in the lower house of the state legislature were dashed as the Democrats gained a 57 to 54 vote edge. The state senate, which is elected concurrently with the governor and whose members serve four-year terms, remains under Republican control. In 1966, Romney helped the GOP to gain a 20 to 18 advantage in that body.

There were few statewide races in Michigan in 1968, luckily for the Republicans. A seat on the Michigan Supreme Court was lost by a small margin, and as a result the previous 4 to 3 GOP advantage on that body was reversed. Republicans were also defeated in contests for the governing boards of the state's three major universities.

In the congressional races, Humphrey was unable to produce any coat tails—though there were worried moments late in the campaign when it appeared the national ticket's deficit would be too big for congressmen such as Marvin Esch to overcome—and all incumbents were reelected. Thus, the GOP retained the five seats it won from the Democrats in 1966 and continued to enjoy a 12 to 7 edge in the House delegation. The poor Nixon showing did, however, end Republican hopes of gaining the seat of Democrat Lucian N.

Nedzi. Peter O'Rourke, a thirty-four-year-old attorney from Grosse Pointe Woods, waged a vigorous and expensive campaign in that district, patterned after the campaign that had produced victory for Don Riegle in the usually Democratic Flint two years before. Nedzi won reelection with over 60 percent of the vote.

With the departure to Washington of George Romney, who built the Michigan GOP into a strong and progressive party, the governorship was assumed by youthful and moderate Republican Lt. Governor William G. Milliken, who enjoys an excellent reputation in the state.

MINNESOTA

A Humphrey loss in his home state could scarcely be imagined. Negative reaction to the Democratic convention by adherents of the state's senior senator, Eugene McCarthy, produced some anxious moments for the Democrats early in the campaign, and the polls showed Nixon and Humphrey in a very tight race for several weeks after Chicago. However, the anticipated Humphrey strength gradually developed and mushroomed in the final days of the campaign.

The labor movement is firmly wedded to its long-time friend, Hubert Humphrey, and turned out a large vote for him. McCarthy Democrats found little in either Nixon or Agnew that attracted them, and most cast reluctant ballots for the Vice-President. Humphrey's choice of Muskie as a running mate helped him heal the intraparty wounds in Minnesota just as it did in other states. In the last days, the bombing halt was obviously of assistance, as was the late prospect of a national upset victory, which tended to rally Minnesotans around a favorite son.

Minnesota was the only Midwestern state where the total presidential vote increased from 1960 to 1968, though

Nixon's ballot total actually dropped. In 1960 Nixon lost the state by only 22,000 votes and made respectable showings in urban Hennepin County (Minneapolis) and Ramsey County (St. Paul). In 1968 Humphrey won 54 percent of the vote in Hennepin County (Nixon, 42 percent and Wallace, 4 percent), though in 1960 Nixon had led Kennedy 51 to 49 percent. In Ramsey County, Nixon had trailed Kennedy 42 percent to 58 percent; in 1968 Humphrey rolled up 63 percent to Nixon's meager 33 percent and Wallace's 4 percent. Statewide, Humphrey took 54 percent of the vote, with Nixon far behind at 42 percent. Wallace did not even manage the 5 percent necessary to retain a ballot position for his party.

Though Nixon ran poorly in Minnesota, he did no damage to the Republican Party. Humphrey had as little extra pull here as Nixon had elsewhere. All five incumbent Republican congressmen were reelected, though the GOP had hoped to pick up at least one of the Democratic congressional seats in the Minneapolis-St. Paul area. Nixon's weak urban showing ended any hopes, and the congressional delegation remained 5 to 3 Republican.

MISSOURI

Richard M. Nixon lost Missouri to John Kennedy in 1960 by 10,000 votes. In 1968, he narrowly defeated Hubert H. Humphrey by 20,000 votes, thanks, in part, to the appeal of George Wallace to habitual Democrats.

Wallace campaigned hard in Missouri. His organizers thought he might register up to 50 percent of the vote in the rural southeastern portions of the state and 25 percent in the state as a whole. In late October, Republican State Chairman Dorman Steelman predicted that if the Wallace vote held, Nixon would win by 100,000 votes. In the urban centers, the Wallace vote collapsed as the unions talked the working man out of his infatuation with the former Alabama governor. In southeast Missouri, where the hearts of the people still belong to the Old South, the Wallace vote was less fickle. The electorate of this region is hard for a Republican to win over, but Wallace denied many of them to Humphrey and made Nixon's task in the remainder of the state much easier. Losing the two urban centers of Kansas City and St. Louis, Nixon fashioned his victory in the suburbs and in the rural counties that had fought for the union in the Civil War.

The Republican Party fielded a strong ticket in Missouri last year, but made little headway. Incumbent Governor Warren Hearnes easily defeated moderate Republican challenger Lawrence K. Roos, who ran an issue-oriented campaign that accented the positive. But Hearnes's assets were too much to overcome. The Democratic governor had compiled a good record in his four years as Missouri chief executive, had worked hard to build his strength in normally Republican areas of the state, and had the services of a strong Democratic organization. In a normally Democratic state, the results were predictable.

Republican chances to gain a Senate seat in Missouri looked promising when the reputation of Senator Edward Long was seriously damaged by *Life* magazine's charges that an unsavory link existed between the Missouri senator and Teamster boss James Hoffa, and when GOP Congressman Thomas B. Curtis decided in the spring of 1967 to try to move up. Against Long, Curtis would probably have triumphed, but Lt. Governor Thomas B. Eagleton defeated Long in the Democratic primary. A McCarthy liberal, Eagleton's youth and vigor provided his campaign with an aura of excitement, in sharp contrast to the more sober scholarship and common sense that characterized Curtis.

Curtis' vote total was higher than that for the Nixon-Agnew ticket, yet in a two-way contest it was still insufficient. Moreover, the House seat Curtis had held for years in the St. Louis suburbs was lost to James Symington, the son of the state's revered senior senator, which was a serious blow that left the GOP with only one seat in the ten-man Missouri delegation.

The big Republican winner in Missouri in 1968 was John C. Danforth, a thirty-two-year-old liberal Republican who won an upset victory in the race for attorney general. A well-financed campaign, an appealing stance on the issues, youth, and enthusiasm were the keys to Danforth's success. He received the support of some 7,000 attorneys, backing from segments of the black community, and the editorial endorsement of both the St. Louis *Globe-Democrat* and the *Post-Dispatch*, two papers with usually antagonistic viewpoints. Attorney General Danforth is the first Republican to win statewide office in Missouri since 1946. Hopefully, he will be able to provide the party with the exciting leadership it so badly needs if it is ever to make serious inroads into the Democratic strength in Missouri.

NEBRASKA

The temperate conservatism of Richard Nixon strikes a responsive chord in Nebraska, and nowhere else in America does his popularity seem so pervasive. It is also persistent. In 1960, Nixon won a higher percentage of votes in Nebraska than in any other state. That record was repeated in 1968 as Nixon won 60 percent of the vote—nearly twice Humphrey's 32 percent. In 1964 Nebraska nearly handed him a write-in victory over Barry Goldwater in the state's presidential primary, and four years later, Nixon wrapped up 70 percent of the primary vote, seriously embarrassing the adherents of Nelson Rockefeller and Ronald Reagan.

Conservatives clearly control the Republican Party in

Nebraska, and the party, in turn, controls the state: the two senators, the three congressmen, and all statewide offices are in GOP hands. (The legislature is unicameral and nonpartisan.) Governor Norbert T. Tiemann is closer to the moderate wing of the party than most other Nebraska Republican leaders, and he won a moral victory at the polls when the voters refused to pass a constitutional amendment that would have repealed the income tax passed by the legislature at his urging. But it is unlikely that he can become the rallying point for a resurgence of progressivism. The GOP progressivism once associated with Senator George W. Norris derived its support from financially hard-pressed farmers and small-town businessmen demanding correction of the excesses of their big-city rivals. However, farm discontent has been blunted somewhat by federal-assistance programs and rising prosperity, and the businessmen are now more worried about labor unions and high taxes than monopolies. A continual exodus of young, well-educated citizens from the state also damages the prospects for moderate Republicanism.

NORTH DAKOTA

Richard Nixon won North Dakota with ease; his 56 percent represented an increase over his 1960 performance of one percentage point—the only such increase in the Midwest. Humphrey was far behind with 38 percent, and George Wallace took the meager remainder—6 percent.

Conservative U.S. Senator Milton R. Young also swept to easy victory over his Democratic opponent, Fargo Mayor Herschel Lashkowitz. Young's victory was the product of his substantial personal popularity, respect for his seniority—he has been in the Senate since 1945—and a general Republican mood, strong in North Dakota in 1968.

Both Republican congressional incumbents were returned to Washington, but their respective success with the voters differed markedly. Representative Mark Andrews, a dynamic young moderate, won better than two thirds of the vote of his district in the eastern part of the state. Andrews carried all but one of his counties, though Nixon failed to carry almost half of them. Representative Thomas S. Kleppe, who represents the western Second District, eked out a narrow win over former Democratic Congressman Rolland Redlin. Without Nixon, he might well have been defeated in 1968.

In statewide races, Republicans made a clean sweep of all state executive offices from lieutenant governor down. The Republican auditor and attorney general were reelected and Democratic incumbents for lieutenant governor, treasurer, and commissioner of insurance were unseated. Democrats made slight gains in the state legislature, but Republicans still control both houses by huge margins.

However, Republicans failed to oust incumbent Democratic Governor William L. Guy, who won another four-year term. The Republican challenger, Robert P. McCarney, was an arch-conservative who defeated Ed Doherty, the endorsed candidate of the party, in a close primary fight. McCarney proved to be an inept campaigner, pledging to reduce state spending but highly secretive as to how he would do it. At the last minute, McCarney's tax proposals became known and Governor Guy bitterly denounced them. Little time remained to defend his plan, and McCarney carried only eleven of the state's fifty-three counties.

OHIO

In 1960, Nixon won 53 percent of the presidential vote in Ohio, but in 1968 he slipped 8.1 percentage points to 45 percent, whereas Hubert Humphrey's 43 percent of the vote was only 3.8 percentage points fewer than what Kennedy received in 1960. Despite all his difficulties, the Minnesota Democrat gave Nixon a much tougher race in Ohio than had the young Massachusetts senator eight years earlier. The presence of third-party aspirant George Wallace complicated matters for both major parties in 1968, as the Southerner took a sizable 12 percent of the Ohio presidential vote.

Nixon provided no help to lesser party candidates, but the potent Republican Party organization of James Rhodes needed little assistance from the national ticket to roll up large victories for most Republican contenders. Of the nineteen Republican members of Congress, only Congresswoman Frances P. Bolton suffered defeat. In that race, Mrs. Bolton's advanced age was probably the crucial issue, as redistricting convinced another incumbent, Charles A. Vanik, to move and challenge her. The Democrats hold only six Ohio House seats in the Ninety-first Congress.

The most significant GOP victory in Ohio was the election to the U.S. Senate of Attorney General William B. Saxbe. A progressive Republican with substantial backing from normally Democratic union members, Saxbe triumphed narrowly over Democrat John J. Gilligan, a liberal Democrat of the "new politics" genre. Gilligan's campaign was issue-oriented and designed to appeal to the younger voter and to independents of the suburbs. A McCarthy man, Gilligan's speeches were filled with references to Vietnam, the needs of black Americans, and the urban crisis. In contrast, William Saxbe used a much more traditional style of campaign, relying on the team effort of the potent GOP state organization more than on the use of issues. Moreover, he was a much more folksy candidate than Gilligan, with a campaign slogan, "At a time like this it should be Saxbe," that emphasized the candidate's down-to-earth, noninflammatory political style. Saxbe struck a positive response from voters seeking a more tranquil society and somewhat suspicious of the combative utterances of the crusading Gilligan. It should be noted that Gilligan's issue focus backfired somewhat. By campaigning hard on his dovish Vietnam proposals he may have won independents, but he alienated many working-class Democrats. Saxbe's positive record on labor matters made defection to him by disgruntled union members all the easier.

SOUTH DAKOTA

This state is Republican territory, though it seldom goes strongly for anybody for President, and the GOP ticket won a clear majority of the presidential vote (53 percent). Humphrey had the votes of 42 percent; Wallace had only 5 percent. Two facts stand out concerning the election results. First, 8.2 percent fewer votes were cast in 1968 than in 1960. Second, the GOP share of the vote declined 4.9 percentage points from 1960, whereas the Democratic ticket ran 0.2 of a percentage point better this time. The implication is that Wallace was hurting Nixon with conservative Republicans more than he was affecting the Democrats. Humphrey may have been losing some working-class Democrats, but he apparently won off setting strength from other quarters.

Democratic Senator George McGovern has won respect in South Dakota for his independence of the establishment of his own party. His reputation as a man of principle who speaks his mind increased his stature with nominal Republicans. Though a colorful and progressive Republican might have beaten McGovern, the platitudes of the drab former Governor Archie Gubbrud couldn't do the job. A 57 percent showing at the polling booths gave McGovern his second term.

Republicans won the gubernatorial contest with the progressive Attorney General Frank Farrar and maintained their hold on both congressional races.

The Republican Party controls the governorship and the legislature. Gubbrud's defeat may help convince Republicans that Democrats can win here unless the GOP offers progressive candidates, and Governor Farrar will be a crucial leader in the attempt to move the GOP away from the right.

WISCONSIN

Nixon won Wisconsin again in 1968, with a percentage-point spread between the two major parties almost the same as in 1960. This time Nixon took 48 percent of the presidential vote, Humphrey trailing with 44 percent, and Wallace with 8 percent. The Wallace candidacy appears to have hurt the two major parties about equally.

Republican Governor Warren Knowles was elected to a third term, defeating the Democratic Attorney General, Bronson La Follette, and Republicans won all state executive offices below governor. Democratic Senator Gaylord Nelson won an easy 62 percent victory over Republican Jerris Leonard, though the GOP leaders had hoped that a Nixon landslide might carry in Leonard. All the congressional incumbents (seven Republicans and three Democrats) were reelected. The GOP now holds the governorship, all other state executive offices, and both houses of the legislature.

The New Deal never broke the back of the Republican Party in the Midwest, and in all the states except Missouri the GOP has been traditionally very strong. Today, of all the partisan state legislatures [1] only Missouri's and the lower house in Michigan are controlled by Democrats; of the congressional delegations, only Missouri's and Illinois's (which is split) do not have Republican majorities.

In the farm belt, Iowa, Kansas, Nebraska, North Dakota, and South Dakota are essentially one-party states. The Republican Party, in a normal election there, has little trouble gaining victory for its nominees from the state house to the courthouse. Yet, even in these Republican bastions, the GOP is not so strong that it can flout the conventional requisites of good issues and good candidates. Over the last decade, Democrats Herschel Loveless and Harold Hughes of Iowa; George and Robert Docking of Kansas; Frank Morrison of Nebraska; and William Guy of North Dakota have succeeded in winning governorships. Hughes, Quentin Burdick of North Dakota, and George McGovern now represent their states in the U.S. Senate.

In the more industrialized regions that surround the Great Lakes, big-city Democratic machines have balanced the more rural Republican bases, and there exists a strong two-party competition in Illinois, Indiana, Michigan, Minnesota, Ohio, and Wisconsin. In all these states, the Democratic Party has managed to grab gubernatorial control in the not-too-recent past. The urban vote is crucial in all these states, and rightist candidates seldom have much appeal to voters who feel an urgent need for leaders who will take positive action to solve the innumerable problems that confront their cities.

All too often in recent years, the GOP has abetted Democratic efforts by permitting some parochial interest in the party to dictate a candidate or issue-stance with little salability to the public. Democratic victory strategies, particularly in the five GOP-dominated farm states, generally involve the portrayal of the GOP aspirant for the target office

[1] Minnesota and Nebraska have nonpartisan legislatures.

as badly out of step with much of his own party's rank and file. McGovern in South Dakota and Nelson in Wisconsin found their reelection campaigns simplified in this way by the Republicans they faced. However, Republican contenders who deny the political middle ground to their Democratic opponents make employment of this strategy difficult, as indicated by the good races run by Stanley and Ruckelshaus against very popular Democrats Hughes in Iowa and Bayh in Indiana, and by the victory of Saxbe over Gilligan in Ohio. Republicans Ray and Farrar also vindicated this tactic on the gubernatorial level in Iowa and South Dakota.

Attention to senatorial politics in the Midwest is particularly important to the Republicans nationally just now. Of the eight Midwest Democratic senators who were not up for election in 1968, only Walter Mondale of Minnesota does not have to face the voters in 1970. In contrast, only one GOP seat, Roman Hruska's of Nebraska, is due for review in two years, and it is considered safe. If the Republican Party has learned its lesson, it may be able to own a majority of the Midwest's Senate seats after the next midterm elections.

CHAPTER 14. The Far West

Richard Scammon classified the American voter in 1968 as "unyoung, unpoor, and unblack." Certainly at least the latter two adjectives applied in the Far Western states, where, outside of California, absence of heavy population concentrations keeps Westerners at a distance from the vast problems of urban life and racial confrontation. It is, in part, this distance that explains the strength of the Republican Party in the western part of the country.

Humphrey apparently wrote off the West (except Hawaii) on the basis of its past election history and its present preponderance of Republican officeholders. Nixon, counting on the trends established by the Eisenhower sweeps of 1952 and 1956 and his own near-complete victory there in 1960, assumed that the area was safe. The opinion polls supported these early assumptions, reporting a 51-28-11 percentage breakdown (Nixon-Humphrey-Wallace) in Colorado, 44-33-7 in California, and 51-16-33 in Alaska up to a month before the election. With a sometime Westerner on the ticket, this should really have made for a banner Republican year.

As it turned out, Nixon did indeed carry eleven of the thirteen states (losing only Washington and Hawaii). He had picked up Nevada and New Mexico since 1960, but lost Washington. This was a good victory, but the smashing landslide everyone had expected failed to materialize. Gaining a 600,000 plurality out of 12 million votes cast, his lead over Humphrey amounted to only 5 percentage points. His margin reached a high of 26 percentage points in Idaho, but it also descended to a deficit of 21 points in Hawaii where in 1960 he had lost to Kennedy by fewer than 200 votes after a recount. Of the states thought safe beyond reasonable doubt, Alaska and California teetered over to the GOP side on the slenderest of margins, and Washington deserted to Humphrey.

Neither candidate spent much time in the West outside of California, which was a mistake for both of them. Westerners appreciate a personal visit from candidates; because of the presidential primaries, Oregonians and Californians expect it. This year they felt every mile of distance between them and the presidential contenders. And when the candidates did stop in, they didn't say anything. One Seattle paper headlined the nearly concurrent appearances of Nixon and Humphrey as "The Politics of Blah."

Consequently, the election campaign in the West tended to emphasize local and state races over that for the Presidency; television was the main contact with the national campaign. The West was considered Nixon country, and it was; but by election day the swing to Humphrey that was immediate and personal to Easterners just was beginning to seep over the airwaves to the West. Washington clearly swung in the last days, and California was swinging. Television almost accomplished what Humphrey had neglected to do in person.

The Nixon strategy was a holding operation from the beginning. If Humphrey could not find active supporters, the numerous Nixon backers seemed disinclined to stir up the voters, even positively. The advertising was bland—huge billboards and newspaper pages simply announced "Nixon's the One," as if it were thought that anything more substantial might offend. In some of the more conservative states, notably Utah and Idaho, the advertisements were of a slightly more rightist bent, but again the aim was to alienate as few people as possible. With the Wallace vote expected to be high (above Humphrey's in Alaska, by some polls), Nixon's organization sought to win back more conservative voters, rather than steal from the Humphrey ranks. The strategy may have helped in Utah or Idaho, although many there doubted Nixon's true conservative credentials, but that staid image could not be kept from leaking into California, Oregon, and Washington, where the electoral treasure is found in the middle of the road.

The sanguine optimism of the "preserve-and-protect" approach proved unfounded on November 5. In July, most Western Republican leaders had gone to Miami satisfied that any Republican could win, and win big, in the West. They backed Nixon as being more party-oriented and more conservative than Rockefeller. Nineteen sixty-four had cured them (most of them) of any hopes for Reagan's viability, although some would have clearly preferred his candidacy. Exceptions to this rule, however, were Governor Dan Evans of Washington, Governor John Love of Colorado, and the Hawaii moderates, all strong supporters of Nelson Rockefeller. As it turned out, the reservations these men shared about Nixon were at least partially borne out, and even some of those who had supported him at Miami came to have second thoughts in November. The overconfidence of the Nixon campaign strategy in the West may have contributed to a perilously close election.

Of course, Nixon did win eleven of thirteen states, but most office-seekers were expecting, and indeed depending on, a huge and deeper Nixon victory. But Governor Tim Babcock of Montana and Max Rafferty in California lost key support from moderates who voted for Nixon. Nixon was able to win for himself, and that was all.

Instead of a large increment of Republican House members, the campaign yielded a net increase among sixty-nine races of only two seats, both in New Mexico. No other Western state had any switching in its line-ups, and the Republican-Democratic ratio shifted only slightly to 33–36. Whatever the presidential outcome, each state split according to local issues and local personalities. In Montana, where Nixon obtained a nine-percentage-point plurality, Governor Babcock went down in the worst defeat of modern Montana history (13.2 percent), largely attributable to Babcock himself and to the third-term handicap.

In Washington, where Humphrey won the state's electors with 47 percent of the popular vote, voters switched to Republican Governor Dan Evans (54 percent) and back to Democratic Senator Warren G. Magnusson (65.9 percent). In Idaho, Nixon took a 26 percent plurality, but voters crossed right back to give Democratic Senator Frank Church an impressive 8.4 percent triumph. Western voters are notoriously independent, and the hope for a lift from above simply didn't materialize.

In Arizona, the Barry Goldwater-Jack Williams team ran considerably ahead of the national ticket. Williams polled 59 percent to be reelected governor and Goldwater 57.6 percent to return to the Senate; their success, rather than Nixon's, carried in Republicans from state house to courthouse. Only such hardy Democratic perennials as Representative Morris Udall and Secretary of State Wesley Bolin survived. The state ticket rode high as Williams polled 270,-000 to Nixon's 256,000. In Utah, 90 percent of the eligible voters went to the polls to defeat a liquor-by-the-drink proposal, but 25,000 didn't even bother to vote for President. Hawaii's popular Democratic Senator Inouye won 83 percent of the vote, and in one of the at-large races for Congress, Spark Matsunaga garnered twice the vote of the popular Republican mayor of Honolulu, Neil Blaisdell. Humphrey polled an impressive 60 percent, but he did not lead the ticket.

There were ten Senate contests in the West. The GOP lost one seat (California), but the Democrats lost two (Arizona and Oregon). These elections, too, were decided on local issues. The Republicans gave up a sure seat from California by rejecting former Senator Thomas Kuchel in the primary, and Max Rafferty proceeded on such a right-wing caper that he almost made the left-leaning Alan Cranston look like a Chamber-of-Commerce stalwart. Californians drew the line in this race, proving to Republicans that they must still attract Democrats in a state with a 3 to 2 Democratic registration. In Oregon's nationally observed race, State Representative Robert Packwood ousted Democratic Senator Wayne Morse. The issue was not Vietnam, however (Packwood was rather dovish too), but Morse himself. Through his crisscross record of Republican to independent to Democrat, and his endorsement of Mark Hatfield for the Senate two years before, Morse had alienated a goodly portion of the voters needed to keep him in office. Packwood garnered a slight majority of the undecided through a finely tuned campaign, knowledge of the issues, and a stunning forensic display on Morse's own ground—a statewide televised debate. He also used skillfully an old statement by Morse to the effect that youth should take preference over age in politics.

Five governors were up for reelection, four of them Republicans (Evans, Washington; Babcock, Montana; Cargo, New Mexico; and Williams, Arizona) and one a Democrat (Rampton, Utah). Two former governors were among the challengers, and both lost. Sam Goddard (Democrat) of Arizona was the more notable, having been one of the most active governors in Arizona history before he was defeated in 1966. Goddard's comeback proved difficult, for he had to campaign against Governor Williams' property tax cut, with rebate checks arriving just prior to the election.

The 1968 election once more indicated the American trend toward ticket-splitting, and nowhere is that trend more pronounced than in the West. In Arizona, with its two to one Democratic registration, the Republicans now hold the governor's office, two Senate seats, two out of three House positions, and a majority in the legislature. In New Mexico, which has been overwhelmingly Democratic for years, a Republican governor was reelected, and Republicans Manuel Lujan, Jr., and Ed Foreman account for half of the nationwide Republican gains in the House. Utah is a very conservative Republican state, yet it reelected Democratic Governor Calvin Rampton. Another conservative state, Montana, ousted its Republican governor and elected Forrest Anderson, the first Democrat to hold the office in sixteen years.

These examples show rather conclusively the lack of party-line strength in the West as a whole, but they also illustrate a trend toward strengthening the Republican Party in traditional Democratic strongholds. Arizona and New Mexico, where Republicans were an oddity until the 1950's, are moving steadily into the Republican ranks (Arizona more sharply so), and California, though narrowly repudiating the hard-line position taken by Rafferty, also elected a thin Republican majority in the legislature.

ALASKA

Alaska voters celebrated their tenth year of statehood with several major upsets and surprises. With a citizenry having an average age of eighteen, and a legal voting age of nineteen, the success of young candidates was not terribly surprising. Neither was the great emphasis placed on

Alaska's welfare (as opposed to "foreign" issues) a new phenomenon. Separated by 500 miles from the nearest state, Alaska encompasses an incredibly diverse hegemony, including semi-urban problems in Juneau, Fairbanks, and Anchorage, vast tracts of tremendous natural wealth, and poverty on a scale that qualifies the entire state outside the capital, Juneau, for federal aid to depressed areas.

Neither presidential candidate made the long trek for Alaska's three electoral votes, nor did the party state committees expend much effort on the national race. Governor Walter Hickel's efforts for Nixon probably offset the state's Democratic trend just enough to carry Alaska for Nixon by a 2.5-percentage-point margin.

The major focus of interest was on the scramble for Ernest Gruening's Senate seat. Having lost the Democratic primary, partly through underestimating his opponent, Gruening sought redress in the general election, running as an independent; but the effort was wasted. Surprisingly, the regular Democratic nominee, Mike Gravel, won, despite Gruening's continuing the fight. Gravel (thirty-eight), a Columbia College graduate and recently moved to Alaska, made his most telling points in the primary, charging that Gruening didn't work hard enough for the state. His slogan was "Alaska First!"

The GOP primary pitted Elmer Rasmuson (fifty-nine), head of the state's largest bank and former mayor of Anchorage, against forty-five-year-old Ted Stevens, speaker of the state house of representatives and an outspoken moderate. Both are Harvard graduates, but Rasmuson was clearly the establishment candidate, well financed by Alaska standards and backed by a forty-man campaign staff. Stevens, on the other hand, traveled the state with one aide in a camper-bus. The two represented different segments of the party, Rasmuson holding the party regulars with his nonantagonistic, Nixon-like campaign, and Stevens, who had spilled a good deal of blood in hammering through an anti-Goldwater convention slate in 1964, speaking out forcefully to youth, independents, and Democrats. He did well with the young, but in the primary Democrats didn't stray and voted for Gravel.

The Rasmuson-Gravel contest was somewhat of a replay of the GOP primary, except that this time the young candidate had just as much money to throw around as the old. Both spent heavily, and had few basic disagreements on the issues. Rasmuson hoped to saddle Gravel with the Johnson-Humphrey unpopularity, but the outcome indicates that the voters didn't buy that line (Gravel, 46; Rasmuson, 38; Gruening, 16 percent). Hickel's subsequent appointment of Stevens rather than Rasmuson to the Senate seat vacated by E. L. Bartlett's death probably reflected his confidence in Stevens's superior pull with Democrats and independents, as well as prior Hickel-Rasmuson conflicts.

With his appointment as Secretary of the Interior, Governor Hickel left the Alaska Republican Party in a strong position for the future, with moderate Secretary of State Keith Miller moving up to the governor's chair.

ARIZONA

Barry Goldwater's candidacy obscured much else in 1968. He spent lavishly on a campaign that was well organized (by Dean Burch and some of the 1964 group) and consummately thorough. His billboards capitalized on his position as an Arizona landmark, and simply stated, "Senator Barry Goldwater. Doesn't that Sound Great?" Every Arizona resident received literature at least once (and often several times) throughout the campaign, which was so well laced with Arizona homespun rhetoric that any issues raised by

Senator Hayden's long-time aide Roy Elson were casually overlooked.

The battle between Governor John Williams and former Governor Sam Goddard was by far the most exciting of the state contests. Goddard, Harvard-educated and from outside the Phoenix area, had held the governorship from 1965 to 1967, during which time he had pushed an ambitious program through a legislature that he characterized as a bunch of "gibbering idiots." Whereas Goddard had backed a $100 million education bond issue as governor, Williams attempted during his term to cut the education budget by 50 percent. And their personal styles contrasted as well—Goddard evinced a more intellectual approach; Williams had the folksy image more closely tied with his constituents.

Williams won easily. One survey found that 70 percent of Arizona voters made their choices on the basis of personal likes or dislikes of the candidates. Obviously this wasn't a year for men with issues.

CALIFORNIA

The only real surprise in California was Nixon's low plurality of 220,000. His strategy of holding the lead without antagonizing Wallace or Humphrey waverers had just the opposite effect. The big margin found early in the campaign—even on October 28, the California poll gave Nixon 50 percent, Humphrey 34 percent, Wallace 8 percent, undecided 8 percent—was nearly frittered away by November 5: Nixon 48 percent; Humphrey 45 percent; Wallace 7 percent. At least part of the credit for Nixon's winning at all should go to the Humphrey forces, who were occupied with intraparty squabbles until late October.

The Rafferty-Cranston contest was somewhat similar to George Murphy's battle with Pierre Salinger in 1964. The major difference was that whereas Murphy, under the direction of Robert Finch, moderated his positions considerably, Rafferty clung to the hard line, refusing even to make conciliatory gestures to Kuchel that might have won him the support of Republican moderates.

In a state where Democratic registration still leads Republican by 55 to 40 percent, even Reagan and Murphy have found it necessary to modify their hard-line positions during campaigns. Toward the end of the campaign, as Rafferty's prospects became darker and darker, Reagan lent him several top staff and backers to give him a more moderate image. They only partially succeeded in curtailing the right-wing pronouncements. The October unrest on college campuses provided a last chance, and Rafferty took a militant position for punitive action, a popular stand. But it wasn't enough.

In 1967 the court reapportionment greatly aided incumbent congressmen, and 1968 provided no net change. The line-up remained twenty-one Democrats, seventeen Republicans. Although the GOP had mounted a massive campaign to elect three new congressmen, voter indifference to congressional issues favored the incumbents decisively, and all returned to Washington.

Governor Reagan stumped the state in 1968 for a GOP legislature, and Jesse Unruh did the same for the Democrats. The Republican victory gave California its first GOP governor and legislature in ten years. The hairbreadth majority in the house (41 to 39) and 20 to 20 line-up in the senate (one Democrat died after the election, making it 20 to 19) could give the "Creative Society" a chance to get off the ground. Progressive Republican John Veneman left the house to become Under Secretary of Health, Education and Welfare, however—a decision which imperiled GOP control, angered Governor Reagan, but considerably strengthened the Nixon Administration.

California Democrats were left disorganized, underfinanced, and fragmented following the election. The Republicans are divided though the GOP is better funded than it has been in a decade. Its future depends on the effectiveness of its new programs. Unruh plans three speeches a week throughout 1969, and San Francisco Mayor Joseph Alioto also harbors further ambitions. Reagan, too, is keying up for 1970, as evidenced in his careful selection of the conservative Congressman Ed Reinke to succeed Finch as his Lieutenant Governor.

COLORADO

Colorado went for Nixon in 1960 by over 70,000 votes. In a state where registered Democrats outnumber Republicans by 335,000 to 252,000, the 330,000 independents hold the balance. In 1968 Nixon again succeeded in capturing a large portion of that bloc, although Humphrey gained fast in the final month according to a *Denver Post* poll. Wallace's showing of 8 percent was in keeping with the general Western results.

The only major statewide race pitted Senator Peter Dominick against former Democratic Governor Stephen L. R. McNichols. McNichols was thought of by some as one of the best governors in state history, but his programs had raised taxes and had thereby contributed heavily to his defeat by moderate Republican John Love. Dominick, whose mixed bag of issues included strong support for educational tax credits, civil-rights legislation, and a national job bank, as well as conservation and anticommunist trade barriers, apparently found the right blend as he won a 59 percent return ticket to the nation's capital.

State Senator Frank Kemp gave Representative Byron Rogers his closest race since 1952. In the heavily Democratic Denver district, he came within 8,000 votes of unseating the sixty-eight-year-old congressman. The rest of the incumbents won reelection, maintaining three Democrats and one Republican in the delegation. The GOP retained control of the state legislature, however, increasing their majority in the senate by four.

Republicans seem to be gaining more appeal in the state's urban areas, and Senator Dominick carried the normally Democratic stronghold of Adams County (just outside Denver), losing the city itself by only 227 votes. Denver has a 43,000-vote Democratic registration edge, and the victory there of appointed Republican District Attorney Mike McKevitt indicates that perhaps the GOP is assuming a new posture to overcome traditional Democratic voting tendencies.

HAWAII

Nineteen sixty-eight was a disaster of unprecedented proportions for Republicans in Hawaii. Republican candidates lost decisively at all levels as the Democratic slate was pulled along by popular Senator Daniel Inouye, Congressmen Spark and Matsunaga, and Congresswoman Patsy Mink. Seventy percent of the contested positions went Democratic. The GOP went into the election a long-time minority and came out more decidedly so.

Nixon's campaign, run by Senator Hiram Fong, depended on Fong's "voter commitment" drive, a sort of chain-letter device. Modest advertising, along the lines of "Remember the good old days with Ike and Dick," was attempted, but there were no funds for a large-scale effort. The only major appearance of any candidate was by Agnew, immediately following his "fat Jap" blooper, a visit the Hawaiians would like to forget.

The GOP factional struggle was only intensified by the election. At the end of the campaign, the conservatives called for the ouster of party chairman Edward Johnston, denouncing him as a liberal and a loser. The moderates issued the following description of the party: "Amidst a kaleidoscope of change and progress, there also stands the mossbacked Republican Party, with the pious rectitude of last century's missionaries, against the tide which is obviously the Hawaii of tomorrow." Criticizing conservative elements, they charged that the party is still the symbol of white-Protestant-landed gentry and the simon-pure clubs of old Hawaii. If the factional struggle continues within the Hawaiian GOP, the concluding epithet of the moderate statement "that the party hasn't been able to offer an echo, much less a choice," will remain valid.

IDAHO

Both the Nixon and Humphrey campaigns in Idaho plugged for the Wallace vote. If they hadn't, it is not inconceivable that Wallace could have won. There was, however, little change in Idaho's traditional Republican domination (other than Church's victory). Nixon gained his largest Western percentage in this conservative bastion, but couldn't pull along senatorial candidate George Hansen, who ran a completely negative campaign. Hansen was one of the few Western candidates who accepted, enthusiastically, the endorsement of Wallace's American Independent Party. The result was a Frank Church victory reaching even into Ada County, which hadn't gone Democratic in twenty-eight years.

One of the reasons Church did so well was that he managed to keep at least partially in tune with the local conservative sentiment with his anti-gun-control stand, his efforts to protect Idaho's water from California's thirst, and an emphasis on his power in the Senate. Hansen, through his arch-conservative stands (opposition to the war is treason, etc.), alienated many of even the normally conservative

Idaho electorate. Frank Church won a big victory, polling better than Nixon.

The victory of First District Representative McClure, who has been described as a muted Hansen, gives credence, however, to the contention that negative conservatism is deeply imbedded in Idaho (ADA rating 0, ACA rating 100 percent). The Second District race provided a pronounced contrast, however, with the more progressive Republican Orval Hansen (no relation to George) winning more or less through a fluke. The AIP candidate took enough votes away from the more conservative Democrat to let Hansen squeak through. He will have to develop something along the lines of Church's rugged independence in order to retain his seat in future elections.

MONTANA

After the conventions, Republicans were confident of Nixon's strength, and the Nixon-Agnew committee informed the local committee that the state was "safe"—all they had to do was hold fast. Their only advertising was overlap from the national media. Yet, Nixon's eventual plurality afforded no change congressionally. The Nixon margin (139,000 to 114,000) was just half that of GOP Representative Jim Battin, who was running only in the state's Second Congressional District.

Tim Babcock was the one gubernatorial incumbent to lose in the West, although the GOP could probably have retained the office had he stepped out of the running. Babcock was very popular up until 1964, when he barely withstood the Goldwater debacle. In 1966, however, he challenged Senator Lee Metcalf and suffered a severe drubbing. Now, with the third-term stigma, and carrying the burden of a recent sales-tax increase, he had even been challenged by his own lieutenant governor, moderate Ted James, in the Republican primary.

In addition to Forrest Anderson's victory in the gubernatorial contest, the Democrats retained their half of the two-man congressional delegation and the office of Secretary of State, and added the offices of Lieutenant Governor and Superintendent of Public Instruction. They retained their control of the state senate and cut the Republican majority in the house by six. Despite the Republican victory in the Attorney General's race, their retention of the State Auditor's post, and their addition of the position of Treasurer, the state GOP definitely emerged weaker from the 1968 contests. Babcock was completely discredited, and Ted James is without a power base; if James and conservative Congressman Battin can team up, a unified party might be able to make a comeback.

NEVADA

Although Nevada was one of the three Western states Kennedy carried in 1960, Nixon expected to take it rather easily. Wallace also was expected to be strong, and Nixon's effort reflected the desire to cut into that vote rather than Humphrey's. As it turned out, Nixon carried the state with a 12,590-vote plurality, but did not succeed in jarring Wallace too much. The 13.2 percent that Wallace garnered in Nevada tied with Idaho for highest in the West.

Young Lt. Governor Ed Fike's challenge to Senator Alan Bible represented a classic geopolitical contraposition: a Democrat from Reno (the Republican stronghold) and a Republican from Las Vegas (the Democratic bastion). The strategy for each was quite simple: carry your home town, plus the area of your party's normal dominance.

Fike proved to be a great hand-to-hand campaigner, and

wore out three pairs of shoes canvassing the state urging the voters to "Give Nevada a voice in the new Administration." He was hawkish on the war, but called for an infusion of youth and, vaguely, for a change in government direction. In a state with a strong conservative Mormon minority and a large right-wing populace, the game was to stress how much more conservative he was than Bible.

Bible played the game too, marshaling his generally conservative record (ADA rating 14, ACA rating 67). He avoided mention of his Humphrey-Johnson connections—although he could not get around his clear support for L.B.J.'s domestic programs—and stressed his senior standing in the Senate and his service-senator slogan, "Keep Building Nevada with Alan Bible." These proved to be potent arguments in a state where 86 percent of the land is federally owned and the second industry of which is government. Bible's only other aids were a film clip with Teddy Kennedy and the following quotation from Senator Mike Mansfield: "Bible is one of the most independent thinking members of the Senate. There have been times when I wished he hadn't been so independent." Independence is a trump card in Nevada, and Jimmy the Greek's 3 to 1 odds on Bible reflected the fact that he had become a rather permanent fixture on the Nevada political scene.

NEW MEXICO

Nixon carried New Mexico with a 12-percentage-point margin in 1968—in sharp contrast to the loss he suffered there to Kennedy in 1960, and the main contest was for the governor's office. David Cargo, who had won two years before by courting the suburban vote, this year sought a winning margin among the Spanish-speaking rural electorate, whereas his Democratic opponent, Fabian Chavez, spent much of his time with the suburban Anglos. Cargo undertook progressive measures during his term and, in the end, gained the Democratic support a Republican must have to win in New Mexico. In 1970, Democratic Senator Joseph Montoya will face the voters and is considered vulnerable if the governor runs against him.

Republicans made real congressional gains in New Mexico in 1968, after forty years of Democratic domination. The state's Democrats have always fared well in the congressional seniority system and have been able to bring lush government contracts to the state. Ironically, the influx of technocrats who accompanied the federal contracts helped vote in Republicans Manuel Lujan, Jr., and Ed Foreman.

OREGON

Nixon carried Oregon (50 to 44 to 6) more because of the state leadership's strong views against the war in Vietnam, and the consequent public disapproval of the Johnson-Humphrey Administration, than because of any special fondness for the Republican alternative. Democrat Wayne Morse first established the respectability of anti-Vietnam sentiment, and Republican Mark Hatfield helped develop it. Even Morse's successful Republican challenger, Robert Packwood, attacked the war.

The Oregon primary had produced a victory for the McCarthy forces, and his supporters—as well as Robert Kennedy's—were the swing votes in the presidential race. Neither presidential candidate appealed to this bloc, but the Nixon staff, working closely with the Packwood forces, was able to link Humphrey with the Johnson Administration's policies and secure the state for the GOP ticket.

Oregon, thanks to Hatfield and Packwood and the moderate GOP governor, Tom McCall, has become the most thoroughly progressive Republican state in the West. Former minority leader in the state legislature, Packwood for several years built up the moderate wing through his annual Dorchester conferences on public issues, which he held at the seacoast. Contacts and organization built there and the respectability the conferences gave to new policy departures gave him a strong thrust against Morse, whom many had come to view as an immovable state tradition.

UTAH

Utah voters remembered this year the endorsement given Richard Nixon by Mormon Church President David McKay in 1960. Though Utah Republicans might have preferred a more conservative Goldwater-type candidate, they were satisfied that such a man couldn't win. Nixon carried Utah with a nineteen-percentage-point margin, whereas Wallace only managed 8 percent of the vote, a great disappointment to Ezra Taft Benson, Jr. and The John Birch Society. The Alabamian's appeal for law and order, just like the issue of urban crisis, seemed slightly remote to the average Utah citizen.

The victory of Republican Senator Wallace Bennett over Milton L. Weinamann is significant only for its closeness. Bennett was expected to win big because of his prominence in the Mormon Church, his position of respect in the state, and his past record (ACA rating 90 percent, ADA zero). His 7.2 percent victory margin was small enough to indicate that either his age (seventy) is working against him, or his ideology is too conservative for modern Utah, or both.

The gubernatorial contest between Democratic Governor Calvin Rampton and Carl Buehner (age seventy-one) matched a popular pro against a negative, poorly managed candidate. Rampton's reelection by 68.6 percent could provide the basis for a rejuvenated Democratic Party in Utah if the GOP doesn't watch closely.

WASHINGTON

Humphrey's victory in Washington surprised many outside the state. Washington, which backed Nixon in 1960, and Eisenhower twice before that, has grown fast in recent years and has an increasingly cosmopolitan electorate, one heavily influenced by a strong labor organization. In the final days of the campaign, Democratic advertising techniques borrowed from the East and not generally used elsewhere in the West were employed by the Humphrey people, while the labor unions got out the working-class vote. Also, as in the East, many normally Republican, well-educated, middle-class districts were evenly split on the Presidency.

Most of the Washington Republican Party organization is state-oriented, and their emphasis in the 1968 campaign was on the state ticket. Running for reelection, Dan Evans mounted a generally high-level campaign marred only by the rather petty revelation of the gambling habit of Attorney General John J. O'Connell, his opponent. But stress continued to be laid on the accomplishments of Evans' first term and his desire to elect a whole "team" of new Republican state officials. Despite the attractive and enthusiastic campaign of Arthur Fletcher, a black, for lieutenant governor, and despite a well-organized youth effort called "Action for Washington," Evans' team made only one addition—progressive Republican Slade Gorton, elected attorney general. The fourth member of the team, progressive Secretary of State A. Ludlow Kramer, was reelected.

The election did, however, reestablish the Evans group's political dominance in the Republican Party. A right-wing effort from within the GOP was waged against Gorton in the campaign's final days. It almost, but not quite, defeated him—something party regulars will not soon forget. Gorton's margin against a law-and-order Democrat was less than half a percent, and the election was decided by the absentee ballots.

Prospects for the Republican Party in generally Democratic Washington depend on the skill of Evans in broadening the party base. Toward this objective, Secretary of State Kramer is working as Evans' agent in urban affairs, and Action for Washington is developing new roles for youth in state government.

WYOMING

The voters of Wyoming were probably more enthusiastic in their support of Richard Nixon than were those of any other Western state. They gave him a strong victory in 1960, and Nixon's efforts on behalf of the state ticket in 1966 were also successful. Wyoming, an out-country plutocracy, is inherently conservative. The voters oppose gun control because of their dependence on big-game hunting as a major industry; they have been angered by federal refusal to allow development of the state's vast oil-shale reserves; and they feel alienated by the federal government itself, whose increasingly urban bias frequently crosses what they consider to be Wyoming's interests. It was this conservatism, coupled with a call for greater consideration for the "forgotten American," which gave Nixon a 26,000-vote plurality (almost double his 1960 margin).

In the campaign itself, Humphrey's forces were disorganized and ineffective. Many Democrats were angered by alleged strong-arm tactics employed by senior Senator Gale McGee in attempting to win over national-convention delegates to the Vice-President. A good number of local party leaders were for Kennedy or McCarthy, and the resulting factionalism persisted through the campaign. Three different chairmen headed the party in one county during the final weeks before November. Although the race was further complicated by the fact that George Wallace ran the best third-party race in state history, Wallace's popularity declined, after a late October appearance, from a high of 20 percent to 9 percent on November 5.

Republican Representative William Henry Harrison was challenged in the primary by John Wold, who won by 1,000 votes after a hard-hitting contest. The controversy stirred up by this race attracted many to register and vote in the Republican primary. This enthusiasm carried over to the general election, where Wold received the largest majority ever given a Wyoming statewide candidate, two thirds of the vote.

In most of the West, the Republican candidate probably has an inherent edge in the a priori political biases of the electorate. As 1968 indicated, however, if the GOP is too complacent or too unresponsive, the Democrats have no difficulty winning elections. Nixon won big in the Far West, but other Republicans on the ticket stood or fell mostly on their own merits. Commenting on the outcome of the November elections in his state, former Senator Thomas Kuchel observed, "Californians cast their votes on their judgment of worthiness of opposing candidates, and their positions on the issues."

In the Southwest, the party is emerging as a strong, generally conservative force. Its representatives in Washington, D.C., vote the ACA line (i.e., Utah's Congressmen Burton and Lloyd, 85 and 74 percent respectively) and seem to fit closely with the temper of their constituents. Prospects for moderate nominations in this area, much less victories, are rather meager for the foreseeable future, although Utah's Bennett may give way to a more progressive candidate in 1974. Much will depend, of course, on how the men in office handle their problems, although many of the region's citizens probably would like to agree with Senator Goldwater's allegation that "there are no issues because the state has no problems." New Mexico is an exception, however. Here it looks as though a moderate party is emerging from years of subordination to a Democratic majority. The state's residents seem more liberal than their neighbors, and make the moderate stance staked out by Governor Cargo and some of the party's other leaders more rewarding than such a position might be in Utah or Arizona.

In the "Wild West" (Montana, Wyoming, Colorado, Idaho), the inbred conservatism was simply made clearer in 1968. The fact that Church, Bible, and Forrest Anderson could win in this area is a tribute, in the case of the senators, to the power and independence that seniority brings. It should be noted, however, that Anderson's election hardly can be looked upon as a very liberal victory, considering that he ran on the slogan, "Tax More, What For?" Outside of these few exceptions, Republicans were reelected en masse to other state posts. The conservatism of this area, more than of any other, is that of frontier America—still without the harsh realities of technological revolution. Among the few bright signs, for moderates, however, is the emergence of Montana's Ted James as a prospect for future contests.

California's Republicans will be affected for years by the outcome of the "Creative Society." Should Reagan and the legislature not make progress in solving some of California's complex problems, they will be open to defeat at the hands of Jesse Unruh and others, who are sharpening their claws for 1970. On the other hand, should they do well, the conservative wing of the party could dominate California politics for some time to come.

In the Northwest (Oregon, Washington, Alaska), the best chance seems to lie in the moderate path. All three states have elected progressive young Republicans to office, and will probably continue to do so as long as the party can supply them. The strength of the party in these states lies not in organization, nor in patronage power, but in the ability to attract pragmatic, attractive candidates to carry the GOP banner. If this can be continued, prospects are bright. If, on the other hand, new faces are not forthcoming, the tenuous hold on these states could easily evaporate. Washington is probably the state most susceptible to Democratic inroads, for it is normally Democratic; but if performance matches increasing problems, moderate Republicans should have the necessary staying power.

One aspect of Western politics that should not go unmentioned is the emergence of young people as an influence throughout the campaign. In Oregon, they made themselves felt campaigning for McCarthy and Kennedy, as well as Packwood and Morse. Also in the West, youth produced a novel sort of organization, Action for Washington, integrating young talent into the Evans "team," raising its own funds, hiring summer interns and full-time staff, even running a political coffeehouse. Youth also made a difference in California during the primary season. Kennedy's death, and McCarthy's subsequent defeat in Chicago, disillusioned many of those previously active and interested; but there is still a residue of political concern that may be activated— by either Republicans or Democrats—in the future. But one must conclude that Richard Nixon failed in 1968 to evoke either youth's interest or its vote.

PART IV. THE REPUBLICAN FUTURE

Today, despite Nixon's victory, the Republican Party finds itself still in a minority position; the 44 percent of Republicans in the U.S. House of Representatives and the 43 percent in state legislative seats probably are the truest representations of the GOP's rating with the American people.

In May 1968, in one of his first radio addresses, Richard Nixon spoke of a "new alignment for American unity"; to those who were already Republicans, he would add the "new liberal," the "new South," the "black militant," and the "silent center." During fall of 1968, presidential nominee Nixon had the opportunity to build his "new alignment" with the rhetoric of his campaign. Though his speech had stated that "We will not seek the false unity of consensus, or the glossing over of fundamental differences," the Nixon campaign strategy projected that very impression, and his new coalition eluded him. Now the problem of building a majority party will be more complex. For in 1969 President Nixon can attract new members to the Republican cause only with administrative acts—words alone are now insufficient.

The question that faces the Republican Party is what action must be taken by the President, and by Republicans in Congress and the state houses, to prove to the electorate that the GOP is capable of governing well and worthy of its support.

CHAPTER 15. THE REPUBLICAN ESTABLISHMENT

The Republican Party entered 1969 only marginally different from what it was in January 1968. There were six additional Republican senators, four more governors, and four more Republican congressmen. Ray Bliss had been eased out of his chairmanship of the Republican National Committee in favor of Rogers C. B. Morton, but it appeared that the status quo within the GOP had not changed substantially. The big difference was having a Republican in the White House, and any initiatives for party innovation were left to the new President.

A political party just returned to the White House seldom busies itself with an overhaul of its organization, or an examination of obsolete sacred cows. There is little motivation for reform; those who have been elected are satisfied, and those who have lost—theoretically, the ones who feel the greatest need for change—soon learn that the incumbent Administration opens new opportunities for their political ambitions. As many defeated (and retiring) GOP candidates for the Senate and gubernatorial posts discovered, they could turn their energies to administrative tasks within the federal government. Furthermore, with a new Administration to form and a country to govern, those who cite shortcomings within the party are likely to be viewed as spoil sports whose warnings deserve to be drowned in the celebrations of victory. Meanwhile, the new President and his supporters have

317

firm control of the party, and the former opposition—
whether young insurgents or Old Guard—is torn between
remaining pure and aloof and climbing aboard the crowded
victory wagon.

Yet, things need to be done; the lessons of 1968 must be
implemented. And there exist power centers within the GOP,
other than the Presidency, that must also initiate change and
build a stronger party.

The U.S. Senate prides itself on being the greatest legislative body in the world. Yet, four years ago, following an
election that reduced GOP representation to less than one
third, the upper chamber was merely a rubber stamp for the
White House. For Republicans seeking progressive alternatives, lone voices such as those of Jacob Javits, Hugh Scott,
Thomas Kuchel, and Clifford Case were barely reassuring.
But, in 1966, there came a group of bright, young Republicans—Baker, Brooke, Griffin, Hatfield, Percy—who gave
substance to the dream of a Republican revival. At this time,
the Senate began to recognize the plague it had brought
down on itself by its hasty approval of the Gulf of Tonkin
resolution in August 1965. Senators of both parties joined to
oppose President Johnson's policies in Vietnam and to reas-
sert their influence over international affairs, and the Senate
began to move once again into the nation's political spotlight.

With a Republican now in the White House, the Senate
contains the Democrats' chief hopes for 1972—Edward
Kennedy, Edmund Muskie, and George McGovern. It also
contains the new Democratic national chairman, Fred Harris
of Oklahoma, and a host of other articulate Democrats, including Harold Hughes of Iowa, Birch Bayh of Indiana, Philip Hart of Michigan, Joseph Tydings of Maryland,
Thomas Eagleton of Missouri, Walter Mondale of Minnesota,
and Mike Gravel of Alaska. Kennedy's move to the post of
assistant majority leader caught the nation's eye, and his

future legislative proposals were foreseen as the program of the opposition. Lacking a significant representation among the nation's governors, and with an aging leadership in the House, the Democratic Party will focus attention on its Senate stars.

The fact remains, however, that one-party dominance of the Senate was eliminated in the Ninety-first Congress, for the Republicans now hold forty-three seats to the Democrats' fifty-seven. And significantly, where Democratic liberals lost, they were replaced by Republicans of progressive persuasion. Although the basic ideological composition of the Senate has not changed, the GOP delegation no longer has the conservative-obstructionist cast it had only four years before. Recently appointed Senators Charles Goodell of New York and Ted Stevens of Alaska, together with the new Republicans elected in November—Cook, Mathias, Packwood, Saxbe, and Schweiker—and other moderates who were returned to office, provide the GOP with a group of attractive young spokesmen who can easily match the Democratic lights on the other side of the aisle.

With Ronald Reagan in charge of the Republican Governors' Association and with the possibility that F. Clifton White will be working out of its Washington office, it appears that the attention of progressive Republicanism will be on the U.S. Senate. The Northeast is the only one of the four regions of the nation that sends a Republican majority to the Senate. This fact, plus the selection of Hugh Scott of Pennsylvania as minority whip, contributes substantially to the progressive image the public presently holds of the typical GOP senator.

The significance of Scott's victory has been widely underestimated, especially in the light of Teddy Kennedy's own advancement. In the view of many, the moderate Republican forces—after an all-out effort—had barely succeeded (by a 23 to 20 margin) in replacing moderate Thomas Kuchel with moderate Hugh Scott. But Scott's backers point to three factors that, in their minds, made his election an important moderate victory.

First, Scott is viewed widely as the best intrachamber strategist among Republican progressives. Thus, though Percy, Hatfield, Brooke, et al. continue to attract attention from the national media, Scott may now be able to unite moderates in successful legislative maneuvers. Indeed, his victory, as Tom Wicker of *The New York Times* noted, proved that the GOP progressives are learning to count votes. Kuchel was less effective as a whip than many had hoped, and Scott may give new cohesion to moderate forces on the Hill.

Second, Scott's victory, unlike Kuchel's, was achieved in a head-on clash with the conservatives. Kuchel was elected whip in 1959, in a compromise among Senate Republicans whereby it was agreed that the top job of majority leader would go to a Midwestern conservative (Everett Dirksen) and the second spot to a California progressive. Ten years later, with Dirksen entrenched as majority leader, the progressives had no chance to repeat the package deal. The media, and most Republicans, assumed that the conservatives, backing Roman Hruska of Nebraska, would triumph in the fight for minority whip—as they had triumphed in nearly every direct ideological collision over the past ten years. But in the caucus, Scott, the moderate strategist, wound up with the votes. Significantly, of the seventeen Republicans who have entered the Senate since 1966, eleven voted for Scott.

Third, Scott's victory was another indication of the slipping prestige and waning power of the Republican leader, Everett Dirksen. Publicly, Dirksen claimed to be neutral, pointing both to his close personal friendship with Scott and his ideological kinship with Hruska. But, behind the scenes, Dirksen's preference for Hruska was well known—many had long believed that the Nebraskan was Dirksen's choice to succeed him as GOP Senate leader—and was made especially clear to the newly elected senators looking for rewarding committee assignments.

The defeat of Hruska is placed in perspective when it is viewed against the background of Dirksen's role in the last Congress. In the battle over the Civil Rights Act of 1968, his purported leadership was largely fictional. Dirksen had long opposed an open-housing bill; only after it had been clearly and publicly demonstrated that a large number of GOP senators, close to a majority in fact, were not in agreement with Dirksen's philosophy did the senator from Illinois shift his position.

The most publicized example of Dirksen's waning power occurred over President Johnson's nomination of Abe Fortas as Chief Justice of the Supreme Court. Dirksen publicly announced his support of Fortas, but a majority of the Republican senators opposed the nomination. Ironically, although his Republican opponents in this battle included such young senators as Griffin and Baker, on this occasion most Republicans who refused to accept Dirksen's leadership were his usual conservative allies. Eventually he gave up his support of Fortas and joined those who opposed cloture. The event was a great embarrassment to Dirksen, for although he ended up on the winning side, he emerged as a leader who had publicly given his word to his friend the President and was then unable to deliver his troops.

No one expects Everett Dirksen to be toppled from his minority-leader post during the Ninety-first Congress. But early indications are that he will not be so important in making or breaking legislation as he was when Johnson was President. President Nixon indicated in the first weeks of his term that he had chosen not to perpetuate Dirksen as sole Republican power broker by passing over Dirksen's noisily touted choice for director of the Small Business Administration in favor of Senator John Tower's candidate for the job.

Dirksen's effectiveness as a leader will now depend on his ability to represent the wishes of all Republicans in the Senate—particularly the younger and newer members. If the progressive Republican senators only recognize and use their power, it will not be necessary for them to follow Dirksen; rather the veteran from Illinois will have to come to them.

The leadership question may be more important two years from now, however, for in 1970 the GOP has an excellent opportunity to control the Senate, for only the third time in thirty-six years. The twin Republican disaster years of 1958 (when right-to-work laws were on many state ballots) and 1964 (when Barry Goldwater was on all of them) have produced a Senate loaded with vulnerable Democrats. Of the thirty-four senators whose terms expire in 1970, almost three quarters are Democrats. As Table 15 indicates, of the twenty-one Senate seats that can be ranked as "vulnerable" or "marginal," sixteen are held by Democrats and only five by the GOP.

Table 15. Rating the Senate Contests for 1970.

(Senate seats held by a party are subjectively classified as: 1) "safe" to be retained, 2) "vulnerable" to capture by the opposition, or 3) "marginal," i.e. that the opposition could win the seat under favorable circumstances.)

State	Rating	Comments
Alaska	Vulnerable Republican	Ted Stevens, a young moderate, was appointed to replace the late E. L. Bartlett and has to face the electorate in two years. Stevens is well known in Alaska. But he must be considered vulnerable in this state that narrowly went for Nixon while simultaneously electing freshman Democratic Senator Mike

State	Rating	Comments
		Gravel, even with the incumbent Democratic senator (his defeated primary opponent) on the ballot.
Arizona	Safe Republican	Incumbent Senator and former Governor Paul Fannin should be a sure bet in this conservative and increasingly Republican state.
California	Vulnerable Republican	George Murphy won in 1964 with 51.5 percent of the vote. His next campaign should be easier, with Republicans controlling the governorship and without a bitter primary fight. Yet Murphy thus far has not greatly distinguished himself in the Senate, and if Democratic Assembly Leader Jesse Unruh challenges him, the ailing Murphy could lose.
Connecticut	Marginal Democratic	Thomas J. Dodd won easily in 1964 with 64.6 percent of the vote. Despite his censure by the Senate, Dodd looks strong enough to fend off liberals in his own party and win against a factionalized state GOP.
Delaware	Vulnerable Republican	John J. Williams has announced his retirement. Republican victories in 1968 should give the party the advantage in 1970, but it will have to work hard to be able to elect Williams' successor.
Florida	Vulnerable Democratic	Spessard L. Holland was first elected to the Senate in 1946. In 1970, he will be seventy-eight years old. Florida voters, who now have a Republican governor and one Republican senator, may well decide

State	Rating	Comments
		that Holland should step aside for another Republican.
Hawaii	Safe Republican	Democrats control both House seats, the governorship, and one Senate seat. Yet Hiram Fong won in both 1958 and 1964 (with 53 percent) and remains personally popular with his constituents. He should win again.
Indiana	Vulnerable Democratic	Vance Hartke won in the two disaster years of 1958 and 1964—in the latter by only 54 percent. Republicans almost upset Birch Bayh in 1968, and they may well topple Hartke in 1970.
Maine	Safe Democratic	Edmund Muskie carried Maine by 2 to 1 in 1964. He may do as well in 1970.
Maryland	Safe Democratic	Joseph Tydings is still young and popular. He won in 1964 by 62.8 percent. He should win again.
Massachusetts	Safe Democratic	Edward M. Kennedy, need we say more?
Michigan	Marginal Democratic	Philip Hart won in 1964 by 64 percent. He will be only fifty-eight in 1970. Unless George Romney returns to Michigan to challenge him, Hart should win. But if Romney tries, it should be a good fight.
Minnesota	Marginal Democratic	Eugene McCarthy said he wouldn't run again as a Democrat. Hubert Humphrey is interested if McCarthy isn't. If Hubert is interested, then Gene probably is, etc. Republicans may gain amidst the confusion.

State	Rating	Comments
Mississippi	Safe Democratic	John Stennis won in 1964 with 100 percent. He won't do any better, but he won't do half so badly either.
Missouri	Safe Democratic	Stuart Symington will be sixty-nine years old in 1970, but there doesn't appear to be a Republican in Missouri who can deny Symington another term if he wants it.
Montana	Safe Democratic	Senate Majority Leader Mike Mansfield should have no trouble back at the ranch.
Nebraska	Safe Republican	Roman Hruska defeated in Nebraska? Not so long as the corn, wheat, cattle, and hogs keep growing.
Nevada	Vulnerable Democratic	Howard W. Cannon won in 1964 by the smallest margin of any senator. It was not an impressive performance for an incumbent Democratic senator midst the Johnson landslide. Odds in Las Vegas are not in Cannon's favor.
New Jersey	Marginal Democratic	The legislative ineffectiveness of Harrison A. Williams, Jr., has rankled many members of his party. The right Republican might be able to defeat him. But who is the right Republican?
New Mexico	Vulnerable Democratic	Joseph M. Montoya won in 1964 with 55 percent. At the age of fifty-five Montoya could be hard to beat, but Governor David Cargo is the man to do it.

State	Rating	Comments
New York	Vulnerable Republican	Recently appointed Charles Goodell is trying hard to get to know all the voter groups in New York and is becoming more and more liberal. In 1970, running on a ticket headed by Nelson Rockefeller, Goodell could be hard to beat. But this Senate seat is the best opportunity the Democrats in New York may have for some time, and they are likely to pick a good candidate. Men, such as Arthur Goldberg and Stephen Smith, wil prefer to challenge him rather than the governor. So Goodell will have a tough fight.
North Dakota	Marginal Democratic	North Dakota is not Democratic territory. Thus, although Quentin Burdick has been elected twice to the Senate—the latter time with 58 percent—he could be beaten by a good Republican in a good Republican year.
Ohio	Vulnerable Democratic	Aged but peppery Stephen Young has indicated that he will retire. Governor James Rhodes cannot run again for governor in 1970, and so is expected to run for the Senate. No one in Ohio can beat Rhodes, but then astronaut John Glenn, who started to run for the Senate in 1964 and is known to be interested in trying again, isn't in the state right now.
Pennsylvania	Marginal Republican	Senate Minority Whip Hugh Scott will be seventy years old in 1970, a little-known fact he never empha-

State	Rating	Comments
		sizes. Scott survived the Goldwater disaster in Pennsylvania—Johnson carried the state by almost 2 to 1—with 50.6 percent of the vote. Republicans have the registration advantage in Pennsylvania, and Scott should have an easier race next time; but the 1964 statistics still say he must be classed as marginal.
Rhode Island	Safe Democratic	John Pastore should win without trouble in this heavily Democratic state.
Tennessee	Marginal Democratic	Albert Gore is much more liberal than the voters of Tennessee, and the Republican Party is gaining strength. Though Gore will probably win, it won't be an easy race for him.
Texas	Vulnerable Democratic	Ralph Yarborough leads the liberal Democratic Party in Texas. Yarborough, sixty-seven, will probably face young Houston Congressman George Bush, whom he beat in 1964 with 56 percent. But Bush is older and wiser now, and Lyndon Johnson is no longer at the head of the ticket to bring out the conservative Democratic vote. Thus, Democratic Texas might wind up with its second Republican senator.
Utah	Vulnerable Democratic	Frank Moss won in 1958 and 1964 with 57 percent. But Utah is a Republican state, and Moss had better run scared.

State	Rating	Comments
Vermont	Safe Republican	Winston Prouty deserves another term. In Vermont, he will get it.
Virginia	Safe Democratic	Accent the Byrd. Play down the Jr. The result: another term for Harry F. Byrd, Jr.
Washington	Safe Democratic	Henry Jackson might have become secretary of defense, but he decided to remain in the Senate. So there he is, and there the senator from Boeing, who received 72 percent of the vote in 1964, will remain.
West Virginia	Marginal Democratic	Republican Governor Arch Moore has a four-year term running until 1972, but he is not allowed a second term and may decide to go job-hunting in 1970. If he does, incumbent Senator Robert C. Byrd could be in trouble. If Moore remains content in the governor's mansion, Byrd can flutter back to the Senate without ruffling a feather.
Wisconsin	Safe Democratic	William Proxmire rises early and runs to his Senate office to stay in shape. Proxmire won in 1964 with only 53.3 percent, but he should keep running successfully in 1970.
Wyoming	Vulnerable Democratic	Gale McGee is a Democrat in a Republican state. He won in 1964 with 54.0 percent. With a strong opponent, McGee can be beaten.

Table 16 provides a regional breakdown of the Senate seats that will be most hotly contested in 1970.

Table 16.

Region	Vulnerable Republican	Marginal Republican	Marginal Democratic	Vulnerable Democratic	Total
New England	0	0	1	0	1
Mid-Atlantic	2	1	2	0	5
Great Lakes	0	0	2	2	4
Farm Belt	0	0	1	0	1
Rocky Mountains	0	0	0	4	4
Pacific Coast	2	0	0	0	2
Peripheral South	0	0	2	2	4
Deep South	0	0	0	0	0
Total	4	1	8	8	21

The table makes it quite plain that Republicans will not be able to produce a majority in the Senate by paying undue attention to either the Deep South or the Farm Belt. The Far West (Rocky Mountains plus Pacific Coast) has the greatest number of seats that will be hotly contested in 1970; in a number of conservative states, Democrats could tumble if the GOP gives the electorate enough reason. The Northeast (New England plus Mid-Atlantic) is important, because the GOP will want to maintain its hold on the New York, Pennsylvania, and Delaware seats. But the Great Lakes region is the area that appears most fertile for Republican gains; there are four seats to be picked up there, half the eight needed for a Republican majority. The four in the peripheral South also look ripe. In all, the GOP needs to hold only four seats rated vulnerable or marginal and to win just half of the Democratic seats similarly rated.

John Tower of Texas has been selected as the chairman

of the Republican Senatorial Campaign Committee, and he will have the major say in determining the strategy for taking over the Senate in 1970. His credentials as a political strategist are in good standing; his personal victories in Texas, his preconvention work for Nixon in 1968, and his reputation among his fellow conservatives attest to his political acumen. One can only hope that in discharging his responsibility for the distribution of funds to senatorial candidates, he will demonstrate equal concern for the requirements of a moderate Republican attempting to win a vulnerable Democratic Senate seat in industrialized Ohio or Michigan as for a safe Republican seeking reelection in Arizona and Nebraska.

The important responsibilities of the senatorial campaign committee chairman, however, are on the banquet circuit. Barry Goldwater was able to parlay his work in this post into a presidential campaign; he also was able to channel about $4,000 of committee funds each month into salary and expenses for his ghostwriter. Conservatives have long held this office, and the across-country travels that go with it have given important exposure to the conservative ideology. Senate moderates will have to extend their influence to this post if they seriously expect to command the leadership of the GOP side of the Senate, and, eventually, to lead the Senate itself.

The GOP members of the House of Representatives, more than any other group in the party, fit the public's mold of the conservative "regular Republican." Because congressmen are less capable of building an independent political image than are governors and senators, they are at the mercy of their leadership. Unfortunately, the House GOP leadership has for many years presented a clearly negative image to the public.

Before the 1968 election, one Republican congressman candidly remarked: "The only thing worse than continuing the old inept Democratic leadership in the House would be to elect a Republican majority so that our own old, inept leadership could be in control." The same crippling seniority system and outmoded procedure that slowed down the Democrats almost to a halt in the Ninetieth Congress also hampers the effectiveness of the minority. Yet, despite their underdog position, House Republicans have appeared to be at least as comfortable in this atmosphere as their old-time Democratic colleagues. Republicans have lacked the motivation and inclination to use their minority position to produce the type of record and image that generates popular support. Their leadership has failed to use minority-staff positions effectively, and progressive Republicans have continually been rebuffed in their efforts to replace cronies with professionals who can provide the party with substantive research and new ideas.

Though 1968 looked like the GOP's best opportunity in fourteen continuous years of Democratic control to regain the leadership in the House, the party proved incapable of the task. On November 6, Minority Leader Gerald R. Ford complained that the GOP would have elected a majority of the 435 congressmen if it hadn't been for George Wallace and the bombing halt in Vietnam. "Unfortunately, we've had some disappointments," he explained.

After the 1966 elections, when the GOP gained forty-seven House seats, there was talk of a Republican majority in 1968—for now the party was only thirty-one seats short of control. However, few recalled that most of the 1966 gains represented the natural revival from the Goldwater disaster, when thirty-eight seats were lost. Despite the lessons of 1964, the House GOP leadership followed a revised "Southern strategy" in 1968: promising challengers and incumbents from districts considered marginal outside the South were given only token cash support from national-party sources. Two other examples of the failure of the leadership to seek new alliances were a somewhat improper and thinly veiled arrangement with the American Medical Association's political-action committee and the excessively negative literature sent out by the Republican Congressional Committee. After the national convention in Miami Beach, the polls and common political sense indicated the need for a change in the House campaign priorities, but no such recognition was forthcoming from the conservative congressional committee chairman, Bob Wilson, or from the committee's executive director, I. Lee Potter, who formulated the original GOP Southern strategy while a staff member of the Republican National Committee.

As one GOP congressman put it: "Two million dollars for four seats! Another few days and we would have had a net loss—including me."

To most observers, the 1968 election results promised a Ninety-first Congress almost identical to the Ninetieth. As in the Senate, public attention focused on the struggle for leadership within the Democratic Party, notably Morris Udall's unsuccessful challenge to Speaker John McCormack. Little note was given to two similar, but less glamorous battles in the House Republican caucus—the naming of a successor to Melvin Laird as House Republican Conference Chairman and the question of whether to continue the Republican Committee on Planning and Research.

Mel Laird is not an easy act to follow. He used his skills to build the Republican conference into the most powerful voice of House Republicans. Yet when Laird left to join the Administration, moderate and independent forces quickly moved to promote John Anderson of Illinois as Laird's replacement. Catching the Old Guard by surprise, they rounded up sufficient support so that the last-minute candidacy of conservative Jackson E. Betts of Ohio never got off the ground.

With a reputation as an unbiased and objective legislator, Anderson has the ability to relate to a wide spectrum of thought within the GOP caucus. Unlike Laird, who competed with the minority leader, he is likely to attempt to move Ford toward a broader and more reasoned outlook. But if Anderson can develop the power of his predecessor and apply it in more consistently positive directions, there is little doubt that he can do much to enhance the over-all Republican image and the power of Republican moderates.

The outcome of the second issue on the agenda of the January Republican caucus was less favorable to moderates. The Republican Committee on Planning and Research, affectionately known as P & R to its supporters, was originally established during the Eighty-ninth Congress in the aftermath of Gerald Ford's leadership coup over Charles Halleck. The changing of the guard had not been complete, however, and Ford was unable to muster sufficient support to dump Minority Whip Leslie Arends or to have young Congressman Charles Goodell replace John Rhodes, a conservative from Arizona, as chairman of the Republican Policy Committee. In a bind, Ford created a new leadership post for Goodell, chairman of the P & R committee—a solution acceptable at that time to caucus opponents.

Under the New York congressman's leadership, P & R soon became a vehicle to skirt senior Republicans on House committees, to overshadow the extremely cautious House Policy Committee, and to do what the Republican Congressional Committee might have done if it had had staff or the inclination. Task forces were established and "constructive Republican alternatives" began slowly to develop.

Some of Goodell's initiatives alienated his more conservative colleagues. Goodell's promotion to the Senate and Nixon's election to the Presidency provided P & R's opponents an opportunity to crush this threat to their positions. At the first caucus, they blocked the naming of a replacement for Goodell and attempted to abolish the committee entirely. They claimed that, with a Republican President in the White House, there was no need for a Republican program or for Republican initiatives in the House. Sensing a close contest, Ford postponed the confrontation.

Leading the pro-P-&-R forces was young Illinois Representative Donald Rumsfeld, himself a candidate for chairman of the committee. At the second caucus, Rumsfeld mustered sufficient support to retain P & R by a vote of 91 to 61. By itself, this result was encouraging, but unknown to most observers the battle was won only after a crippling compromise. Henceforth, chairmen of P & R's task forces would be required to clear any studies with whichever ranking Republican on the House committee had jurisdiction in the area. The effect of the compromise was to allow the Old Guard to veto any new idea that did not meet the orthodox interpretation of Republican philosophy.

The caucus then went on to choose Representative Robert Taft, Jr., of Ohio over Rumsfeld for P & R chairman, 76 to 74. Many Republican members thought that three members of the House leadership from Illinois would be one too many, so Rumsfeld's defeat was not unexpected. Taft, though a moderate, is extremely cautious, and is not likely to wage an outright battle with the senior colleagues who gave him his margin of victory. His potential, much like Anderson's, rests with his ability to communicate with most members of the caucus and to marshal support from all factions. Only time will tell whether he will be able to continue a hobbled P & R as one of the few opportunities for positive expression open to House Republicans.

Ironically, as moderate House Republicans were winning a leadership contest and losing a procedural one, progressive Democrats were doing just the opposite. While Congressman Udall was soundly beaten by Speaker John McCormack, McCormack was forced to allow the Democratic caucus to act on committee assignments rather than retaining that function for the leadership alone. Thus, Old Guard Democrats were stripped of an important source of power. Forward-looking Republicans might learn a lesson from their like-minded colleagues on the other side of the aisle and concentrate as much on procedural improvements as on who appears before the cameras.

With organizational matters settled, House Republicans could begin to consider their new relationship with the White House. The election of Richard Nixon put congressional Republicans in a position that they as a group had not experienced for eight years and that 70 percent of the members had never experienced at all. The success of the Nixon Administration and the future hopes of Republicans to control the House are closely intertwined. The GOP needs a successful Administration to make gains in the House, and Nixon will need skillful Republican leadership on the Hill to mold a successful Administration.

To increase their ranks in the House, however, Republicans must do more than support and guide the Nixon Administration. First, they must demonstrate that they are deserving of public support and trust, and second, they must revise their campaign priorities and procedures.

The first goal is by the very nature of House Republicans a long-range one. These men will have to recognize that serious domestic problems exist and must be attacked. They will have to convince themselves and their largely rural constituencies that the problems of the cities are on their very doorsteps and threaten to destroy their security and way of life. There are many older Republicans who have already made this recognition and commitment. But only when this group represents a majority will the House GOP become truly national in scope.

Republicans on the congressional and state levels are ten years ahead of the Democrats in the use of modern campaign techniques. But such modern research tools as in-depth polling, electronic data-processing, and sophisticated fund-raising methods can rarely produce victory if the initial focus and strategy of a campaign are warped. It did not make any sense for the Republican congressional com-mittee to adopt the widely discredited Southern strategy in 1968 when the facts showed that most marginal seats were in the Northeast and Midwest. It did not make any sense for the committee's public-relations operation to encourage candidates in marginal seats to carry the torch for Richard Nixon when he would obviously run behind them in their districts. It did not make any sense for this same group to encourage House candidates to make strong attacks on Hubert Humphrey during the last few weeks of the cam-paign, when it was clear the Democratic candidate was making tremendous gains. It did not make sense that while candidates in marginal Northern districts, such as Toledo and suburban Detroit, had to beg for funds, impossible contests in the South were being well financed.

The future of the Republican Party in the House is clouded. The election of 1970 may be decided on factors totally beyond the control of GOP House members—such as an unfortunate low point or an exceptionally high standing in Nixon's popularity. Importantly, the absence of any coat tails on the national GOP ticket in 1968 means that there should not be a historical slippage in the congressional ranks of the President's party in 1970. A popular Administration should produce conditions favorable to a large gain in Republican strength if a practical campaign strategy is developed and followed. In the long run, however, nothing short of major attitude changes on the part of many members, meaningful alterations in the exercise of power, and imaginative leadership will give House Republicans the power to govern that they expected to receive in November 1968.

After four years as Republican national chairman, Ray C. Bliss "resigned," despite efforts—led by State Party Chairmen John Andrews of Ohio, Don Ross of Nebraska, and Peter O'Donnell of Texas—to convince President Nixon and his advisers to keep the professional technician at the helm. Obviously, President Nixon was either interested in a different type of national committee operation or in having his own man at the helm—or both. The question is what efforts the new chairman, Rogers Morton, will make; where will he place—or, more to the point, where will Mr. Nixon tell him to place—the priorities for the National Committee?

It appears that those who argued for a replacement for Bliss were tempted by the opportunity to dismiss a man whose prime quality was his ability to avoid ideological warfare from 1964 to 1968 and to replace him with a more telegenic personality on the banquet circuit. This recalls memories of the fall's campaign tactics, when image ranked more important than substance and when a well-produced speech or show was considered to be sufficient for winning legions to the Republican cause. But there already are plenty of public speakers in the U.S. Senate, and more importantly, the GOP image will not be formed on the rubber-chicken circuit, but rather by the actions of the party's leader in the White House. In the past eight years, John Bailey, the Democratic national chairman, contributed little, either positively or negatively, to the public's view of the Democratic

Party; the most significant image-makers were John Kennedy and Lyndon Johnson, the incumbent Democratic presidents.

The chief function of the Republican national chairman is not to convince voters that the GOP is the better of the two political parties, but rather to open the organization to all citizens who—having been convinced of the soundness of the Republican programs and policies by the Republican President and members of Congress—wish to participate in the party's activities. Blacks will not join the Republican Party or vote for its candidates unless Mr. Nixon makes them feel comfortable with the GOP; but once he has, the work of the national committee's minorities division can make it easier for blacks to vote Republican. Similarly, if the Republican Administration adopts an antilabor stand, neither speeches nor quiet homework will win union leaders or the rank and file to the GOP banner. Over the next four years, the job of Congressman Morton will be not to construct the GOP's public image, but rather to take the best advantage of the image built by the Republican government.

The national chairman's principal duty is to make sure that Republican candidates win. Naturally, the first step toward this goal is the selection of candidates who have the credentials necessary for victory at the polls. In March 1968, the Republican National Committee sponsored a research conference at which Professor Alvin Dozeman of the University of Connecticut discussed this problem. His thesis was that the GOP must pay increasing heed to non-Republicans:

To the extent that these independents fail to register with either party, party registrants—those who run the party, control its caucuses and conventions—are less and less representative of the whole electorate.

Thus, something less than 30 percent of the people—Republican identifiers—have the responsibility for selecting candidates who must appeal to more than 50 percent of the electorate. If Republicans choose a candidate with whom only they are happy and feel comfortable, they have probably lost the election. The Republicans, as the minority party, cannot win elections unless a number of independents and Democrats vote for the Republican candidate.

It is in this regard that the national committee can perform an important function. If it can convince local party committees that its candidates must have an appeal to others than those who attend the local Republican caucuses, it will have taken an important step toward a party with majority status. The seminars, meetings, speakers, and conferences that the national committee arranges for local party officials can have a significant impact on their attitude toward the candidates they run for office.

Another important step in expanding the party's constituency is to open its auxiliary organizations to the entire spectrum of American public opinion. In recent years, both the Young Republicans and the Federation of Republican Women have been so tightly controlled by their respective conservative cadres that they have lost contact with the main body of the electorate. The ironic failure of the Young Republicans to attract youth to the GOP was demonstrated by the fact that the parent national committee felt it necessary to initiate the "Opportunities Unlimited" program that brought vigorous young Republican politicians to college campuses.

A first step in opening up the Young Republicans to the outside world necessarily must be to make this politically autonomous but financially dependent organization answerable to the national chairman for its ideological excesses and intraparty backbiting. Certainly, the conservative leadership of the Young Republicans understands that fiscal subsidy inevitably entails political accountability. Chairman Morton should explicitly inform the Young Republicans that he does not intend to sponsor anti-Republican activity with Republican funds. Another, simpler reform would be to lower the maximum age for Young Republican membership from its faintly ridiculous current limit of forty to a more youthful thirty.

To a large extent, the national Republican Party is a federation of fifty state parties. The Republican National Committee exists not so much to direct these local groups, but to service them. However, the type of aid that the national committee staff in Washington provides can have a significant impact on the direction of local party units. Candidate conferences and campaign-technique seminars are already a standard part of the national committee's program. The success and popularity of these programs would indicate that they could profitably be extended and expanded into a full-fledged Republican college. This school would absorb, for months, the complete time of candidates, local party chairmen, campaign managers, political activists from nonpolitical organizations, and young people interested in politics. An institution of this sort would make significant gains toward swelling the ranks of the army of skilled Republican workers. The existence in Britain of Swinton Conservative College and the Kierhardic (Labor) College extends the grass-roots participation in the parties' political activities.

The national committee presently supplies research material for use by local candidates, but the content is limited to either reams of statistics or to catalogues of the Democratic Party's deficiencies. There is a need to make positive ideas and programs available for use by Republican candidates. Every GOP senator and congressman has his own pet project, and the Republican National Committee would significantly improve its research service if it distributed information on these programs to candidates running for national office. Similarly, there exist many excellent ideas at the state and local levels that have been proposed by Republican officeholders; the Republican Governors' Association distributes such information to nonincumbent gubernatorial candidates, but the national committee should expand this function to the state-legislature and local levels.

A natural vehicle for the dissemination of unusual and innovative Republican initiatives is the monthly newsletter of the Republican National Committee, an organ that traditionally has given its readers little more information than they could pick up from the pages of the *Chicago Tribune*. The committee would perform a valuable public and partisan service by opening the newsletter to Republican officeholders of all persuasions who would like to sell their ideas to their party.

Such intraparty services will be of little use, however, unless the Republicans who hold public office prove the GOP worthy of the public's trust, and unless the party nominates candidates whose vision is not so narrow that it repels a majority of the electorate. Progressive Republican candidates have proven that GOP victory is possible in urban centers as well as in agricultural districts—with black citizens as well as white. But if the GOP is ever to win majority representation in the U.S. Congress, state legislatures, city councils, and county commissions, it must nominate those candidates whose concerns coincide with those of their prospective constituents.

CHAPTER 16—R.M.N. vs. E.M.K.

Republicans are now asking themselves what will happen in 1972 if the Democratic presidential nominee is the youthful, dynamic, and personable heir to the Kennedy mystique, Edward M. Kennedy. Will the Kennedy legend be able to sweep him into the Presidency and make him the youngest occupant in White House history? Can such a candidate, with appeal to all the "old politics" elements of F.D.R.'s Democratic coalition (except the South), win a commanding majority by gaining the support of the "new politics" groups of the educated young and the suburban elite? Will a Democratic ticket be able to combine the party's traditional strengths with a large enough group of those who are alienated from the Republican Administration, thus denying the GOP a decisive mandate to govern the nation?

Like most Presidents who enter the White House for the first time, Richard Nixon looks forward to eight years as the nation's leader. At the minimum, he wants to keep the option of a second term open. President Nixon in 1972 may not have the advantage of facing a disunited Democratic Party, as he did in 1968. He will, however, have the advantage of incumbency. He will be able to set the pattern, establish the ground rules, and create the issues for the 1972 campaign; the initiative will be his during the next few years.

The exact strategy for Nixon's reelection campaign may

not be decided for a couple of years—perhaps not until the 1972 Democratic convention. Right now, Nixon's game must be one of waiting—and seizing on apparent Democratic weaknesses in order to develop a successful strategy for reelection. As he begins to set the thrust of his Administration, one of the important factors that enter into the establishment of the priorities for his government is the political climate (as can best be projected) of 1972. President Nixon's time is limited, and its allocation must be somewhat affected by the necessities of ensuring the possibility of eight years in office. After all, it was Lyndon Johnson's narrow devotion to the war in Vietnam that caused him to lose sight of what else was happening in the nation. So let us take a practical look at what is likely to be the nation's political scene in 1972.

From today's vantage point, it would appear that Edward Kennedy is the leading contender for the 1972 Democratic nomination. Some even claim he could have had the prize in 1968, if he had only asked for it. Such speculation is a tribute to his acceptability to both the old and the new factions; Mayor Daley was said to be holding Illinois for a Kennedy nomination, and Senator McCarthy told Stephen Smith that he was willing to release his delegates to Kennedy. The Massachusetts senator's history of cautious and conventional respect for established power figures coupled with his liberal policy positions accounts for his broad support.

After the 1968 campaign, he moved quickly to capitalize on the Kennedy charisma. The significance of his victory over Russell Long for Senate majority whip is not alone the value of the new office he holds, or merely the fact that he ousted a senator with twenty years' seniority. It is rather the fact that he undertook a political challenge—whose outcome was by no means assured and in which he had more to lose than to gain—executed the necessary maneuvers masterfully, and emerged successful. Now Kennedy sits high in the Senate leadership and, under the fatherly tutelage of Majority Leader Mike Mansfield, appears to be developing into an official spokesman for the Democratic Party.

Already, the youngest Kennedy brother is further ahead of the pace set by either John in 1957 or Robert in 1965. He has a distinct advantage over the other prospects of his party, for his voter identification is matched by no one.

At the age of forty, Kennedy could easily afford to stay out of the 1972 presidential sweepstakes. He will, at the point of decision, have to balance two handicaps: the possibility of the decay, with time, of the Kennedy myth, against the difficulty of defeating an incumbent President. If Richard Nixon can establish a firm-enough grip on his office and the nation in the next three years, strong enough to convince Edward Kennedy not to seek the Democratic nomination, he should be strong enough to win reelection. And if he is popular enough to deter the challenge of an ambitious, charismatic Kennedy, Nixon should be able to defeat any Democratic nominee.

Though the most publicly recognized Democratic possibility for 1972, Kennedy is not the only one. The dark horse, whose quiet, reasonable style stole the show in the fall 1968 campaign, Edmund S. Muskie has discovered that national campaigning is "tremendously stimulating." "I liked it," he commented after the election, and indeed it appears that the senator from Maine has the "presidential bug"—he calls it the "faint flickerings of ambition." Yet Muskie's timidity with respect to the challenge to Senator Long awarded the first round to Kennedy. In the style of John and Robert Kennedy, Muskie appears to have decided to ignore the Senate, choosing instead to travel the banquet circuit—as did

Richard Nixon from 1964 to 1968—in an effort to seek national exposure and to develop his constituency.

And there is Edmund Muskie's running mate, the affable and talkative titular leader of the Democratic Party. Hubert Humphrey did win back the grudging respect of some of his liberal critics with a spirited, if not imaginative, campaign and a surprisingly close finish. He is likely to talk a lot, be consulted from time to time, take part in some party appointments (as he did in the selection of Senator Fred Harris as chairman of the Democratic National Committee) and position statements, and may return to the Senate—his real home—in 1970. It appears that Humphrey has learned some lessons from 1968. An early indication of this was his postelection speech to the Illinois Democratic Study Group, an organization of liberal Democratic state legislators. Though Daley ordered a boycott of the meeting, the 1968 Democratic presidential nominee seemed willing to nip at the hand that once fed him, for he flatly stated that "I intend to encourage the formation of groups like this all over the country, in all fifty states."

Given his present status, however, it is hard to imagine Humphrey as a power in the party per se. As Murray Kempton and Norman Mailer argue, in politics power is property; and right now Hubert Humphrey has very little political property. However, he may conceivably be in the fold again of those who *do* have political property but are annoyed or alarmed by the rise of other power centers that exclude them. Humphrey may be watched, therefore, not so much as a source of power in the immediate future, but rather as a receptacle for it within the party.

Though Kennedy, Muskie, and Humphrey are in the forefront of speculation, there exist others who cannot be ignored. South Dakota's Senator George McGovern may be more ambitious than was indicated by his modest, last-minute holding action at the Democratic convention. In-siders suggest that he did not seek the 1968 nomination merely to provide an outlet for Kennedy doves who couldn't stomach McCarthy and that he was not seen smiling sweetly with nominee Humphrey on the convention podium simply for the sake of party unity. He, too, is angling for field position for 1972, and one indication that the Kennedy "machine" may not be monolithic and that not all of his brothers' supporters have moved automatically to support Edward Kennedy is the fact that at least one member of the Kennedy Administration who was subsequently a close aide of the New York senator is now working quietly for McGovern with an eye toward 1972.

Still, the Democrats are in a worse position today than the GOP in 1964 in terms of the number of available po-tential contenders for the Presidency. They have some im-portant men in the Senate, but at the gubernatorial level they lack the personalities the Republicans possessed. Only Governor Richard Hughes of New Jersey has any national prominence, and he must retire in 1970.

The 1970 elections are of course fertile ground for the development of new Democratic leaders, but it appears that there is little opportunity for new ones to sprout in 1970 and be in full bloom by 1972. In the big states especially, the Democrats have scant reason for optimism. There are no nationally significant contests in Illinois. In Michigan, the Democrats are far too weak to offer a successful guber-natorial challenge with national implications. In Ohio, any race by John Glenn must face the prospective opposition of the popular and capable John Rhodes. In New York State, the Democrats might make strong challenges in 1970, but it is doubtful that Arthur Goldberg will become a presidential contender, and Stephen Smith would have to accept a secondary role to the ambitions of brother-in-law

Edward Kennedy. Such states as Pennsylvania and New Jersey are in no position to yield any new Democrats of national prominence in the next four years.

Only in California does the potential for new presidential figures appear. Although Jesse Unruh lost his powerful post as Speaker of the state assembly in 1968, he did emerge as an important Democratic power broker in his capacity as chairman of the California delegaton to the Chicago convention. A man who has practiced the "old politics" with great success in his home state, he became a champion of the "new politics." In 1970, both Ronald Reagan and George Murphy must stand for reelection. Unruh may decide that his best chance lies in a race against George Murphy and thereby forgo his long-time ambition to become governor of California. Alternatively, Mayor Joseph Alioto of San Francisco could emerge as a candidate—and possibly a successful one—in either spot. Coming from the nation's most populous state, Unruh or Alioto could help to place the Republicans on the defensive in exactly the areas of the GOP's greatest weakness—among the ethnic, black, and intellectual voters. Either could conceivably attract a large share of the suburban white vote.

And last, always lurking in the background and possibly the most astute of all, is Lyndon B. Johnson. Still eligible for that second full term that he might have won in 1968, Johnson left the White House with much of his popularity restored. He is much concerned about his place in history and would not be opposed to rewriting it from the best office of all, the Oval Room of the White House. He will certainly attempt to influence the Democrats and could weigh carefully any opportunity to regain firm leadership of the party.

Other Democratic senatorial personalities, such as Joseph Tydings of Maryland, Birch Bayh of Indiana, and Fred Harris of Oklahoma, must be classified more as potential vice-presidential candidates. They lack either the large state constituencies or the prominent backgrounds essential for a convention victory.

It appears, too, that Eugene McCarthy, the enigma of 1968, must be eliminated from presidential consideration. Depicted by the media—and not without reason—as a lonely antihero and antipolitician, his behavior, though confounding his allies as much as his enemies, has maintained a certain internal, if not entirely predictable, consistency. McCarthy was as much the product of the movement that bears his name as he was its creator; in his candidacy, he sought not so much to lead the forces opposed to Johnson and the war as to offer them a voice. The act of announcing his candidacy was perhaps one of the few major acts during or after his campaign that was consistent with conventional political tactics.

McCarthy's withdrawal from center stage—which began with his late-October announcement of support for Humphrey—became complete with his vote for Russell Long and his astonishing switch from the Senate foreign relations committee to the government operations committee, made with the knowledge that hawkish Gale McGee would replace him. The "new politics" may never again have so obvious a cause or be in so desperate need of a leader as was the case in early 1968; without such a vacuum, it appears that such heroes as Sir Thomas More do not flourish.

It might then be concluded that the 1972 Democratic convention will be dominated by three major factions. First, there will be the remnants of the F.D.R. coalition led by Hubert Humphrey and Lyndon Johnson. A second important group will be the proponents of the "newer"—or at least glossier—politics, who nonetheless seek their base of power among the established party forces. This faction will be led by Edward Kennedy, Edmund Muskie, and George Mc-

Govern. The third key force will be the power brokers, such as Jesse Unruh and the big-city mayors whose support will be required to ensure victory.

One may reasonably assume that, when the American people go to the polls in 1972, they will be electing their President on the basis of the traditional electoral-college system. The momentum for electoral reform that was developing before November 1968 has been blunted by the fact that a constitutional crisis was averted when Richard Nixon won more than 270 electoral votes. A strategic tangle has been caused by the inability of the reformers to agree on a specific solution, and even if one were settled on it would face the formidable constitutional requirement of a two-thirds approval by the Congress and ratification by three fourths of the states. The prospects for the adoption of *any* corrective amendment appear dim indeed.

As it did in 1968, the continuation of the electoral college in 1972 may work slightly in Nixon's favor. The states he carried in 1960 showed a net gain of eight electoral votes in 1968 as a result of the 1960 census. Between now and 1972, the 1970 census will again record population shifts that give increased electoral votes for Nixon's states (such as California, +6, and Florida, +2) at the expense of states carried by Humphrey (such as Michigan, —1, New York, —1, and Pennsylvania, —2).[1] However, these shifts will not be of enough magnitude to affect the 1972 outcome in any substantial way; the net gain for the states carried by Nixon in 1968 is only four (the same as the net loss for the states won by the Democratic ticket).

A crucial question that must be considered by both Demo-

[1] A discussion of the distribution of the seats in the Ninety-third Congress and the consequent projected allocation of electoral-college votes in the 1972 election is found in Appendix B.

crats and Republicans as they plan for 1972 is whether George Wallace will again enter the presidential race. It seems clear that the Alabamian had surprisingly little effect on the 1968 presidential election. Though he did accomplish the goal of making himself an important national figure, his 13.5 percent of the national vote represented a smaller share than Robert M. La Follette's Progressive Party garnered in 1924, nor is much of his following transferable en bloc to another candidate. More importantly, Wallace neutralized the exact area of the nation for which he had hoped to gain bargaining strength—the Deep South. His campaign effectively removed the hard-core racist vote from active solicitation by either of the two major parties in 1968, though there is some doubt as to whether the Nixon strategists understood this point. If Wallace does run again in 1972, the result should be the same. It is unlikely that a Wallace candidacy would be able to improve on his 1968 showing of five Southern states (Alabama, Arkansas, Georgia, Louisiana, and Mississippi) with their forty-five electoral votes, though without Thurmond working hard for Nixon, South Carolina and its eight electoral votes may go for the American Independent Party too. However, unless the national mood of alienation becomes substantially deeper in the next four years, so as to give the Southern demagogue more significant appeal in the North—and for such to be the case the nation would be so agitated that all predictions would be off—the real effect of his candidacy will be to remove the reactionary fringe from the ranks of both major parties.

For the remainder of the states, the ethnic population breakdown is an important key to projecting which political party they will support. From a detailed analysis of this breakdown (See Appendix A) the strengths and weaknesses, on a state-by-state basis, of the Republican and Democratic tickets in 1972 can be forecast. In Tables 17, 18 and 19, are listed those states which can be considered "Strongly Republican," "Strongly Democratic," and "Toss-Up" states respectively.

Table 17. Strong Republican States.*

State	Electoral Votes	State	Electoral Votes
Arizona	6	New Mexico	
Colorado	6	(Kennedy in 1960)	4
Florida	16	North Dakota	3
Idaho	4	Oklahoma	
Indiana	13	(Stevenson in 1952)	7
Iowa	8	Oregon	6
Kansas	7	South Carolina	8
Kentucky		South Dakota	4
(Stevenson in 1952)	9	Tennessee	11
Montana	4	Utah	4
Nebraska	5	Vermont	3
Nevada		Virginia	12
(Kennedy in 1960)	3	Wyoming	3

* All 22 states (with a total of 146 electoral votes) went to Nixon in 1968 and to the Republican tickets in 1952, 1956, and 1960, except where indicated.

Table 18. Strong Democratic States.*

State	Electoral Votes	State	Electoral Votes
Connecticut	8	Michigan	20
District of Columbia	3	New York	42
Hawaii	4	Rhode Island	4
Massachusetts	14	West Virginia	6

* All 8 states (with a total of 101 electoral votes) went to Kennedy in 1960 and Humphrey in 1968.

Table 19. Toss-Up States.*

State	Electoral Votes	State	Electoral Votes
Alaska	3	New Hampshire	4
California	46	New Jersey	18
Delaware	3	North Carolina	13
Illinois	25	Ohio	25
Maine	4	Pennsylvania	27
Maryland	10	Texas	26
Minnesota	10	Washington	9
Missouri	12	Wisconsin	11

* Sixteen states, with a total of 246 votes.

Table 17 reveals that President Nixon begins the 1972 race with a clear lead in twenty-two states that have 146 electoral votes. In contrast, the Democratic nominee can count on seven solid states (plus the District of Columbia) for 104 votes. In fact, the Democrats, on the presidential level, face the prospect of finding almost their entire basis of support in the Northeast. Even with a Midwestern, somewhat populist candidate in 1968, the Democratic Party was unable to improve on its 1960 showing in the nation's midsection. Indeed, the East is in danger of isolating itself from the rest of the country—and in so doing isolating the national Democratic Party.

Though President Nixon should be able to carry a near majority of the fifty states (the twenty-two listed in Table 17) with relative ease, their low populations will award him only slightly more than half the electoral votes he would need for a second term. At least 124 more votes must be added from the sixteen "toss-up" states (in Table 19), which hold almost half, 246, the total electoral votes.

The importance of the states listed in Table 19 can be seen from a comparison of the 1960 and 1968 elections. In

1960, Richard Nixon carried only seven of these sixteen with only 90 electoral votes, whereas Kennedy won nine of the states with 149 votes in the electoral college; in 1968, however, Nixon won ten with 156 votes compared to six states and 87 votes for Hubert Humphrey.[2] The Democratic ticket carried all the strong Democratic states comprising Table 18 in 1960 and again in 1968, and Richard Nixon won all but two of the states listed as strongly Republican on Table 17 in 1960 and every one of them in 1968. In both presidential elections, the winning electoral-vote margins came from the "Toss-up" states comprising Table 19, and it is here, too, in all probability, that the 1972 election will be won or lost.

A majority of these states lie in the Northeast and the Midwest region that surrounds the Great Lakes. When added to Nixon's 146-vote base, the 137 electoral votes of these ten states (Maine, Minnesota, New Hampshire, Wisconsin, Ohio, Delaware, Illinois, Maryland, New Jersey, and Pennsylvania) would put the Republican President thirteen votes over the magic number of 270. On the other hand, if Nixon won none of these states, he would fall fifteen votes short of a second electoral-college majority. These states have indicated a preference for progressive, pragmatic Republicanism, and the metropolitan regions located in many will require special attention if the Republican Administration wishes to hold its job after four years.

This fact is reinforced when one considers the pressures that exist on the Democrats. With Wallace in the race and the GOP doing well at the presidential level in the border states, the Democrats will have to ignore the South and con-

---

[2] In neither case do the electoral votes add up to the 246 listed in Table 19. This is a result of the fact that in both 1960 and 1968 the distribution of electoral votes was different from the projection for 1972.

centrate on those states with a high ethnic vote. As the meager list in Table 18 indicates, however, this will be woefully insufficient. The final success of any Democratic ticket in 1972 must lie in a strong appeal to the white, middle-class vote, especially in the suburban areas that are nominally Republican but have responded to liberal Democratic personalities, such as Eugene McCarthy or John Kennedy.

These factors all favor a Catholic Democrat with appeal to the middle class, i.e., Edward M. Kennedy (or Edmund Muskie). The potency of another Kennedy candidacy in a three-way contest cannot be ignored by Nixon. Starting with a united Democratic Party, the Massachusetts senator would concentrate on holding three blocs of the electorate: the ethnic groups (Catholics and Jews), the black voters, and the upper-middle-class intellectuals and the young. He would place immediate priority on holding the five toss-up states with the eighty-two electoral votes that were carried by his party's ticket in 1968: Maryland, Minnesota, Pennsylvania, Texas, and Washington. Adding them to the eight basic Democratic states that comprise Table 18 would give Kennedy 187 votes. Next, Kennedy would aim his sights at five other key states: Illinois, Ohio, Wisconsin, Missouri, and New Jersey. Except for Wisconsin, which Nixon won comfortably, all of this group went narrowly to Nixon in 1968, possibly because of Wallace. All five were the subject of close contests between Nixon and Kennedy in 1960, and their 91 electoral votes would give the Democratic ticket 8 more than the 270 needed. Victories in California, Delaware, and Maine by Kennedy would be helpful but not vital to a winning Democratic strategy; in these states, a vice-presidential running mate such as Jesse Unruh could help him.

If Wallace decides to ignore the Presidency in 1972, Republicans may be put at a slight disadvantage. With Nixon in the White House, the GOP will not be the natural beneficiary of antiblack antagonisms. Still, the race issue could well become blurred, especially if the Democrats attempt to modify their liberal strategy somewhat in order to win back the Deep South and some border states. Arkansas, Alabama, Mississippi, Louisiana, and North Carolina would all be prime targets for the Democratic ticket; here the potential black vote is 30 percent or greater and, if a charismatic candidate were to bring it out in force, only 30 percent of the white vote—the bulk of which is still nominally Democratic—would be needed for a majority.

In such a two-way contest, Nixon might be tempted to move too far to the right to attract the vocal Wallace legions looking for a new champion; in the process he would isolate himself not only from the black and the economically liberal ethnic vote, but, even more importantly, from the middle-class moderates. The forty-five electoral votes that Wallace won in 1968 will tempt the GOP in 1972, but a strategy run from the White House to ensure their loyalty could well sacrifice Illinois, Ohio, and New Jersey—a total of sixty-eight votes. In such a race, a liberal Protestant candidate such as McGovern, or even Lyndon Johnson, would make a strong Democratic candidate. Still, the basic battleground for 1972 remains the same, concentrated in those few states that Nixon won or lost so narrowly in 1968.

Nixon's success will depend on his ability to counter Kennedy in any one of three areas: the black vote, the ethnic vote—both of which are traditionally Democratic—and the middle-class vote, which though basically Republican is now necessary for a national Democratic victory. Though Nixon would find it difficult to do much worse among the first two groups in 1972 than in 1968, the Democrats should have little difficulty in improving on Hubert Humphrey's fundamentally weak appeal to the white, middle-class voter—

Mr. Nixon's "Forgotten American." The Republican position for 1972 leaves, at this stage, little room for slippage. At the same time, there remains great opportunity for gain in those areas where the party was weakest in 1968.

CHAPTER 17. The Vulnerabilities of the Democratic Party

The old F.D.R. coalition—with its resilience and tenacity in the face of new social currents and political realignments —is the crux of both the strength and the weakness of the Democratic Party as it faces the future.

The closeness of the popular vote for President and the retention of Democratic control of the Congress leave the party in considerably better health for the short run than was the case with the Republican Party after the 1964 rout. Despite the end-of-the-Democratic-Party-as-we-know-it predictions following the Chicago convention, the party has not gone the way of the Whigs any more than the Republican Party did four years earlier. The inertia and staying power of political structures and power centers are perhaps the most consistently underrated forces in American politics—even now, as rapid and dramatic change is becoming the watchword of our society.

In nominating Hubert Humphrey, and doing so amidst nationally televised repression and intolerance both in the convention hall and on the streets outside, the Democrats rendered themselves incapable of appealing to a new coalition, one more relevant than the essentially anachronistic power group on which they are still compelled to rely. Despite public support for Senators Kennedy and McCarthy, the toppling of an incumbent President by his own party, the massive publicity given the "new politics," radical social upheavals, public disgust with the Democratic nominating process, and Humphrey's loss of the election, the Old Guard which controlled the party at the start of 1968 still holds a strong position.

That gives the Nixon Administration the opportunity to accomplish what the Nixon campaign failed to do: to build a lasting coalition among constituencies for change while the Democratic Party struggles with the internal conflicts posed by power centers whose self-interests resist innovation within the party.

The dilemma of the Democratic Party, then, is that, while the old coalition is dying as a means of maintaining the party's majority status, that deterioration is not yet reflected in the institutional make-up of the party. In other words, the Democrats are guided by a coalition that can no longer deliver enough votes.

The ironical reason for this is that though the Democrats lost the Presidency, they did not do so convincingly enough to thoroughly discredit the urban machines, the labor oligarchs, and other regressive forces that stand as the chief barriers to a genuine reconstruction of the party. Where political parties are concerned, it generally takes considerably more than "writing on the wall" to mandate real structural change—and sometimes even a massive trauma such as the 1964 GOP disaster does not guarantee the necessary reevaluation. Except on the Southern "wall," where inroads by both Nixon and Wallace highlighted the political "writing" in bold relief, the omens of the 1968 election returns may prove to have been entirely too subtle to produce real reform within the Democratic Party.

The 1964 election campaign—which was supposed to have offered voters a "real choice" for the first time in decades—actually offered voters no choice at all. That is, the Goldwater candidacy was so extreme and the Johnsonian "consensus" so broad that L.B.J.'s programs and policies were never really tested in the fire of reasonable debate. For entirely different reasons, the campaign of 1968 produced the same result: The ambiguity and vagueness of the Nixon campaign and the trite irrelevance of the Humphrey rhetoric combined to leave the most fundamental issues confronting our society untouched and unexplored in any detail.

Thus, a major barrier confronting a Democratic resurgence is the fact that an increasingly outdated party ideology has gone untested and unrepudiated in two consecutive presidential elections. Hubert Humphrey, for one, believes that his resurgence at the end of the 1968 campaign demonstrated that "the goals and objectives of the Democratic Party were not repudiated." Significantly, even the insurgent liberal and reform-minded factions of the party appear unaware of the extent to which their traditional programmatic liberalism is inadequate as a response to current issues.

Many Democrats seem to think that if only there had been no Vietnam war, with its resultant skewing of national priorities and squandering of national resources, the battles on the domestic front could have been won by increased funding for Great Society and new frontier retreads of old New Deal programs.

They are wrong. The war has clearly been a major source of our national discontent and anguish, and its seemingly endless escalation under the blanket of governmental deception no doubt intensified the sense of helplessness, frustration, anonymity, and powerlessness that has swept the ghettos, the campuses, and, in different ways, Wallace's lower-middle classes and McCarthy's suburbia. But the individual's feeling that he has no significant impact on his environment or future will remain a fact of our mass society long after the war has ended. Ancient Democratic dogmas about progress through centralized power and federal appropriations will be no more capable of responding to this issue than when they appeared in Lyndon Johnson's Great Society programs or in Hubert Humphrey's presidential campaign.

The face of the Democratic Party is sure to change over the next four years, but unless the basic philosophy, structure, and thrust of the party undergoes a similar change, the party cannot reasonably be expected to become a vehicle for effective government or a plausible rallying point for the voter groups whose allegiance it traditionally has sought. An examination of the prospective roles some of these key groups may play in the coming years is instructive.

THE SOUTH

The national party is ideologically opposed to most Southern ideas and politicians; yet Southerners still have significant influence, Senator Long's defeat by Edward Kennedy notwithstanding. The national party failed even to punish all but one of its Wallace supporters among the Southern congressmen, yet it still cannot count on the Southerners' support in a national campaign.

MINORITY GROUPS, ESPECIALLY BLACKS

These groups may stay with the Democratic Party, though with decreasing energy and enthusiasm. Although they would be very difficult for the Republican Party to convert en masse, a growing number of their young activists are stressing independence from (and contempt for) *both* major parties. The black and other minority turnout may well increase, but any improvement the Democrats might make in over-all numbers would probably be offset by the fact that Nixon will get a better *percentage* of this vote the next time out.

YOUTH

Party rhetoric indicates that the Democrats intend to make a big effort to attract and hold the young voters—and they will have to. The Young Democrats have been decimated in the Johnson years, with the college Young Democrats at one point separated from their official parent for opposing the Vietnam war policy. On the issues themselves, Johnson's party provided the two most direct causes of youth's alienation from society today—the war and the draft. As for the future, Humphrey is opposed to the volunteer-army concept and Kennedy is at best ambivalent on it. If President Nixon successfully ends the war and the draft, the Democrats will be hard pressed to salvage any credit as a party.

As with the blacks and other minorities, it may be overoptimistic to anticipate large-scale conversions among youth to a Republican Party lacking the glamour of the new frontier. But though it may be too much to hope that young people will develop real enthusiasm for Richard Nixon in any great numbers, ending the war and the draft will go a long way toward neutralizing the outright hostility toward the GOP that has been the Democratic Party's trump card in seeking the minorities' support.

LABOR

Edward Kennedy, already busy with private hatchet-burying efforts with George Meany and other former labor enemies of his late brother, can win broad labor support for the Democrats, but, with the rank and file becoming more prosperous, it will never again be as deliverable as it was in the past. More significant is the fact that in such matters as foreign affairs, economic priorities, and racial policies, labor is hardly a progressive influence on the party and is likely to help alienate it from the other kinds of people the party wants, in particular the nation's youth.

THE INTELLECTUALS

This, of course, is not a voting bloc of any significance, but it is an influential group that in the past has been Democratic and on which Democratic candidates have traditionally been intensely dependent for manpower and energy—and for the vitality of their ideas. This is much less so today, as a consequence of the bitterness born and bred of the war, the Chicago convention, and the Johnson Administration in general. With L.B.J. more or less absent from the scene and with Richard Nixon—the traditionally highest ranking object of hatred in the liberal Democratic demonology—as President, the alliance of the intellectuals with the Democratic Party may well be renewed. But the ADA has become more and more a collection of the late middle-aged and old left, and the vitality of the alliance will never reach the peaks of the past.

THE MIDDLE CLASS

This is the big group in America, and it is perhaps the biggest problem the Democrats face. Whereas the left wing in America was very angry about many things in 1968 (and now), and is unlikely to be easily mollified by anybody, the middle-class WASPs (or perhaps more accurately, the suburban-class whites) were merely nonideologically unhappy—chiefly about the war and civil disorders. If the war is ended and civil disorder checked, their Republican partiality should be maintained.

So dying but not yet dead (except in the South), the old coalition still made a game effort at recovery in the bizarre political year of 1968. And, because it was held together, not so much by the positive attributes of the Democratic Party as by the negative aspects of the GOP campaign, the Democrats may find it comforting to believe they lost in 1968 simply because the country was moving to the right. Consequently, as the Democratic Party seeks to rebuild itself and recover its versatility, it appears likely that this legacy of its past, a source of strength when the coalition flourished, will prove a heavy burden.

To be sure, the rhetoric of reform and face-lifting will be pervasive—committees, commissions, reports, and recommendations will flourish as the party attempts to "reconstruct" itself without hurting anybody's feelings. But tempted by the narrowness of its defeat in 1968 to believe that the party will not long be out of power, reformers and regulars alike are already angling for position and influence within the party hierarchy as it now stands, devoting precious little energy to the kinds of structural and policy changes that would make possible a return to power on a lasting basis. The cult of the personality may, in fact, dominate party affairs to the exclusion of most ideological battles, now that the presence of a Republican Administration has removed from their shoulders the two issues which most polarized them: Vietnam and Lyndon Johnson.

Kennedy and Muskie, despite their attempts to cultivate the new politics image, will, at least in part, still play by the old politics rules. Their partisans are much more likely to attempt to woo those already in established power than to risk their wrath by trying to overthrow them. At the same time, the bosses will want to discover the winner early enough to be first on the bandwagon. The result will be a fusion of the new personalities with the old power sources. Grass-roots revitalization at the base of the party—such as characterized the "McCarthy movement" from New Hampshire to Chicago—will have to fight hard to make its way. Those few on the Democratic left who understand the need for structural change as opposed to mere face-lifting appear to have leaders in Senators Hughes and McGovern, but lack a useful enemy target (such as L.B.J. or the war). They will be hard put to find muscle, money, or politically aware constituencies to support their thrust for a bottom-up revitalization of the Democratic Party.

The faster-than-expected ascent of Edward Kennedy as a figure equally attractive to party establishment and insurgents makes genuine structural reform and power redistribution within the party even less likely, except on a token or public-relations basis. Why restructure a party if you can gain power within it as it stands? The great appeal of the McCarthy campaign for many of its followers—aside from the obvious issue of Vietnam—was that McCarthy was so much an anathema to virtually all party "leaders." His quest for the nomination could have been successful only over the dead bodies of virtually every boss and establishment figure in the Democratic Party. This very facet of the McCarthy campaign, of course, guaranteed its failure, but it was the long-shot hope of fundamental grass-roots reform that kept his children's crusade going.

By the same token, of course, some reforms might be more easily achieved since the old leaders could be more willing to go along with changes which do not imply a McCarthy candidacy and which present no immediate danger to their position.

A politician cannot be expected to turn upon the very coalition that elected or nominated him and preside over its destruction in the name of party reform. Though the strategy by which power was pursued need not be the strategy by which it is wielded, it may well determine certain ways in which that power is *not* wielded.

If Mayor Daley, for example—long known to be an ally of the Kennedys—plays an important role in a successful Kennedy bandwagon for 1972, he would not thereby necessarily be in a position to dictate government policy on a broad scale, any more than Strom Thurmond has been playing such a role in the Nixon Administration. But within the context of intraparty dynamics, his position would be immeasurably enhanced, just as Thurmond's has been.

Thus, if Edward Kennedy plays the role of tranquilizer for a nervous and edgy Democratic Party—soothing and "unifying" a family of political interests whose goals are fundamentally in conflict (urban machines and labor leadership vs. blacks and young intellectuals, for example)—the short-run advantage may be outweighed by the long-run failure to assemble a new coalition capable of governing the nation and sustaining itself. This was the kind of imposed "unity" that was prescribed for the Republican Party after 1964, and it remains of questionable value for the Democratic Party today.

The Democrats' apparent preference for token change within their party would seem at first to be contradicted by the election of Edward Kennedy over Russell Long as Senate Democratic whip—but the importance attributed to it actually confirms the opposite. Despite ideological overtones (Southern hawk against Northern liberal dove, etc.), Kennedy's victory was a personal one. No other liberal could have won. In some ways, it appears to be the rough counterpart of the GOP's Ford-for-Halleck switch in the 1965 Congress.

Senator McCarthy's allegation that the Kennedy victory would produce the shadow of reform while discouraging its substance has more than a grain of truth to it, McCarthy's widely acknowledged anti-Kennedy bitterness notwithstanding. The whip post is not a power center. The ousted incumbent, Russell Long, had long since exhausted the patience of his colleagues, both Northern and Southern, with a combination of unorthodoxy and orneriness epitomized by his embarrassingly vehement defense of Senator Dodd during the Senate floor debate on Dodd's censure. Long was thus the perfect foil for the legendary Kennedy machine (which in this case went into action virtually overnight) and the self-fulfilling belief that a Kennedy can't be beaten.

Ultimately, it appears to have been personal dynamics within the Senate establishment itself, rather than awareness of the need for party reform, that was decisive for Kennedy. One of the most significant factors at work for him was the failure of powerful Southern senators, notably Senate patriarch Richard Russell of Georgia, to mount an energetic campaign on Long's behalf. They did not go so far as to vote for Kennedy, but neither did they push hard for Long. It appears, therefore, that the Kennedy victory was less the tip of a revolutionary iceberg within the Democratic Party than a relatively harmless switch of personalities in a post that Kennedy can use as a public platform, but that has little impact on the power distribution within the Senate establishment or the party.

A much more significant contest for power within the party than the Senate whip fight was the insurgency of Arizona Congressman Morris Udall against the aging John McCormack for Speaker of the House—certainly a more important position than Kennedy's. Udall had youth, energy, aggressive liberalism, and a mood for change on his side in this contest against the seventy-seven-year-old representative of the old establishment; but the speaker had the votes, even on a secret ballot, 178 to 58. Udall did not even gain half the votes of the once energetically liberal Democratic study group.

With Johnson in the White House, McCormack could remain in the background guiding the President's legislation through the Congress; but now he will not be working with a partisanly friendly White House. He may not be the Speaker at the time of the 1972 elections, but his presence at the head of the Democratic leadership in the House of Representatives will contribute to the national image of the Democratic Party. As one young liberal Democratic Congressman put it: "The trouble with John McCormack is that he is completely out of touch with modern American politics."

At the local level, too, many of the forces of "reform" continue to be divided, disorganized, and deluded while old power figures solidify their faltering positions. In the New York State Assembly, for example, leaders of the Reform Democrats (a party within the party, whose feuds among themselves almost overshadow their animosity for the hated regular Democrats) abandoned incumbent Minority Leader Moses Weinstein in order to support their long-time foe, Stanley Steingut—one of the last of the old-time political bosses in the New York State Democratic Party.

Personality dynamics and angling for position raise serious questions about the composition of the party leadership in the years ahead. The new national chairman, Fred Harris, is attempting to establish his own mark on the party apparatus, and, although he is an old friend of the Kennedys, his presence does provide the Johnson-Humphrey axis with a continuing voice in the party inner circles. The former followers of Senator McCarthy, and to a lesser extent of Robert Kennedy, will not have the field to themselves, but they are not going to be silent. And if Harris creates the impression that he is exploiting his post to advance his own career, he risks precipitating a bloody free-for-all among all the factions.

Lyndon Johnson may be gone, but he is hardly likely to allow himself to be forgotten. An activist President, he will doubtless be an activist former President. If he continually speaks out on national questions, he cannot help but have an effect on the tenor of the party. In fact, it is not unlikely, given his bent, that he will be as helpful to President Nixon as General Eisenhower was to him during his own Administration—and on questions where the Democrats may be divided. And for the rest of his life, L.B.J. will probably be defending the record of his Administration—vociferously— which will help remind voters of a period many other Democrats would just as soon have them forget.

On an organizational and financial basis, the Democratic Party structure appears to be ill prepared to deal with potential schisms and conflicts. Financially, the Democrats face a crisis of monumental proportions. The surface has not even been scratched on the $6 million deficit left by the general election campaign or the preconvention campaign deficits that have been assumed by the national party: $1 million each for Humphrey and Robert Kennedy, something greater than $500,000 for McCarthy, and less than $35,000 for McGovern.

Any party—the Democrats even more so than the Republicans—has a hard time raising money when it is out of power. Unless a really strong grass-roots anti-Nixon movement arises, the party apparatus will be sorely underfinanced for some time. Candidate-oriented funds may be easier to come by if, for example, Edward Kennedy begins early to look like a sure thing, but that will be of little assistance for the huge task of rebuilding the official party machinery.

Another factor compounding the Democrats' economic plight is the likelihood that the cozy relations L.B.J. managed to develop with the financial and industrial communities of the country, relations seriously undermined in 1968, will almost totally disappear in the coming months. Additionally, for those who do maintain a residual personal loyalty to L.B.J., a tax-exempt foundation set up for the Johnson memorial and library (Lyndon Johnson's "place in history" again) will be a more attractive receptacle for their tributes than non-tax-exempt political donations to the Democratic Party. The impact of this shift in the monied interests at a time when the financial squeeze is tightening will certainly be felt by the 1970 congressional campaigns, at the least, and the effects may well last through the 1972 presidential elections.

The financial problem is complicated by the fact that the Democratic National Committee was already seriously understaffed when the Humphrey campaign began. It is no secret that the Johnson Administration permitted (and even encouraged) the national committee to fall into almost complete disrepair as the President preferred to keep the reins of power close to himself in the White House. Registration campaigns of any size were cut from the budget long before the 1968 campaign was under way.

Besides the financial problem, the Democratic National Committee is ailing organizationally and structurally. A complicating dilemma is the question of whom to recognize as the official Democrats in Southern states where integrated insurgents challenged the regulars at the convention. (That question was *not* settled in Chicago). Furthermore, many individual departments of the national headquarters are in poor condition. The very effective Louis Martin, for example, is leaving the minorities division—a serious blow to efforts in that area.

While the struggle for position goes on at the top of the party among personalities essentially without distinctive policy disagreements (e.g., Muskie vs. Kennedy), and in the absence of a national thrust for the party from the White House or the national committee, the local Democratic parties will probably continue to determine the tone and structure of the party. In Illinois, for example, now with two GOP senators and a Republican governor, that control will still be Mayor Daley's.

And in New York, with Republicans in control of everything (governor, both senators, both houses of the state legislature, and New York City's mayoralty) and despite its being a normally Democratic state, we can expect to see reformers feuding with each other and making deals with the regulars while the party's potential strength lies unappreciated. In New York City in particular, when Democrats have a chance to regain city hall in 1969, the "pragmatism" of expediency has taken its toll on principle and enlightenment, with regulars and reformers alike scrambling to close in on John Lindsay's right flank. First to throw his hat into the mayoral ring was ambitious reform Democrat Representative James Scheuer, an early McCarthy backer with impeccable "liberal" credentials and a 100 percent ADA rating of his voting record—none of which discouraged him from basing his early campaign on old Democratic platitudes, calls for "firmness" and order in city government, and plans for a book capitalizing on the crime-in-the-streets issue. (Scheuer aides launched a search for a new title for the book, fearing that the original proposed title, "To Walk the Streets Safely," was a bit too unsubtle.)

The fact is that though the Democrats have several promising and attractive figures in the U.S. Senate, they are especially weak at the state and local levels. Although they still control many of the legislatures, they have only twenty of the governors, a drop from thirty-four in 1960. Furthermore, there do not seem to be any leaders among the present Democratic Governors, now that Iowa's Harold Hughes has moved to the Senate. Whereas after 1964 the GOP had the likes of Rockefeller, Scranton, and Romney, among others, as a counterbalance to Democratic control of the

White House, the Democrats at this point have hardly one governor of national stature. Perhaps the 1970 elections will produce some new leaders, but for a party whose emphasis has traditionally been on the federal government, this would take a great deal of effort.

Reform movements cannot succeed within the Democratic Party without the support of those considered presidential contenders for 1972. Yet if the Democratic Party's renovation turns on individual stars, it could appear little more than a tactic for winning the nomination in four years. The personality cults may consequently diminish the possibility of real reform that is necessary to revitalize a party narrowed by a dwindling base of national support and controlled by an ideology and political coalition that grows increasingly outdated.

The banishment of the Democrats from the White House places both parties in unfamiliar positions. In one sense, the Democrats now have the advantage enjoyed until recently by the GOP, freedom from the responsibility of governing—and the consequent opportunity to develop a new rhetoric and a new image. The Democrats are unencumbered by the messy task of ending the war, finding funds for the cities and making the government function. This is a short-run advantage, however, and is partially balanced by the GOP's advantage of its patronage resources and the opportunity to wage a campaign against opposition control of Congress in the 1970 elections.

Although the Nixon Administration cannot claim much of an electoral mandate, the temper of the nation may well be in its favor. The Democrats will have a hard time developing a strategy against the President. They cannot afford to hit too hard; it is unlikely that a good rousing personal campaign against Nixon can be stirred up so soon after the one directed against Johnson (mostly by non-Republicans). The radicals will be nasty, to be sure; but their approach is less likely to catch fire now, and it may even be counter-productive—much as the excesses of the John Birch Society have always been of great assistance to Liberals.

Now, the initiative belongs to the GOP. The Democrats can only respond to the way in which Republicans exercise that initiative. The Democrats can—and surely will—highlight GOP failures, and gain as much attention as possible in doing so. But in the long run, nationwide speaking tours and Senate floor speeches are a poor substitute for the White House as a vehicle for projecting an image of a party that can solve the nation's problems. If the Republicans take the right initiatives, the Democrats will end up looking like the "me-too" party. Journalists have already noted that Senator Harris and other Democratic leaders are worried about their inability to regain the policy initiative. To take one example, Robert Kennedy had recognized the need for involvement of the private sector in the confrontation with urban problems; now others in the Democratic Party have taken up the call. But the idea is one of basic Republican origin, and the Republican in the White House can render the speeches of the leading Democrats hollow.

With a Republican President, the GOP's image will no longer be what the Democrats say it is—nor what the Republican Party, through its campaign technique, permits the public to assume it is. Rather, the GOP image will be based principally on the record of the Nixon Administration.

CHAPTER 18. Priorities and Policies for a Republican

In his campaign for the Presidency, Richard Nixon hinted that his Administration would mark a new era in Republican politics, a departure from the Eisenhower years as complete as the transfer of the Presidency from William McKinley to Theodore Roosevelt. Even as he exhorted the party faithful to "win this one for Ike," Nixon rejected the prospect of a return to the passive leadership of the Eisenhower Administration. Of his radio addresses during the campaign, the best were those that focused on the character of government that America now required. Nixon declared that the next President "must take an activist view of his office. He must articulate the nation's values . . . and marshal its will." He promised,

> a cabinet made up of the ablest men in America, leaders in their own right and not merely by virtue of appointment—men who will command the public's respect and the President's attention by the power of their intellect and the force of their ideas.

While quietly chiding the party's previous inclination to govern from a narrow base, the candidate promised to create an open administration, "open to new ideas, open to men and women of both parties, open to the critics as well as those who support us."

With Nixon's narrow triumph in the popular vote, it was

generally assumed that the President-elect would use the power of appointment to build the kind of open and broad-based coalition government he spoke of in the campaign. His first appointments appeared to do just that. Paul McCracken (chairman of the Council of Economic Advisers), Henry Kissinger (national security), Lee DuBridge (science), and Daniel Patrick Moynihan (urban affairs) have been widely acclaimed both for the talents and original viewpoints they bring to the new Administration. Whereas McCracken and DuBridge were identified with more traditional Republican policies, Kissinger and Moynihan stood out as good bridges to Rockefeller Republicans and Kennedy Democrats.

When the Nixon team finally took shape, it was clearly better qualified and more broadly based than the Nixon-haters had feared. Nevertheless, it was discernibly narrower than he had led many of his sympathizers to hope it would be.

President Nixon's cabinet selections bore little resemblance to Eisenhower's "nine millionaires and a plumber." By his own definition of a broad-based government, "one including not only executives and administrators, but scholars and thinkers," Nixon presented a diverse picture: three businessmen, two lawyers, two academics, and five elected officials, three with extensive experience as business administrators. But the collective picture was striking more for what it was not than for what it was. Glamorous names such as Shriver, Brooke, and Rockefeller were absent. Nor was there a Negro, a Jew, a woman, a Democrat, or a young person among the appointees. The announcement of the reappointment of the District of Columbia's Mayor Walter Washington just before the cabinet unveiling only highlighted the uniformity of the other appointees. Those who were already Republicans were represented by Malvin Laird, the new South by William Blount, and the "silent center" by perhaps everyone; but in the new Nixon alignment, "black militants" and "new liberals" had been left out.

Every man appointed was either a close personal associate of the President-elect, a key political supporter, or an advocate of policies already outlined in detail during his campaign for office. Reporter Chalmers M. Roberts, among others, has described Richard Nixon as "a loner," and although Nixon did delegate authority and responsibility to his campaign staff during the fall, real power was rarely extended beyond those who were old, close friends. Nixon's closed style of decision-making may have taken a new form, but its existence remains. The President placed his closest allies in the most sensitive and powerful cabinet positions.

Nixon's cabinet selections, like his choice for Vice-President, gravitated toward the political center, carefully avoiding the extreme of a Lindsay or a Reagan, in a general sense skirting anyone with a powerful constituency of his own that might prove divisive. He tipped his hand shortly after the election when he declared, "America needs to hear the vital voices of the broad and vital center. The center is under savage attack. It must be held at all costs." Neither his cabinet selections nor, indeed, his other major appointments pose a threat to that vital center.

The merits of the cabinet are clear, then. Unlike John Kennedy, President Nixon has not been hindered early in the Administration by continually having to size up his advisers, learning their strengths and weaknesses, and testing their judgment. He is comfortable with them, appreciates their proven loyalty, and shares a considerable portion of their opinions. Cabinet meetings do not often reflect the "ferment of ideas" Nixon promised in his speech on "The Nature of the Presidency," but more John Mitchell's concept of the campaign directed by an orderly board of directors. Nixon's men are all business with very little show.

They are perfectly suited to be his arms and legs as well as his eyes and ears, truly, as the London *Economist* called it, a "cabinet of Nixons."

One of the journalistic fashions of the day is to contrast the Democratic Party as one of ideas and innovations with the Republican Party as one of managerial and administrative skills. Under this rubric, which rather condescends to the Republicans, we are given to believe that the Johnson Administration will be known for its hundreds of new programs, and the Republicans for implementing them.

Such generalizations are dangerous, despite their partial truth—Republicans, as they turn their attention from politics to governing the nation, may be tempted to acquiesce in their own myth and restrain their impulse to creativity. The fact is that eight years out of office did give the Republican Party some ideas of its own, both natural born and adopted: the volunteer military, revenue-sharing, social volunteerism, the negative income tax. Any of these that Mr. Nixon successfully implements must be called an innovation, and if some turn out not to be very controversial, that will be simply because the Democrats have withheld their attack.

On the urban front, the Nixon Administration's energies appear to be focused, as was the Nixon campaign's rhetoric, on the reordering of government agencies to get more for every dollar spent; "a more efficient Great Society" was the way one observer described the Republican Administration. To investigate and attempt to solve urban problems, Nixon created the Council for Urban Affairs, whose members include the Vice-President, Attorney General, the Secretaries of Agriculture, Commerce, Labor, HEW, HUD, Transportation, and Arthur Burns, Counselor of Domestic Affairs. Moynihan serves as the council's executive secretary, but the President presides over the council himself.

With coordination as the key to the new council, the emphasis will most likely not be on greater expenditures, but on getting more efficient allocation of funds. None of the council members is a big spender. Moynihan and others point out that after the last eight years of legislative activity, there are more than 400 domestic programs, each with its own budget and bureaucracy, as compared to forty-six in 1960. The elimination of unnecessary dead weight in new legislative programs through careful planning might save enough for the council to embark on Moynihan's programs for job-training and income maintenance. Other members of the council, particularly Finch and Romney, look for aid from private business and independent civic groups to supplement federal funds.

Some pressures for increased expenditures will undoubtedly develop. If Finch wants to overhaul the nation's welfare system, he will need substantial funds. A committee set up by Nixon to report on welfare before the inauguration urged the federal government to assume a much greater share of the burden and to impose minimum standards of payment for the nation's 8.5 million welfare clients. The cost would add between $1.4 and $1.9 billion annually to the federal budget. Republican anticrime bills, if passed, will increase the strain on federal revenues. State needs for additional money, through revenue-sharing or increased bloc grants, will put more pressure on the national Administration for funds. Governor Rockefeller's 1969 state of the state message—and his presentation before the Council for Urban Affairs—as much as declared that New York could not survive financially without help from Washington. With twenty-nine other Republican governors also asking for funds, and with a Republican Administration committed to the idea of tax-sharing, the federal government may be forced to undertake a new plan.

It appears, however, that the greatest pressure will be to check domestic expenditures. Secretary of the Treasury David Kennedy has indicated that in efforts to cut inflation, federal expenditures will be kept down. But most importantly, funds for domestic programs will have to compete directly with increases in military spending. In the introduction to the Brookings Institution's *Agenda for the Nation,* a study on the urgent issues that confront the new Administration, Brookings' President Kermit Gordon wrote:

> It is quite possible that the decisions of the new administration and the new Congress on the post-Vietnam defense budget will be the single most important factor in determining the scale on which the nation attacks its internal social problems.

In fact the domestic- vs. defense-spending question is probably the most fundamental issue that must be faced by the Nixon Administration. It must be settled, for an ever-large defense bill is the greatest obstacle to domestic peace and progress.

In his statement on Vietnam to the Republican national convention in August 1968, Nixon recognized that "The war must be ended." But even the conclusion of the Vietnam conflict will not resolve the question of funding priorities. Though it was long felt that the end of the Vietnam war would bring a "fiscal dividend" of $25 to $30 billion, it now seems that it will be far less, for some of the war's costs have been delayed for the future. "We will have big military inventories to build up again," argues Senator Dirksen, indicating that new Pentagon requests will find a receptive ear on Capitol Hill. Moreover, with the press of war the Joint Chiefs have held back on several advanced weapons systems that they "must" now acquire and, in fact, the generals will tell the President that the commitments have already been made. New model Polaris submarine missiles are planned, as are new bombers, and biggest of all, the anti-ballistic missile system, which could run from a trifling $5.5 billion to over $200 billion for "complete defense." As Senator Charles Percy has noted, the anti-ballistic missile system could be equivalent to another Vietnam war in terms of the large amounts of federal funds that the weapon would drain from urgent domestic programs.

Powerful lobbies such as the 2.5 million-member American Legion, the munitions makers in the Army Ordnance Association, the Reserve Officers Association, the Association of the U.S. Army, the Air Force Association, the Navy League, and all the weapons-systems manufacturers can be counted on to advise the President that their claims on the public treasury are primary and irrefutable. Many in Congress will couple this sentiment with the scare tactic that any other decision represents a return to isolationism. But the most important support for increases in military spending is likely to come from within the Nixon cabinet.

Many news analysts passed off Nixon's celebrated "security gap" speech of October 24 as a parallel to Kennedy's phony missile-gap issue of 1960. Instead it was the capstone of a campaign in which Nixon promised repeatedly to restore "clear-cut U.S. superiority" in weapons. "Whoever is President for the next four years," the candidate remarked on one occasion, "may be in the very difficult position of having to negotiate from weakness, rather than strength. That's why I would restore the strength of the U.S. That must be the first priority." Nixon's post-election task force on national security confirmed his stand, making maintenance of nuclear superiority its main recommendation and attacking "the euphoric hope" that peace could be reached by replacing superiority with parity as advocated by former Secretary of Defense Robert McNamara. The United States, it said, "must be prepared to crush all threats to the peace, with force if required," including nuclear weapons.

Some of Nixon's statements might possibly be attributed to campaign rhetoric designed to win over key states (particularly Texas, which benefited greatly from defense contracts during the Johnson Administration). Yet, on November 3, Republican campaign headquarters announced that Nixon hoped to be spending $87 billion a year for defense by 1972 ($10 to $15 billion for rebuilding Vietnam and $72 to $77 billion on non-Vietnam spending). The projection marked a substantial increase on spending from the 1968 level of $74 billion total, which included a $21 to $26 billion increase for non-Vietnam costs.

In Secretary of Defense, Melvin Laird's own manifesto on defense, *A House Divided: America's Strategy Gap* (1962), the theme was that the United States had become needlessly defensive in relation to the Soviet Union. He called for a firm policy of deterrence, training for guerrilla warfare, and reduction of taxes with acts of nondefense spending. On December 13, 1968, Laird was asked at a news conference what he had meant when he stated in his book that "the credible announcement of first-strike initiative is the real way to effective disarmament discussions with the Soviet Union." Taking his cue from Nixon, Laird replied that the passage was "written in a period of confrontation. We are now in a period of negotiations and I think that that should be considered as we face the future."

Shortly after taking office, Nixon announced his intention to downgrade pentagon systems analysis instituted under McNamara and to revive the National Security Council, a presidential advisory board that played a key role in the Eisenhower years.

The Security Council may be a more oderly forum for decision, but it may also amplify the voice of the military. The

President's decision to deploy an ABM system may reflect this influence. Among cabinet-level appointees, only U.N. Ambassador Charles Yost, who pointed out the dangers of military advice in broad issues of foreign policy during the Cuban missile crisis, is likely to oppose the tendency. Indeed, there may be a bias in the Nixon government that favors inexpensive cures for domestic ills while relying on expensive military hardware to ensure international security. But there is also reason to hope that the fall's campaign rhetoric will not bind the priorities of the Republican Administration.

The development of a space-age Maginot Line only accelerates the arms race, requiring our enemies to find new weapons to circumvent our new defense. Indeed, it may be possible actually to improve our security by spending less. Carl Kaysen, who served under President Kennedy as deputy special assistant for national security affairs and who now heads the Institute for Advanced Study at Princeton, argues this very point in his essay on "Military Strategy, Military Forces, and Arms Control," which appears in *Agenda for the Nation.*

> The new political and technical realities point to the futility of a quest for security primarily through increased military strength and to the increasing importance of political factors and arms control arrangements and agreements . . . In plain words, the course of arms limitation restrictions in deployments and arms control is not only cheaper than that of continuing competition in arms and military confrontation; it is safer.

This apparent conflict between "economy" and "security" is an old problem for the Republicans. Ironically, fiscal conservatives in Eisenhower's treasury kept a tight rein on defense expenditures, to the disappointment of none other than Henry Kissinger. Writing in the October 1956 issue of *Foreign Affairs,* Kissinger charged that Secretaries George M. Humphrey and Charles E. Wilson had known success so much of their lives that they could not imagine making an ultimately fatal decision. Kissinger warned against selling national security short. "They may know in their heads, but they cannot accept in their hearts, that the society they helped to build could disappear as did Rome or Carthage or Byzantium." The same might be said of some of the successful men at the top levels of the Nixon Administration today, though the unperceived threat may now come from within. As some members of the GOP government have noted, the fact that every American family does not live in comfort and security in its own home is a result not of Soviet missiles but of the structure of American society.

During the 1968 campaign Richard Nixon promised to "marshall the moral authority of that office [the Presidency], to set priorities." Actually the most potent aspect of his leadership will be the priorities he sets for his own government. The Nixon Administration will have to recognize the true magnitude of the domestic problems that confront the nation, and adjust its financial and manpower priorities in relation to the magnitudes of these problems. This does not mean simply initiating new legislative programs, for though the number of domestic programs increased by a factor of ten during the Kennedy-Johnson years, the funding of such programs rose only from $10 to $25.5 billion. Nor are larger funds the sole answer. Urban ills and the pervasive feeling of governmental impersonality must be addressed systematically in a comprehensive effort to use existing programs, modify others, and develop new ones that ensure progress.

It will take a long time for the Republican Administration

to use the wealth of legislative authority given it to make the federal bureaucracy respond to President Nixon's desires. The President does have four years, and certainly at the end of his term he should have the government well under control, with both inherited and new programs bearing fruit. But there are problems that must be attacked now. First the cities and then the colleges have erupted in protest over the inequities and impersonality of American society, and the government ignores these pressures at its own peril.

There appear to be several courses of action that will buy time for the GOP Administration. The most important (after a Vietnam disengagement) is the release of local governmental funds to attack the multitude of domestic problems at their sources. As the economy expands, the monies collected by local government lag far behind the national growth rate, while federal-income-tax revenues, because of the progressive rate structure, run ahead. If President Nixon can immediately implement a method for funneling money back to the states—either directly or indirectly—he will have made a special contribution to the country's stability over the next two years.

There are a number of forms that such a redistribution of federal-tax monies can take. The official Republican position for several years has favored federal-state tax-sharing by which funds are returned directly to state governments to be used as they see fit. Municipal governments also need money, however, and the mayors of the nation's cities have argued that some of the tax-sharing funds should be rebated directly to urban government.

The current procedure for providing federal financial assistance to states and localities is the narrow categorical grant administered by occasionally competing federal bureaucracies. A city that has planned a multipurpose project often must get funds approved by three or four different federal bureaus, and the mayor involved can face frustrating delay or complete disappointment. Revenue-sharing with local government would solve this problem, of course. But a government-wide policy that required bureaus and agencies to cooperate in the funding of local projects would also be a significant help. Halfway between revenue-sharing and the current categorical grants are bloc grants for general government purposes, such as education. Nixon may consider these if Congress balks at direct revenue-sharing.

Another way to get funds to state and local government is through nationalization of the welfare program, as proposed by Vice-President Agnew, or through adoption of a negative income tax. Because under such programs the funds would go directly to the people, state and local welfare programs would be eliminated and the monies assigned to this budget category could be diverted to other pressing problems, such as crime, housing, or transportation.

The Republican Administration should be aware that with the GOP holding three-fifths of the state houses, the political effect of any program of financial relief would be extremely beneficial. Indeed, one of the salient claims to power made by Republicans in the recent past has been their concern for decentralization and particularly for progressive state government as a balance to an aggressive federal establishment. Partly as a result, thirty Republicans now occupy gubernatorial mansions. The Administration would be as mistaken to ignore such legitimate partisan considerations as to pursue them wantonly.

One of the main reasons for the high rate of gubernatorial political mortality is that governors have to raise taxes. In the next two years, thirty-seven governorships are up for reelection, twenty-four of which are currently held by Republicans. And in the ten largest states where the GOP controls eight gubernatorial chairs, the terms of seven Republican governors expire in 1970. Many of these states are in the "toss-up" category for the 1972 presidential election and thus essential to a Republican victory. If, in the backlash over financial troubles, these states are lost to the GOP in 1970, it will be a disaster for Mr. Nixon as well as for his party. The strong Republican base in the state houses can be maintained, and the loyalty of the gubernatorial wing of the GOP to Nixon can be assured, by relieving some of the tax burden of the states.

As President Nixon establishes the priorities for his government, he cannot afford to ignore the problems of the constituency that elected him in 1968—taxes, crime, and the individual's sense of anonymity and powerlessness. Though federal spending on the crime problem probably is of limited utility, it is an important symbol to Nixon's forgotten American. Funding the Crime Control and Safe Streets Act of 1968 to its full authorization of $300 million would be significant, especially if the money were spent for training, community relations, officials, and new correctional techniques, and not for more riot equipment that the police really do not need. But the Justice Department itself has little authority to tackle "crime in the streets"—muggings, robbery, assault, burglary. Consequently, in the long run, the money and effort spent to make the nation's capital a crime-prevention showcase may be the most important contribution the Nixon Administration can make in this area. Washington's police will have to experiment with enforcement techniques, different recruitment practices, community-relations efforts, cooperation with other police forces in the metropolitan area, and with the allocation of resources, including the division of labor among patrolmen, detectives, meter maids, and police cadets. It may take all of Nixon's first term to bring down the District's crime rate. However, if a careful program is mapped out, with detailed evaluations made of every initiative and the results distributed to all local law-enforcement agencies across the country, the Republicans may earn a reputation as the party that can truly cope with crime.

Contrary to Democratic campaign rhetoric, a successful crime-control program need not entail a curtailment of personal liberties. This distinction must be made clear by the Nixon Administration by scrupulous observance of the constitutional rights of the individual with regard to electronic surveillance, interrogation, bail, and arrest procedure, as well as free expression. These safeguards will doubtlessly be unpopular with a public impatient for a crackdown on crime. But the President's oath to uphold the Constitution does not contain an escape clause for cases of political expediency. (Nor can the Nixon government be equivocal on civil rights, especially when it has laws to enforce. The early positions taken by the Secretary of Health, Education, and Welfare, Robert Finch, with respect to Southern school districts, and Northern ones as well, are encouraging.)

Another initiative that will find acceptance with Nixon's campaign constituency is tax reform. Ignored by Lyndon Johnson were numerous proposals that could still have the effect of making most Americans happier about paying generally the same amount of taxes, with no loss to the treasury. There should be no illusion that tax reform will substantially decrease the burden placed on the middle-income American; but it must at the same time be recognized that the middle class will protest in the polling booth against a government that refuses to close the kind of loopholes that permitted twenty-one Americans with incomes over $1 million, and an additional 134 in the $200,000 to $999,999 bracket, to pay no taxes in 1967. There will always be complaints about taxes, of course, but if there is no tax reform in the next four years, the Democratic presidential nominee in 1972 may himself be appealing to the forgotten American.

The final complaint of the "average" American that found voice during the 1968 campaign was the individual's feeling of futility with respect to the power of government. If Nixon can make the voters believe that he is their personal President, he will have solved the fundamental problem that caused Lyndon Johnson's downfall. Trust is not developed with a program or a policy, but rather emerges from a personal attitude of the President and his advisers. Responsiveness does not eliminate the responsibility for leadership, but rather demands wise leadership that avoids the perils of decisions which result solely from an over-commitment of personal prestige.

The whole concept of citizen volunteerism can help eliminate this sensation of importance. It is an idea that has won enthusiasm from all sides of the Republican Party and is unassailable, really, from almost any ideological position. In one radio speech of the campaign, Nixon stated that "as the nation's first citizen, the President should be the chief patron of citizen efforts. I intend . . . to point out where the needs are, to encourage and reward citizens' efforts to meet those needs." In fact, as President, Mr. Nixon already is moving toward establishing a nationally organized clearinghouse of volunteer action at costs that would seem small when compared to the new free manpower the President hopes to enlist. Adequate precaution must be taken, however, to ensure that the government does not place so many constraints on the projects it supports that the true volunteer nature of the efforts disappears.

There are other decisions that the Administration could make to establish itself as a responsive government. The eighteen-year-old vote and the volunteer army are two examples advocated by Nixon himself during the campaign. Largely on account of the government's Vietnam war policy, the young people of America have felt particularly alienated from the national government. Permitting more of them to participate in the democratic process will not appreciably alter the political balance, nor should the President expect a big political benefit in 1972 in the event that Edward Kennedy is his opponent.

An all-volunteer military would cost several billion dollars, though much of this would be balanced out by eliminating what is now an unfair tax forced on conscripts through artificially low wages. If the elimination of the draft and the adoption of the eighteen-year-old vote are coupled with a meaningful program of volunteerism, the idealism of youth could find its outlet within the productive elements of American society.

It is, of course, premature to judge the Administration on the basis of the few personalities who hold cabinet rank or surround the President. A pundit once said that a conservative is a liberal who has come to power. Perhaps the opposite will be true in the Nixon Administration. Soon after John Kennedy took office in 1961, he realized that the missile gap did not exist; maybe Richard Nixon will discover that the same is true with respect to the "security gap." Perhaps men with a previously conservative bent will discover that, when charged with responsibility for administering the law, they cannot ignore the civil liberties of those who have long been denied them. By the same token, when given the assignment of holding the nation together, men who previously slighted the problems of the cities may recognize urban decay as the biggest issues they face.

In fact, Richard Nixon is in some ways the Republican Disraeli. Long a champion of party orthodoxy, brilliant, enchanted with imagery, and almost too-smart-by-half, defeated and defeated, he has, late in his career, reached the top. And for what? To reassess, perhaps to recompose himself. As Disraeli, hero of the rotten boroughs, brought electoral reform and gave it a conservative stamp, Nixon, the darling of the small towns who didn't carry a major urban center, may yet save the cities.

We tend to forget, for example, that the debate over the reorganization of the war on poverty is not nearly so significant as the Republicans' decision not to dismantle it, for one would have guessed dismantlement was their intention when the programs began. The same holds true for model cities. After the election, the program's bureaucrats expressed fear that the new Administration would terminate their operation altogether; they may find it expanded, instead, under a sympathetic director. If a willingness to reconsider in power the positions one took out of power is a sign of political maturity, Mr. Nixon can be said to have achieved it.

If Nixon does reach out for the urbanite—for the young, the poor, the black—he must still, like Disraeli, bring along his old constituency—the pensioners, farmers, tradesmen, professional people, the bulk of the country outside the East. He surely cannot secure the support of the radicals of the opposition left—though he can hope to discourage them— and he probably cannot retain the "aginers" he had in 1968, nor attract Mr. Wallace's troubled congregation.

This huge, growing country is choking at the collar, hot and tired with adolescent indignation and sanctimony. The problem isn't simply racism or poverty or international communism or even war, but a frustration that comes with rapid change, with fast-paced technology, prosperity, and growth. How do we catch up and gain control, as individuals and as a country? How do we set priorities, mobilize our resources, and recapture our destiny?

The answers are not simple. They are not merely economic; some are political and even spiritual. "To a crisis of the spirit," said the President in his inaugural address, "we need an answer of the spirit." Some have measured that address against John F. Kennedy's, which is a mistake, for this was a document of a different sort, words of calm encouragement rather than a call to sacrifice. The latter, in these times, would have been like a shot of adrenalin to a man suffering from the tremors.

"What the nation needs now," wrote David Broder of the *Washington Post,* "is not a 'super-President,' real or imagined, but one who will restore the sense of public participation in public business which has been so conspicuously lacking in recent years." Nor is the present business of the Presidency a mere businesslike weighing of desires and income. Rather, it is a matter of delicate balancing, proximate solutions, compromises, art. It means personal presidential lessons in taste (not to be confused with glamour), intellectual precision, and proportion.

Many progressive Republicans concluded that they lost the campaign. They may be surprised that now, so soon, they too must bury the old grudges. They may wonder how Richard Nixon finally will do, but they cannot afford to sit by until they find out; to the extent Mr. Nixon is a progressive today, they have a stake in his success, expected or not. One can imagine, for example, how Democrats may throw the Nixon speeches on the power of volunteerism back at him in 1972; but he won't suffer the criticism alone. The new community of the public spirit that he seeks includes progressives among its investors; the President is not alone in his responsibilities and risks.

These then are some of the lessons of victory from 1968— in particular the requirement that a permanent political majority be built on positive actions rather than on an appeal to ephemeral moods. They are lessons that must guide the new Republican government as it sets the priorities that control the nation's energies.

APPENDIX A.   Ethnicity and Politics

The extent to which a state's ethnic composition has been able to generate empirically valid correlations with voting patterns during recent presidential elections is remarkable.

On the accompanying graph, the vertical axis represents the percentage of white Protestant population in a state, and the horizontal axis measures the percentage of Catholics. Each state has its location on the graph. The higher it is, the greater its percentage of Protestants; the more to the right it is, the greater its percentage of Catholics. Thus, a quick look shows that such Southern states as Mississippi, South Carolina, Alabama, Georgia, and North Carolina—nearly all the way over to the left—have very few Catholics.

If there were only white Protestants and Catholics in America, all the states would fall on the solid diagonal line that runs across the graph. (That is because this line includes all the points at which the horizontal and vertical coordinates add up to 100 percent.) No state can be above this line in theory (because the sum of Protestant percentage and Catholic percentage would be greater than 100), and none can be on it in practice, because there are people in every state who are neither Catholics nor Protestants.

The population of Louisiana, for example, is about 30 percent white Protestant and 38 percent (white) Catholic. The remainder in this case are blacks, but in states with significant Jewish populations, Jews are included with

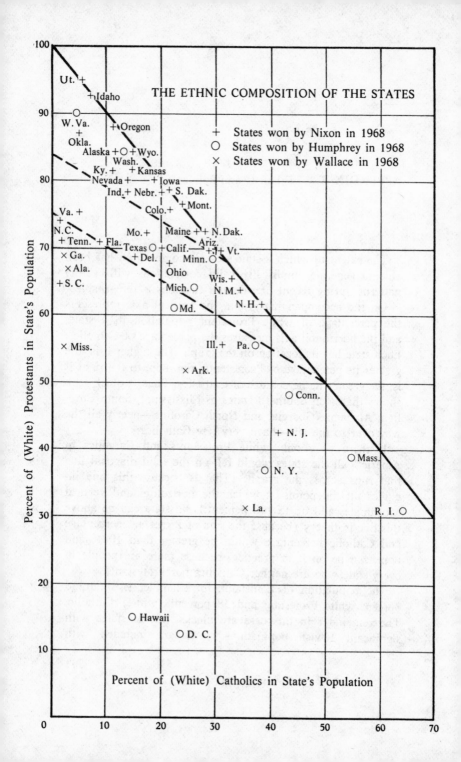

THE ETHNIC COMPOSITION OF THE STATES

+ States won by Nixon in 1968
○ States won by Humphrey in 1968
× States won by Wallace in 1968

Percent of (White) Protestants in State's Population

Ut. +
+ Idaho
○ W. Va.
Okla. +
+ Oregon
Alaska + ○ + Wyo.
Wash.
Ky. + + Kansas
Nevada + + Iowa
Ind. + Nebr. + + S. Dak.
Colo. + + Mont.
Va. +
N.C. +
+ Tenn. + Fla.
Mo. +
Maine + + N. Dak.
Texas ○ + Calif.
Ariz.
+ + Vt.
× Ga.
+ Del.
Minn. ○
× Ala.
Ohio +
+ S. C.
Wis. +
Mich. ○
N. M. +
○ Md.
N. H. +
× Miss.
Ill. + Pa. ○
× Ark.
○ Conn.
+ N. J.
○ Mass.
○ N. Y.
× La.
R. I. ○
○ Hawaii
○ D. C.

Percent of (White) Catholics in State's Population

0   10   20   30   40   50   60   70

blacks. This residual category is not explicitly plotted on the chart, but the distance that separates a state's position from the diagonal boundary indicates the size of that state's population that is neither white Catholic nor white Protestant. Those states located near the diagonal boundary, such as Maine, North Dakota, Montana, Iowa, and Washington, have their populations composed almost entirely of Protestants and Catholics and, conversely, have few blacks or Jews.

In a presidential election, the Republican Party can poll very well among Protestants and a substantial minority of Catholics. Unfortunately, Republicans get markedly less support from blacks and Jews. Suppose, for instance, that a Republican candidate receives 60 percent of the white Protestant vote and 30 percent of the Catholic vote but no votes from the remaining groups. Simple arithmetic tells us that in such a situation he would be able to win in a state that consisted entirely of Protestants—he would receive 60 percent of the vote. Or in a state that had a population that was 70 percent Protestant and 30 percent Catholic, he would win 51 percent of the vote; he would receive 42 percent of the total vote from Protestants (by winning 60 percent of the vote from the 70 percent Protestant population) and 9 percent of the total vote from Catholics (by winning 30 percent of the vote from the 30 percent Catholic population). However, in a state that was 50 percent Catholic and 50 percent Protestant, this 60–30 formula would be inadequate for the Republican to carry the state; his 60 percent majority of Protestants would be insufficient to compensate for the 70 percent majority of the Catholic vote that the Democrat would win.

To get an idea of what all this implies for presidential campaigns, it is convenient to divide the states into three groups. On the chart, all those states located above the upper dotted line can be carried by a Republican who wins 60 percent of the Protestant vote and 30 percent of the Catholic vote, and shall be referred to as Group I states. Of course, this is not the only formula that could bring a Republican victory in these states; because all of the states in Group I are composed of greater than 50 percent Protestants, a candidate could win merely by carrying 100 percent of the Protestant vote and ignoring the remainder of the electorate. However, in Group I states, the formula of 60 percent Protestant and 30 percent of the Catholic vote *guarantees* victory.

States in Group I, as follows, are hence "ethnically favorable" to Republicans:

Alaska	Maine	South Dakota
Arizona	Minnesota	Utah
Colorado	Montana	Vermont
Idaho	Nebraska	Washington
Indiana	Nevada	West Virginia
Iowa	North Dakota	Wyoming
Kansas	Oklahoma	
Kentucky	Oregon	

These twenty-two states, however, are small ones from the viewpoint of a presidential campaign strategist—the largest is Indiana with thirteen electoral votes—and during the 1960's they were allotted only 130 electoral votes.

Yet, most of them, located in the Midwest and Rocky Mountain states, are traditionally Republican strongholds. Thus, the 60 to 30 formula is not merely an abstract mathematical concept but in a sense defines those states that are solidly Republican. It should be noted that of the Group I states, only four did not cast their ballot for the Nixon-Agnew ticket in 1968; two of these defectors (Minnesota and Maine) were the home states of the Democratic nominees, Humphrey and Muskie, whereas the other two (West Virginia and Washington) are the most unionized states in the nation. Of the remaining states, only four failed to give clear majorities to the GOP ticket. (Nixon also carried all but three of these Group I states in 1960.)

If the Republicans can do better than the 60–30 formula, they can win more states. For example, if the GOP can win two=thirds (67 percent) of the Protestant vote and one-third (33 percent) of the Catholic vote (but again no votes from blacks or Jews) it can expand the number of states it can carry to include all those above the lower dotted line on the chart. Because the "ethnically favorable" states are themselves insufficient for a presidential victory the GOP ticket must do significantly well in these Group II "ethnically neutral" states (in the 1960's they accounted for 173 electoral votes):

California	Missouri	Texas
Delaware	New Hampshire	Virginia
Florida	New Mexico	Wisconsin
Michigan	Ohio	

Note that whereas Nixon carried nine of these eleven crucial states in 1968 for 127 electoral votes, to Humphrey's two states and 46 electoral votes, Nixon took only six of them in 1960 for 95 electoral votes, to five states and 64 electoral votes for Kennedy.

Group III, those states located below the lower dotted line on the chart, are "ethnically unfavorable" to Republicans. They either contain a large number of Catholics, such as the industrial states of the North (Massachusetts, New York, New Jersey, Illinois), or a large number of blacks, such as the states in the South (Mississippi, South Carolina, Alabama), or both (Louisiana). This group is extremely important, for it includes eighteen states, accounting for 235 electoral votes in 1968:

Alabama	Illinois	New York
Arkansas	Louisiana	North Carolina
Connecticut	Maryland	Pennsylvania
District of Columbia	Massachusetts	Rhode Island
Georgia	Mississippi	South Carolina
Hawaii	New Jersey	Tennessee

For a Republican presidential candidate to win, he must either carry almost all of the states from Groups I and II or he must make significant gains into ethnically unfavorable Group III. In 1960, Nixon was only able to carry one Group III state. But in 1968 he won five states from Group III with a crucial seventy-six electoral votes, while Humphrey took eight states and Wallace the remaining five.

Thus, in a sense, it was an "old politics" election—one whose results were basically defined by the ethnic characteristics of the states. Nixon won a solid base of 100 electoral votes from the Group I states. He added 127 votes by taking most of the Group II states—i.e., by doing better than the 60 to 30 formula and winning something equivalent to 67 percent of the Protestant vote and 33 percent of the Catholic. Finally, he completed the 270-plus total he needed by adding seventy-six votes from five Group III states—two from the industrial North (New Jersey and Illinois), where the defection of the working class to Wallace helped, and three from the South (Tennessee, North Carolina, and South Carolina), where the Democratic Party is on the decline.

The correlations found on this chart are applicable to more than just one election, and are particularly helpful in attempting to predict future voting trends. In Chapter 16, the fifty states were rated as "Strongly Republican," "Strongly Democratic," and "Toss-up" for the 1972 presidential election

(Tables 17, 18, and 19; below, Tables 1A, 2A, and 3A give a more detailed rationale for these categorizations. In each of them and within each ethnically characterized group, the states are roughly ranked according to Nixon's potential there, with the most favorable ones on the top of the list. Among ethnically favorable states in Table 1A, for instance, Utah and Idaho are more inclined to vote for Nixon than are Oregon and Nevada; in Table 2A, among the ethnically unfavorable category, the Republican President has a better chance of carrying Connecticut than of carrying the District of Columbia. One should be cautioned against reading too much into such rankings—and even the clear distinctions made between the three tables—for certainly many of the relative judgments are subjective. For instance, it would not be implausible to argue that New Hampshire belonged at the bottom of the ethnically neutral category in Table 3A (Toss-up). Similarly, someone could credibly contend that North Carolina belongs at the bottom of the ethnically unfavorable group in Table 1A rather than at the top of this category in Table 3A. No claim to the absolute validity of these tables is made—but the relative significance of the tables does permit conclusions to be drawn.

Table 1A lists those states that are strongly Republican and that should provide President Nixon's base of electoral votes in 1972. Most of these states are predominantly white Protestant and are consequently in the ethnically favorable category. These are the Rocky Mountain and Great Plains states plus a few from the peripheral South that have grown increasingly Republican in the past few elections. With the exception of 1964, nearly all the ethnically favorable states in Table 1A have voted for the GOP ticket since 1952, and in fact almost all of them delivered popular majorities for the Nixon-Agnew ticket in 1968. It seems safe to state that a Republican Administration that merely calms the nation down (i.e., ends the Vietnam war and reduces civil dis-

	State	Electoral Vote	Nixon-Humphrey Percentages, 1968	Nixon-Kennedy Percentages, 1960
	Utah	4	57–37	55–45
	Idaho	4	57–31	54–46
	Wyoming	3	56–36	55–45
	Kansas	7	55–35	60–39
	Nebraska	5	59–32	62–38
	South Dakota	4	53–42	58–42
	Arizona	6	55–35	56–44
"Ethnically	Indiana	13	50–38	55–45
Favorable"	Oklahoma (Stevenson in 1952)	7	47–32	59–41
17 states	Kentucky (Stevenson in 1952)	9	44–38	54–46
95 votes	North Dakota	3	56–38	55–45
	Colorado	6	51–41	55–45
	Montana	4	51–42	51–49
	Iowa	8	53–41	57–43
	Vermont	3	53–44	59–41
	Oregon	6	50–44	53–47
	Nevada (Kennedy in 1960)	3	47–39	49–51
"Ethnically	Virginia	12	43–33	52–47
Neutral"	Florida	16	41–31	57–49
3 states 32 votes	New Mexico (Kennedy in 1960)	4	52–40	49–50
"Ethnically	Tennessee	11	38–23	53–46
Unfavorable"	South Carolina (Kennedy in 1960,	8	38–30	49–51
2 states 19 votes	Stevenson in 1952 & 1956)			

* All went to Nixon in 1968, and to the Republican tickets in 1952, 1956, and 1960, except where indicated.

Table 2A. Strong Democratic States *

	State	Electoral Vote	Nixon-Humphrey Percentages, 1968	Nixon-Kennedy Percentages, 1960
"Ethnically Favorable" 1 state 6 votes	West Virginia	6	42–50	47–53
"Ethnically Neutral" 1 state 20 votes	Michigan	20	41–48	49–51
"Ethnically Unfavorable" 6 states 75 votes	Connecticut	8	44–50	46–54
	Rhode Island	4	32–64	36–64
	Massachusetts	14	33–63	40–60
	Hawaii	4	39–60	50–50
	New York	42	44–50	47–53
	District of Columbia	3	18–82	——

* All went to Kennedy in 1960 and Humphrey in 1968.
Within Group III, states where Nixon has the best opportunity are listed near the top.

Table 3A. Toss-up States *

	State	Electoral Vote	Nixon-Humphrey Percentages, 1968	Nixon-Kennedy Percentages, 1960
"Ethnically Favorable" 4 states 26 votes	Alaska	3	N 45–43	N 51–49
	Washington	9	H 45–47	N 51–48
	Maine	4	H 43–55	N 57–43
	Minnesota	10	H 41–54	K 49–51
"Ethnically Neutral" 7 states 127 votes	New Hampshire	4	N 52–44	N 53–47
	Wisconsin	11	N 48–44	N 52–48
	Ohio	25	N 45–43	N 53–47
	California	46	N 48–45	N 50–50
	Missouri	12	N 45–44	K 50–50
	Delaware	3	N 45–42	K 49–50
	Texas	26	H 40–41	K 49–51
"Ethnically Unfavorable" 5 states 93 votes	North Carolina	13	N 40–29	K 48–52
	Illinois	25	N 47–44	K 50–50
	Maryland	10	H 42–44	K 46–54
	New Jersey	18	N 46–44	K 49–50
	Pennsylvania	27	H 44–48	K 49–51

* Within each group, the states most apt to lean Republican are listed at the top, gradually blending into the states most apt to lean Democratic at the bottom.

order) should ensure these seventeen states for Richard Nixon, no matter whom the Democrats nominate, for a solid ninety-five electoral votes in 1972.

Today, white, middle-class Protestants comprise the largest voter group in America, and the category is growing dramatically—especially if you realize that white, middle-class Catholics are fast becoming their political kin. They were the forgotten Americans to whom Richard Nixon appealed in 1968, and they present as big a problem to Democrats today as the so-called ethnic blocs do to Nixon. Indeed, of all the ethnically favorable states, only West Virginia with its high labor vote can be considered solidly Democratic. As such it is listed in Table 2A with other strongly Democratic states.

The Democrats find their power base in those states with strong ethnic populations. Five of the ethnically unfavorable states plus the District of Columbia, with a total of seventy-five electoral votes, can be classified as strongly Democratic. In contrast, the Republicans start out as clear favorites in only two ethnically unfavorable states—South Carolina and Tennessee. Many states that are ethnically unfavorable, however, are toss-ups. These states (which have half their category's electoral votes) are listed in Table 3A.

Of the ethnically neutral states, there are three (with thirty-two votes) which any Democratic nominee, Ted Kennedy included, would find almost impossible to win—New Mexico, Virginia, and Florida. Though these states have a higher ethnic group percentage than do those in the ethnically favorable class, they have turned increasingly Republican in recent years. The Democrats are strong in only one ethnically neutral state at the national level—Michigan. The vast majority of the ethnically neutral states, with over two thirds of the group's electoral votes, must be rated as Toss-ups.

APPENDIX B. Congressional Seats in the Ninety-Third Congress

Exactly how the apportionment of seats in the U.S. House of Representatives is to be adjusted in response to population changes is determined every ten years following the decennial census; it is done by applying a congressionally approved formula to the population of each state. The Constitution provides that each state is entitled to one representative and that the rest of the House shall be apportioned "according to population." Among statisticians, there are five accepted methods of apportioning "according to population," but the Congress has chosen since 1940 to use only the method known as "equal proportions" (Title 2, U. S. Code, Section 2a).

A mathematical explanation and defense of the method of equal proportions will be found in Lawrence F. Schmeckebier, *Congressional Apportionment,* published by the Brookings Institution in 1941. In 1950, a committee of the American Political Science Association recommended retaining the apportionment system, and there appears to be no pressure for change at the present time. Consequently, when the results of the 1970 census are used to compute congressional apportionment, we can reasonably expect that the method of equal proportions will be continued.

The first Congress to have its seats apportioned on the basis of the 1970 census will be the Ninety-third Congress, which will not convene until January 1972. An accurate projection of the distribution of seats can be made now, however, for the Bureau of the Census maintains projections of individual state populations. Taking these projections *(Current Population Reports,* Series P-25, GPO, 1967) and using the method of equal proportions, the predicted allocation of congressional seats shown in accompanying Table 4A was obtained. The electoral-college votes that will be accorded each state for the 1972 presidential election can be obtained by adding two to the number of congressional seats allotted to each state. Note that the principal gainers are Florida, with two new seats, and California with six. In the 1970's California will have a delegation of forty-four, almost double the twenty-three seats it held in the 1940's. The bulk of the losses comes for the big industrial states—Illinois, Michigan, New York, and Ohio all lose one seat, whereas Pennsylvania loses two.

Table 4A. Predicted Allocation of Congressional Seats
for 1972.

State	No. of Seats	Change from 1962–1970
Alabama	8	
Alaska	1	
Arizona	4	+1
Arkansas	4	
California	44	+6
Colorado	4	
Connecticut	6	
Delaware	1	
Florida	14	+2
Georgia	10	
Hawaii	2	
Idaho	2	
Illinois	23	−1
Indiana	11	
Iowa	6	−1

State	No. of Seats	Change from 1962–1970
Kansas	5	
Kentucky	7	
Louisiana	8	
Maine	2	
Maryland	8	
Massachusetts	12	
Michigan	18	−1
Minnesota	8	
Mississippi	5	
Missouri	10	
Montana	2	
Nebraska	3	
Nevada	1	
New Hampshire	2	
New Jersey	16	+1
New Mexico	2	
New York	40	−1
North Carolina	11	
North Dakota	1	−1
Ohio	23	−1
Oklahoma	5	−1
Oregon	4	
Pennsylvania	25	−2
Rhode Island	2	
South Carolina	6	
South Dakota	2	
Tennessee	9	
Texas	24	+1
Utah	2	
Vermont	1	
Virginia	10	
Washington	7	
West Virginia	4	−1
Wisconsin	9	−1
Wyoming	1	

APPENDIX C. Other Publications by the
Ripon Society

BOOKS

Election '64
From Disaster to Distinction
Southern Republicanism and the New South
The Realities of Vietnam
Ripon's Republican Who's Who at Convention '68
The Politics of Moderation, the Ripon Papers, 1963–1968

PUBLICATIONS

"A Call to Excellence in Leadership," January 1964
"The Republican Party and Civil Rights: A Continuing Commitment," prepared by the Ripon Society for the Critical Issues Council of the Republican Citizens Committee, April 1964
"The Idea for the Ripon Society," June 1964
"A New Republican Mandate," preliminary analysis of the 1964 elections, November 1964
"The Republican Governors' Association: The Case for a Third Force," December 1964
"A Republican Civil Rights Platform for 1965," June 1965
"A Second Mandate to Republicans," an analysis of the 1965 elections, November 1965
"China '66: Containment and Contact," a Ripon policy statement, April 1966

"Citizenship for Cuban Refugees," a Ripon legislative proposal, May 1966

"Government for Tomorrow," a proposal for the unconditional sharing of federal tax revenue with state and local government, November 1966

"The Potential to Govern," Ripon statement on the 1966 elections, November 1966

"Politics and Conscription," a Ripon proposal to replace the draft, December 1966

"The Rights of the Mentally Ill," February 1967

"The Negative Income Tax," a Republican proposal to help the poor; report and recommendations for congressional action, April 1967

"Overkill at Omaha," analysis of the Young Republican National Federation 1967 Convention at Omaha, Nebraska, June 1967

"Multilateral Foreign Aid," a better way to foster development, January 1968

"The SMIC Boondoggle," a Ripon analysis of the influence of the Southern military-industrial complex in the Johnson Administration, February 1968

"Here's the Rest of Him," a report on Ronald Reagan, June 1968

"Urban Papers," six Ripon position papers on urban financing, neighborhood information centers, welfare, jobs, education, and housing, August 1968

"The Draft's Agony of Conscience," a Ripon position paper, October 1968

"The 'Complex' Society Marches On," an analysis of the influence of the military-industrial complex, 1937–1969, January, March, and April 1969

"Nixon at the Crossroads," presidential action for human rights, February 1969

"Biafra and the Bureaucrats," February 1969

Information on receiving any of the above publications, or copies of other Ripon books, or on subscribing to the Ripon *Forum* and other future publications of the Ripon Society may be obtained by writing to:

The Ripon Society
14a Eliot Street
Cambridge, Mass. 02138
Tel. (617) 491-4180